indonesia

1991

The Role of the Indonesian Chinese in Shaping Modern Indonesian Life

Proceedings of the symposium held at Cornell University
in conjunction with the Southeast Asian Studies Summer Institute
July 13-15, 1990

Sponsored by the Joint Committee on Southeast Asia of the
Social Science Research Council of Learned Societies
with funds provided by the Ford Foundation

© 1991, Cornell Southeast Asia Program

Interim Editor: Virginia M. Barker
Editor: Audrey Kahin

Guest Editor: Suzanne A. Brenner
Associate Editors: Roberta Ludgate and Dolina Millar

Editorial Advisory Board

Milton L. Barnett		James T. Siegel
Martin F. Hatch	Stanley J. O'Connor	John U. Wolff
George McT. Kahin	Takashi Shiraishi	O. W. Wolters

Submissions: Submit manuscripts in a typewritten or computer-keyed, *double-spaced* format with footnotes and other stylistic conventions in accordance with *The Chicago Manual of Style*, 13th ed. Double space footnotes and group them at the end of the article. Include a short statement of your institutional affiliation and status to be used in the "List of Contributors" if the article is published.

Address: Please address all correspondence and manuscripts to *Indonesia*, Cornell Modern Indonesia Project, 102 West Avenue, Ithaca, NY 14850.

Computer submissions: Submissions on disk facilitate and accelerate the publication process. The editors will request disk copies and FAX, telex, and telephone numbers when your manuscript is accepted for publication.

Reprints: Contributors will receive ten complimentary reprints of their articles and one complimentary copy of the issues in which their articles appear. They may order additional reprints at cost *at the time the manuscript is accepted for publication*.

Abstracts: Abstracts of articles published in *Indonesia* appear in *Excerpta Indonesica*, which is published semiannually by the Centre for Documentation on Modern Indonesia, Royal Institute of Linguistics and Anthropology, Leiden.

Subscription rates: US $18.00 per year or $9.50 per issue. For mailings outside the United States, add US $5.00 per year postage. Order from Southeast Asia Program Publications, East Hill Plaza, Ithaca, NY 14850

ISBN 978-0-87727-851-1

Cover: By Astri Wright, a Ph.D. candidate in the History of Art Department, Cornell University. The design was inspired by Chinese elements in Cirebon batik.

Contents

The Role of Indonesian Chinese in Shaping Modern Indonesian Life: A Conference in Retrospect ... 1
   Leonard Blussé

Placing the Chinese in Java on the Eve of the Twentieth Century ... 13
   James Rush

A Critical View of the Opium Farmers as Reflected in a *Syair* by Boen Sing Hoo (Semarang, 1889) ... 25
   Claudine Salmon

The Chinese of Indonesia and the Development of the Indonesian Language ... 53
   Dédé Oetomo

Forms of Censorship in the Dutch Indies: The Marginalization of Chinese-Malay Literature ... 67
   Hendrik M. J. Maier

Towkays and Tycoons: The Chinese in Indonesian Economic Life in the 1920s and 1980s ... 83
   Jamie Mackie

Becoming an *Orang Indonesia Sejati:* The Political Journey of Yap Thiam Hien ... 97
   Daniel S. Lev

The Social and Cultural Dimensions of the Role of Ethnic Chinese in Indonesian Society ... 113
   Mély G. Tan

The Role of Elites in Creating Capitalist Hegemony in Post–Oil Boom Indonesia ... 127
   Yoon Hwan Shin

China and Indonesia Make Up: Reflections on a Troubled Relationship ... 145
   Michael Williams

Acknowledgments

This symposium would not have been possible without substantial support from the Social Science Research Council. Funds for the symposium were also provided by Indonesian donors: Yayasan Prasetya Mulis, P. T. Summa International, and the newspaper, *Kompas*.

Thanks are owed also to the many people at Cornell—staff, faculty, and students—who made it possible for this symposium to take place. They are too many to list separately, but I would like to mention a few who were crucial to the success of the program. Of the faculty, Professor Takashi Shiraishi spent a great deal of time and mental energy helping me to formulate the intellectual focus of the symposium and keeping the contents in focus throughout the various changes that were required in the eighteen months of preparation. Of the students, I should thank particularly Sarah Maxim, who took personal responsibility for many of the logistics of the program in the days preceding and during the symposium. Among the staff a particular vote of thanks goes to Maria Theresia Centeno, the SEASSI coordinator, who with admirable courtesy took responsibility for correspondence with the participants and saw to it that their personal needs were taken care of before and during the symposium and also to Tammy Bloom of the Cornell University Conference staff, who never left the scene of the symposium and spent many hours of her own time to make sure that every aspect of the facilities, catering, and registration proceeded smoothly. Finally, I would like to thank Suzanne Brenner, who at considerable sacrifice of time and energy helped edit the symposium proceedings in a timely and intelligent fashion.

John Wolff

THE ROLE OF INDONESIAN CHINESE IN SHAPING MODERN INDONESIAN LIFE

A Conference in Retrospect

Leonard Blussé

Long before anyone could imagine that the Republic of Indonesia and the People's Republic of China would reestablish diplomatic relations in August 1990, the idea was conceived to convene a conference on the cultural heritage and the social and economic roles of the Indonesian Chinese. This idea was brought to fruition in the symposium on the Role of the Indonesian Chinese in Shaping Modern Indonesian Life, which was held at Cornell University in conjunction with the Southeast Asian Studies Summer Institute, July 13–15, 1990.

The motivation behind the symposium was to analyze how Chinese culture, as it was introduced by Chinese migrants throughout the centuries, converged with Indonesian culture. Although in Java the Chinese intermarried with the native people, and some even married into the nobility and converted to Islam, and although they were profoundly influenced culturally by the peoples with whom they came in contact (they began to speak Malay or the regional languages as natives within a few generations), nevertheless, they are still looked upon by the natives (*pribumi*) as a nationality apart. Despite the generations of shared history and cultural experiences, the Chinese Indonesians also think of themselves as a separate group. Wondering why this should be so and unable to formulate an adequate answer to this question, the organizers of the symposium committed themselves—a "demonic commitment" as John Wolff put it—to the creation of a platform where Chinese Indonesians from different walks of life—writers, filmmakers, politicians, businessmen, social scientists, and historians—would be given the opportunity to air their views on the issue free from any political connotations.

The cultural identity and the position of the Chinese population group within Indonesian society is a contentious one. The *masalah Cina* (Chinese problem) issue has been hotly discussed within Indonesian society itself and has inevitably resulted in such crucial questions as whether the Indonesian Chinese are entitled to maintain their own cultural identity or should instead seek integration or even assimilation into Indonesian culture.

It was evidently not the organizers' intention to carry on this debate at the symposium. Rather, they wished to find out how Chinese Indonesians evaluate their position and what it feels like to be a Chinese Indonesian or a Chinese in Indonesia. What motivates these people? What cultural heritage has this highly diverse group descended from farmers, traders, and coolies, *peranakan* or *totok,* to offer to Indonesian culture at large? How, where, and when has Chinese cultural influence transposed into Indonesian culture? In other words, it was felt that this meeting should not be devoted merely to cultural affairs but should also deal with existential issues.

It is almost miraculous that during the whole conference, which, after all, was held in the United States, the heartland of political science, almost no political questions were raised or forecasts given about the future of Sino-Indonesian relations. The conference may actually have been the last large academic meeting at which the different aspects of Indonesian Chinese culture will have been discussed in isolation from the so-called "China factor." Yet the selection of conference papers assembled in this special issue of *Indonesia* will certainly contribute to future discussions about the role that should be assigned to the Chinese Indonesians within the renewed political, economic, and cultural relations between China and Indonesia. The public interest displayed in the conference exceeded the wildest expectations of the organizers, even causing some initial worry about how to run a conference with a large audience of several hundred people who clearly also wanted to have their say on the subject.

In consideration of the wide coverage received in the Indonesian press, the organizers decided not to publish the conference proceedings in book form, a long, drawn-out procedure that normally takes three years to accomplish, but to persuade the editors of *Indonesia* to publish a special issue on the theme instead. This decision implied that papers must be selected because of limited space. It also saddled this author with a problem for, although in my concluding remarks to the conference I could philosophize and elaborate at will about some of the main issues that were generated during the debate, it was clear that this approach would not do here. It would not do justice to those contributors who, perhaps, drew most public interest during the conference but whose spontaneous, intimate presentations did not lend themselves easily to publication. As a result, the aim is to incorporate, or at least refer to, all papers in the following observations on the conference without necessarily trying to recapitulate or summarize all that has been said. I hope that in the following retrospect of the conference some of the enthusiasm that characterized the whole operation will be transmitted.

In his inaugural address about the position of Indonesian Chinese in Indonesian life, Prof. Wang Gungwu came straight to the point by posing the questions Have the Indonesian Chinese played an active or passive role in shaping Indonesian life? and Has that role been positive or negative? In this context he rather dramatically paraphrased Hamlet's words "to be or not to be . . . a Chinese (in Indonesia)." Professor Wang, who in the past has coined the term "merchants without empire" to describe the historical Chinese presence in the Nanyang, now elaborated this analysis further by referring to "wealth without power." Discerning four key periods of change, he discussed the Chinese presence abroad from the era of the Malay trading rulers, via the *zaman kompenie* to the colonial state and, finally, contemporary Indonesia. He observed that over these four periods the Chinese have been very adaptable and sensitive to political changes. They adapted themselves well to local conditions and developed a general Sino-Malay culture of their own. In the post-1880 period, other options were made available. The China factor became more important as a result of better transportation, and in the 1920s, Western education provided "modern alternatives."

With his remarks on the China factor, Professor Wang briefly touched upon the issue of "Chineseness" among overseas Chinese, an issue that was taken for granted during the conference and not quite conceived as it should have been, that is, as a recent reinvention of tradition and identity for nationalist objectives.

Chinese moving into the Nanyang during the Ming and Qing dynasties often did so to escape the embrace of poverty and the paramount presence of the metropolitan bureaucracy in China's southeastern coastal provinces. This phenomenon did not elude the imperial authorities, who outlawed these emigrants en masse again and again throughout the seventeenth and eighteenth centuries.

When by the end of the nineteenth century a tide of nationalistic feeling was mounting everywhere in Asia, the overseas Chinese in Southeast Asia could no longer afford to shun their ancestral roots and sought to renew their political ties with the homeland. As a result, the China factor, that is, a distantly looming China as an ever-present factor within the balance of power of local politics, was introduced into the Southeast Asian arena. But there were also moves from the other side. Appeals to the Nanyang Chinese, first by the Manchu government, then by ardent nationalists like Kang Yu-wei or Sun Yat-sen and, later, by the Republican government did not fail to stir a response. Soon these patriotic feelings were consciously played upon by Chinese community leaders to improve the status of the ethnic Chinese within colonial society itself. Schools were established where the national language, *guoyu*, was taught to Hokkien dialect speakers and *baba* who had forgotten their mother tongue and had already been speaking Malay for generations. As a result of the teaching of Chinese culture and values around the turn of the century, Chineseness was "reinvented" by the overseas Chinese, and nowhere were the effects of this reorientation on the homeland more sweeping than among the Chinese living in the Netherlands Indies.

James Rush set the scene by demonstrating how, on the eve of the Dawning of the East, peranakan society was embedded in colonial society by its leaders. Surveying the position of Chinese communities within Javanese society, the internal structure of the communities, and the changes that they underwent as a result of externally generated economic, political, and social influences, he focused on the role of the Chinese community leaders and their ties with the colonial elite before these great changes were to happen.

For his analysis of the configuration and the dynamics of the *cabang atas* relationship between the Chinese elite, the Dutch officials, and the priyayi elite, Rush has mainly drawn on the archival sources of the Dutch colonial administration. Yet, one could also envisage the position of the Chinese population groups within colonial society by focusing on the social structure of the Chinese community itself and inquire what cultural heritage the Chinese migrants brought along and what cultural ballast they chose to leave behind, as Professor Wang suggested in his introductory speech. Coming from a southeastern Chinese rural setting with severe ecological constraints and fierce competition between the local lineages, they found their way overseas via these same kinship organizations, merchant guilds, or *huiguan*.

When the *orang baru* from Fujian or Guangdong came to Java, all along the *pasisir* he found firmly embedded peranakan communities with a sociocultural structure that, apart from various adaptations to local Javanese culture, differed in one important respect from the community in the home province. In China, society was made up of four layers according to the Confucian hierarchy, with the literati on top, the merchants at the bottom, and the farmers and artisans in between—the so-called *shi-nong-gong-shang* relationship. In overseas Chinese society, an upside-down reflection of the situation in the homeland was observed. Contrary to the situation in China, where literati of the local gentry, as agents and guardians, functioned as community leaders and intermediaries between the local community and the agents of the metropolitan government, in Java, in the absence of an educated local gentry, the most successful entrepreneurs assumed the leading position of *kapitein* or *majoor*.

Instead of witnessing a social elite nurtured by Confucian teaching to play its role in the ritual of Confucian bureaucracy, the peranakan of Semarang saw their paramount patrons involved in frantic fights for tax farms, such as the opium monopoly, to an extent that would make Clifford Geertz's Balinese cockfighters blush with embarrassment. Claudine Salmon portrayed later during the conference how contemporaries perceived these auctions.

I would suggest that it was this particular state of affairs that engendered a peculiar branch of "little tradition" culture among the "People of Tang," as overseas Chinese society styled itself. Free from the all-pervading metropolitan constraints of Confucianism, it was remarkably open to Javanese culture.

In traditional Southeast Asian colonial society, peranakan society thus functioned as a safety valve, a passageway for the newly arrived from China, a function that can scarcely be exaggerated and requires further study. Only in moments of massive immigration, when mounting waves of immigrants could not be absorbed by the traditional social networks, such as the lineage organization or the temple organization, as happened, for instance, in the 1890s, was peranakan society no longer equal to its task as a cultural mediator.

What would happen if totok Chinese immigrated en masse, without being absorbed by already existing peranakan communities embedded in local society, became manifest from the situation in northeastern Sumatra, which had never harbored a sizable Chinese community. When the coolie laborers swarmed out from the labor concentration camps, euphemistically called plantations or tin mines, they established solid totok communities in Medan and Bangka. They even almost swamped Java's pasisir communities at a moment when, as Rush explains, for a variety of reasons the power structure of peranakan society was passing through an identity crisis.

I venture these comments to set out the conditions under which, from the turn of this century onward, Chineseness was reinvented on Java, either through Chinese education from the mainland, which enabled the peranakan to bypass and disparage Javanese as well as peranakan society, or by the Dutch language educational model of the "Hollands-Chinese scholen," which eased the peranakan elite away from the Javanese cultural sphere. The Dutch curriculum even introduced its own brand of Confucianism in austere Calvinist guise into the lessons on Chinese traditional culture. It is telling that from the turn of the century many educated peranakan sought to express themselves either in Dutch or in guoyu.

The reconfirmation of Chineseness will not be elaborated further here. It will suffice to state that historically peranakan society has functioned as a cultural filter to Indonesian society, cushioning the impact from Chinese culture, and, on the other hand, has tended to absorb the cultural shock for the newcomers.

A variety of factors, such as the increased scale of immigration from China, the rise of nationalism in the Chinese community, the influx of Chinese women from the homeland, resulting in a steep increase in totok marriages, and finally, the Dutch efforts in the late colonial period to wean peranakan society from the cultural and political propaganda of the homeland, contributed to the alienation of peranakan society. The apothegm, "Cina wurung, Londa durung, Jawa tanggung" (no longer a Chinese, not yet a Dutchman, a half-baked Javanese) applied to Kapitein Cina Tan Jin Sing of Yogyakarta in 1813, might just as well have been used to characterize the intellectual upper echelon of the peranakan elite on the eve of *kemerdekaan*. Colonial society with its rigid hierarchy was divided into three racial layers: the whites and *gelijkgestelden* (Asians with European legal status) on top, the *Vreemde Oosterlingen* (Foreign Orientals) in the middle, the native peoples below. As soon as the broad basis of this society started to shift, the house of cards fell apart. Especially those Chinese Indonesians who had received higher education saw their career prospects dim when for political reasons they had to make room for pribumi Indonesians. Considering the massive emigration of lawyers, economists, and medical practitioners of Chinese ethnicity from Indonesia to Europe and the United States during the 1950s and 1960s, it may be sensible to realize what a tremendous brain drain occurred at a moment when Indonesia needed expertise most. One should like to paraphrase Lenin: one expert is worth twenty nationalists.

The conspicuous presence of the Chinese in Indonesian economic life formed the subject of the contributions by Jamie A. C. Mackie and Yoon Hwan Shin. Whereas Mackie discussed the changing roles of the Chinese in Indonesian economic life by comparing the towkays, merchants, and small-scale businessmen of the 1920s with the large-scale tycoons of the 1970s and 1980s, sketching a development from small family firms to corporatized big conglomerates, Shin focused on the relationship between the rise of big business in Indonesia during the 1980s and the dissemination of new ideologies to support the growth of a new national capitalist class. After the failure of the planned economy (*geleide*) approach and the pribumi-oriented economic policies for economic development, the government has now chosen to depend on private investment and initiatives. Why Chinese Indonesians are such successful entrepreneurs remained somewhat obscured. Shin maintained that ethnic Chinese Indonesians, through their ties with international banking interests and influential politicians, have carved a niche for themselves in the new capitalist class. Mackie argued that Chinese businessmen indeed have managed to obtain help and facilities of various kinds from state instrumentalities in the name of promoting national development, but he added that behavioral and cultural factors should not be dismissed either.

"Forces That Have Shaped My Creative Life" was the title of the informal talk that dramatist and critic N. Riantiarno was scheduled to give during the evening session of the first day. Riantiarno said he was happy to have been invited but felt quite puzzled about what he should talk about. He did not feel he was a Chinese, but rather an Indonesian from Cirebon saying "All I know, as founder of Koma theater, about the Chinese in Indonesia is that there are lots of rich Chinese around but few who want to sponsor my productions." Questions as to whether he felt himself to be *kasno* (a person who hides his Chineseness) or *kirno* (a person who denies his Chineseness) he deemed irrelevant, "What one creates is what counts."

As it turned out, none of Riantiarno's plays except one, *Sampek Engtay*, had any Chinese cultural roots. To his surprise, *Sampek Engtay* drew sizeable crowds of Chinese Indonesians wherever it was performed. Occasionally, he even had noticed people among the audience who had dressed for the occasion in traditional Chinese clothes. All this somewhat bewildered the dramatist, who "just wanted to concentrate on making Indonesian theater."

How do Chinese-Indonesian businessmen experience their own function in Indonesian society? The gallery of eminent entrepreneurs who took the floor in the morning session of the second day of the symposium each presented tales of his own career, which generally bore out Mackie's observations on the growth of conglomerates and Shin's remarks on the growth of a capitalist elite.

The panel on Chinese in Business and Politics was opened by Christianto Wibisono with a short talk on the profile and anatomy of Indonesian conglomerates. Having categorized the conglomerates into state-owned, bureaucratic (set up by former officials), crony capitalist (formed on the basis of special licensing and favors), and the conglomerates of the genuine private sector, Wibisono felt that the relative weight of Sino-Indonesian business within the Indonesian economy might be the direct result of the government's reliance on the private sector for development. This policy has encouraged Chinese investment from Singapore, Taiwan, and Hongkong by way of the Sino-Indonesian conglomerates.

Mochtar Riady, head of the Lippo Bank and the Bank of Central Asia conveyed his message to the conference through close friend and associate, Mr. Priasmoro Prawiroardjo. The paper began by stating that Confucianism acted as a brake on development but nonetheless went on to emphasize that the sage's tenets might be applied as a "moral code of materialist enjoyment." The late Herman Kahn, the high priest of neo-Confucianism for business purposes, would have heartily concurred with this latter observation. Perhaps the most striking point of the paper was that it was read by a Javanese, who stressed that he had a lot in common with the author: "Riady and I are close in age. I am fifty-eight; he is sixty. He owns the bank; I work there . . . that is the only difference." This multiethnic veneer notwithstanding, the paper itself was a Sino-centric exercise in entrepreneurial philosophy stressing the need for the (Chinese) private sector to take the initiative in solving problems the Indonesian government cannot grapple with.

Edward Soeryadjaya, in his personal, matter-of-fact style, gave the greatest insight into what makes the peranakan entrepreneur's heart beat. Explaining that his was not exactly a "from rags to riches" story because his father, William Soeryadjaya, head of the Astra Group, the second largest conglomerate in Indonesia, had enabled him to set up a business of his own with a loan of "only a million dollars," he described how he built his own conglomerate in the seventies and eighties and dwelled at length on the extraordinary contract that his bank, the Summa Bank, has recently signed with the Nahdlatul Ulama (NU) organization. When prodded about the rationale underlying this unusual collaboration between a Catholic capitalist and a fundamentalist Islamic organization, Soeryadjaya retorted that he had not sought the relationship himself, but on the contrary, it was he who had been approached by Abdurrahman Wahid, a high-ranked ulama. From his own point of view, Soeryadjaya saw the deal as purely commercial. The latest January 1990 requirements of the Deregulation Package stipulate that all private banks should set aside 20 percent of their loan portfolios for small businesses and rural and cooperative loans. Presented with the opportunity for establishing what could possibly amount to some two thousand rural banks in conjunction with the NU, he saw his dilemma of how to reach enough customers to attain the 20 percent minimum level and thus comply with the government regulations now automatically solved.

Regarding questions about his peranakan background, Soeryadjaya saw no reason to hide that in making a career in business it might be quite convenient to look Chinese, even though he feels 100 percent Indonesian. He confessed that he would not even be able to tell from which village his Chinese ancestor came five generations ago, and frankly, he could not care less. He also added that he had married outside his own community by wedding a Sundanese woman. Soeryadjaya's contribution was much appreciated because of its frank presentation and utterly commonsense approach.

Harry Tjan Silalahi, former secretary general of the Roman Catholic party and now director of the Center for Strategic and International Studies (CSIS) only marginally touched on the relationship between politics and business, expanding instead on his own political career and the issue of nation building. He maintained that attempts to preserve the (ethnic) Chinese population group as a *suku* might actually endanger the process of Indonesian nation building; "Chineseness" should gradually disappear and merge into the Indonesian national culture. He elaborated on this theme further by explaining what political events in the past had driven him to play a leading role in the *assimilasi* movement. Raised as a devout Catholic peranakan in a Javanese environment, recipient of a Dutch language education, and adopted into a Batak family, he feels himself a child of several worlds. He chose a political career because he saw it as his personal responsibility to act as a beacon for those Chinese Indonesians who have felt utterly lost since the political upheavals of the 1960s. Silalahi's plea for assimilation, of course, had a familiar ring to those who have known him as a politician over the past twenty-five years. At this congress it sounded like a declaration of faith mixed with an *oratio pro domo*.

The assimilasi versus *integrasi* dispute blazed up that same afternoon when Daniel Lev presented a paper about his friend, the late human rights lawyer Yap Thiam Hien, a presentation so extraordinarily well tuned to the conceptual world of Yap that, at times, it bordered on being a personification of the main character, especially when countered by Harry Tjan's comments. If for the Lev-Silalahi duo, judging from their performance, a bright future in show business is in store, the undertone of their quick-witted exchanges dealt with an extremely serious existentialist issue: For the sake of solving ethnic tension should the Chinese unconditionally give up their own cultural identity to fade away in the pribumi majority culture, as Tjan would suggest, or has the time come for ironing out ethnic differences and reaching a general consensus on cultural matters, rendering it unnecessary for this minority to sacrifice its identity and even religion for the sake of survival? The dilemma is vividly portrayed by the different ways in which Harry Tjan and Yap Thiam Hien each have attempted to serve the needs of their fellow men. In many ways Tjan, the Catholic looking after his flock, represents the traditional community leader, always cognizant of the group's acute needs for protection or assistance, bending like resilient bamboo in times of hardship.

Yap Thiam Hien, on the other hand, did not feel the need to stand up for the Chinese community per se but felt called upon to defend individuals who suffered unfair legal treatment. His unyielding stance, rooted in his Calvinist background and legal training, might be likened to a solitary oak tree anchored by the Bible and the *Burgerlijk Wetboek*. The question of human rights as such was hardly touched upon during the conference—William Skinner went as far as to complain of a "conspiracy of silence." I believe, however, that Lev's approach to the life and times of Yap Thiam Hien actually came to grips with the issue in a much more subtle manner than had otherwise been possible. As Lev pointed out, Yap Thiam Hien's career went through different stages. At the outset fully conscious of his own peranakan identity, he became gradually less concerned about ethnicity. He was not against personal assimilation as such but against the forced assimilation of a group. These concerns actually made him transcend the bounds of the Chinese community.

In this respect, it is rather telling that most of the verbal dispute about the assimilation or integration issue is going on within the generation of Dutch language trained Chinese Indonesians who are over fifty years old. By a strange irony of fate, the Dutch, who over the years have obtained a reputation for their overlegalistic behavior in political matters and are rightly criticized on that account, almost see themselves outdone by their own disciples, Yap Thiam Hien not excluded. If this man of principles, who was so vividly and convincingly portrayed by Dan Lev during the conference, had possessed the freckled face of a Frisian—a particularly headstrong race eclipsing even the Scots—he might have gone unnoticed in this author's home country.

How the discussion occasionally borders on petty bickering about labels became clear on the last day of the conference when a heated argument developed on the term *Cina*, which the government has adopted to address the Chinese minority. Several participants held the opinion that this was a humiliating label and preferred to be designated as *orang Tionghoa*. Quite understandably, one member of the audience, a Batak who briefly fell out of her role as a radio reporter, wondered aloud what all the bickering was about. Raised amidst the Chinese of Medan, she asked whether the latter should not first stop referring to pribumi Indonesians as *hoanna* (barbarians) before starting to complain about discriminatory labeling by the government.

It is time that scholarship came to grips with the artificial garments of Chineseness, rips them off, and observes the educational systems that have shaped and transformed the outlook of the peranakan elite. The only way in which the Chinese of the Netherlands Indies could escape from the colonial situation was to walk the highway of higher education, and if Chinese students, upon having Dutch academic education, found most alleys blocked in post-liberation Indonesia, this explains much of the frustration reigning in those circles.

What would seem to be of prime importance in solving ethnic friction is to gain a better understanding of the perception of difference that underlies ethnicity, a difference that is the result of the sociopolitical history of a society. The SEASSI conference, which addressed particular features and contributions of Indonesian Chinese culture, may indeed contribute to such a better understanding. The perception of difference in the cultural sphere should, however, have a meaning other than the one some prominent members of the audience would have liked to apply to it. One of the participants, for the practical purpose of solving the assimilation problem once and for all, proposed dividing the four million or so Indonesians of Chinese descent into brackets varying from those who are so well assimilated that they can no longer be distinguished from pribumi, those who are in the process of being assimilated, and the hard core who still speak Chinese and cling to their own cultural values and await assimilation by "persuasion," to solve the masalah Cina.

This approach, however functional it may seem from the point of view of the administrator, who derives pleasure from social engineering and the application of grids on society, would seem in the final analysis to be utterly unrealistic because it conceptualizes the Chinese presence in Indonesia as an internal problem, an issue that can be isolated and dealt with properly.

In the decade after 1965, when relations with the People's Republic of China were interrupted and the PRC itself was in turmoil, the delusion that the Chinese problem could be solved in isolation from the international context took root in Indonesia. This was not only wishful thinking, it also was, historically speaking, a fallacy, for Indonesia was not and never will be a closed society. From time immemorial, Chinese migrants have come to the Nanyang in search of better opportunities. They will always continue to do so, even more as China aims for an export market and Indonesia opens further to the world market.

It should be understood that the perception of how differences come about between ethnic groups calls for a multidisciplinary approach. Resentment between groups may crystallize along lines of religion, language, or differences in physical appearance. These antipathetic feelings can easily develop into deep-rooted passions. From this perspective it is clear that the assimilasi policy, with its call to abandon Chinese names and adopt Indonesian ones instead, really may have been used as a defense mechanism to control and defuse passions. At the root of the confusion of tongues about assimilasi and integrasi is that some people quite mistakenly see the assimilation policy as an end instead of as a means for solving a dilemma.

The moot question, however, remains how passions within a society can be reduced in the long run within the kind of fluid society that contemporary Indonesia has become. In Indonesian society, with its overlapping and interlocking interests inside and outside the country, it remains for the nation to move to a plural solution and reach consensus on the ethnic issues. A one-way action aimed at the more or less coercive loss of cultural and even religious identity is a terrifying trap, as one of the commentators, Charles Hirschman, pointed out. It was indeed in Germany, where the Jewish middle class was most consciously seeking to assimilate within German nationhood, that *shoah* occurred.

Daniel Dhakidae's observation that Indonesia's newspapers seem to be aimed at exploiting "human interest stories" rather than acting as vehicles of change was interesting in itself, but the focus of his paper remained very much on today's situation, and there was every reason that one would have liked him to discuss the history of the Chinese-Malay language papers, like *Sin Po*, which were withdrawn from circulation. Onghokham addressed the question of what impact ideologies about the Chinese may have on contemporary Indonesia and sought "to bring out the realities of Chineseness within the present day (Javanese) patrimonial state and society." In doing so, he focused on inner- and outer-group concepts so characteristic of traditional societies. As an example, he alluded to stereotypes that are commonly connected to successful Chinese merchants, such as belief in *tuyul* spirits, "children who are not human beings and who steal for the merchant to make him rich." Even more fearsome spirits are the *babi-pepet*. Impishly rubbing his cranium, Ong described tuyul as stocky, bald-headed creatures, drawing a murmur of recognition from the audience.

Makers of policy tend to carry out remedial action in ethnic conflicts by drawing on the results of the sociological study of ethnic relations. Even if this knowledge is acquired with the practical aim of influencing policy, it should be remembered that it relies heavily on scholarly research in the cultural and historical fields, which is generally carried out for its own sake. The contributions of Henk Maier on the Malay language policies of the Dutch colonial government, Claudine Salmon on Chinese-Malay *syair*, Myra Sidharta on the perception of the Dutch in Sino-Malay novels and Dédé Oetomo on vernacular spoken in the cities of Java, stigmatized "low Malay," all show how much path-breaking and important work can be done on peranakan history and literature.

In Indonesian studies, one of the great developments of the past few years is the (re)discovery of Chinese-Malay literature and the pioneering function it has performed in the development of modern Indonesian literature. The Sino-Malay novel emerged from the 1870s onward, paralleling the establishment of the first Chinese-owned printing presses. When the Dutch colonial administration meant business by establishing a mass-oriented educational system, it introduced its own brand of national "civilized" standard Malay and saw to it that this was used in all textbooks and the Balai Poestaka literature. In his paper, Henk Maier convincingly showed how no efforts were spared to extirpate the "low Malay literature," which was seen as a menace to the illiteracy campaigns. This debate is not without precedent. As early as the seventeenth century, the Dutch gave considerable attention to the translation of biblical texts and whether these should be rendered into "high" or "low" Malay. In that instance, high Malay was also chosen.

What printed Chinese-Malay literature looked like in its early phase was illustrated by Claudine Salmon in her paper on an 1890s poem in which the proceedings of an opium farm auction are ridiculed. As Benedict Anderson commented, the development-oriented policies of the colonial administration went hand-in-hand with "cultural policing" to dampen the scandalizing and alarming aspects of a native gossip-ridden mass press that it found difficult to control. Furthermore, he drew attention to the fact that the mocking tone of Claudine Salmon's syair and of the many "fun-poking" novels cited by Myra Sidharta should not be seen exclusively as a Chinese-Malay feature in Indonesian literature. They were actually part of a much broader phenomenon throughout Indonesian literature aimed at making fun of the colonial authorities with their ponderous "white man's burden."

The importance of all these papers, including Dédé Oetomo's, is that they show how peranakan Malay, peranakan literature, and the peranakan frame of mind suffered the merciless onslaught of colonial bureaucracy, which perceived in them a possible menace to the state-building process. Indeed, there is nothing new under the sun!

In the final session of the conference a balance was struck among the cultural, economic, and political policies that have been implemented by the state to solve the masalah Cina. Mély Tan and Leo Suryadinata independently produced two papers on basically the same theme: Indonesian policies toward the Chinese and the Chinese response toward these policies. Mély Tan outlined how Chinese language education, the use of Chinese characters, the display of Chinese cultural elements, and the public worship of Chinese religions were banned in 1967. She showed how these draconic measures provoked different responses from the Chinese ethnic groups, varying from integration movements to assimilation movements. But what interested her most was how the post-1967 educated generations of Chinese Indonesians look at intermarriage and how their language patterns and use have altered as a result of the educational policies.

Leo Suryadinata dwelled on some of the paradoxical effects of the 1967 regulations. In the New Order era, the economic strategies aimed at reducing the economic strength of the Chinese actually favored them, whereas the requirement that all Indonesians belong to an organized religion resulted in the establishment of new religions such as the "Confucian religion," *agama Khonghucu*. Chinese who were persuaded to adopt Indonesian names did so but often made sure that their original Chinese surnames could still be recognized.

If the regulations aimed at eliminating Chinese cultural and religious identity have provoked countereffects and bypasses, the language policies seem to have reaped results. The younger Chinese generation speaks and, what is more important, thinks in the Indonesian language. It is within this context that the rediscovery of Malay-language peranakan culture should be of current interest.

As the conference neared its end realization dawned that, although the initial questions of the organizers perhaps had not all been satisfactorily answered, participants had at least gained new insight into the complexities of the study of peranakan society. This recognition prompted the following observations.

Before the great clearing-up of peranakan culture by the Dutch and Indonesian bureaucratic administrations successively reaches the stage of mopping-up the last remaining vestiges, ways and means should be found to study this unique cultural sphere that is equally at the center and the periphery of Indonesian culture. The call is not for an antiquarian quest for an idealized society but for profound research into the dynamics and configurations of Chinese communities embedded in Indonesian cultures.

As a scholar with a cause but without political aspirations one should not only search for and analyze rare manuscripts and books but should also focus on the institutional effects the Chinese educational system, the Dutch colonial school system, and finally, the Indonesian educational system have had on reforming, or drawing a veil over peranakan culture. The study of peranakan culture indeed deserves far more. It asks for dignified treatment by the national and local governments of historical sites, even if only as a reminder of a Chinese presence on Java and other islands. Most monuments of peranakan architecture are destroyed by ignorance rather than by concerted action. This author does not believe in the conspiracy of the state in this respect. Yet it has always seemed rather curious that a monument like the large stone slab of the Chinese hospital of Batavia, which dates back to the eighteenth century and states the names of all the Chinese board members of that institution, should be lying horizontally in the inner court of the National Archives with its text facing the ground so that no visitor can see it. Almost all the photographs in Claudine Salmon's paper by now have historical value, as the sites that she photographed only a few years ago have since been obliterated. Economic progress demands sacrifices, but cultural ignorance eradicates. Many historic buildings in and around the *kraton* of the sultan of Madura at Sumenep, designed and built by the peranakan Lauw Pra Ngo in the 1780s, threaten to collapse. There are many more examples like these. It is to be hoped that the conference organized in the summer of 1990 at Cornell will contribute to the rediscovery of the actual legacy of peranakan culture, a culture of which Indonesia should be proud. Wang Gungwu opened this conference by referring to the issue "to be or not to be." I conclude by quoting once more from Shakespeare's *Hamlet* and say with Polonius to Indonesia's Chinese:

> This above all—
> To thine ownself be true;
> And it must follow, as the night the day,
> Thou canst not then be false to any man.

Placing the Chinese in Java on the Eve of the Twentieth Century

James Rush

To place the Chinese in late nineteenth-century Java one must find them first.[1] Finding them is by no means easy. Until now, scholars of the Chinese in Indonesia have touched on this period only lightly.[2] Many primary sources remain underexplored, and in some important cases they are meager. Aside from peranakan Chinese writings of the late century—only now being explored with vigor[3]—few Chinese records remain. And what is, to my knowledge, the best collection has been transmitted to us only indirectly, that is, Liem Thian Joe's *Riwajat Semarang* of 1933, based largely upon the archives of the Chinese Council of Semarang and augmented by Liem's own collections and the peranakan talk stories of his day.[4] A rich store of information may await the collector of oral histories. But one hundred years is too long to expect *facts* to come through undisturbed, especially in large families where polygamy and the dispersal of various branches around the world have complicated

---

[1] A fuller discussion of the Chinese in late nineteenth-century Java is presented in James Rush, *Opium to Java: Revenue Farming and Chinese Enterprise in Colonial Indonesia, 1869–1910* (Ithaca, N.Y.: Cornell University Press, 1990). This sketch draws upon additional materials, but it does not break new ground. Instead, it addresses the topic broadly to comport with the symposium for which it was written: "The Role of the Indonesian Chinese in Shaping Modern Indonesian Life." Despite the title, the emphasis here is on central and east Java. Batavia and its hinterland are underrepresented, a serious gap because the largest single community of Chinese in Java was settled there.

[2] See G. William Skinner, "The Chinese Minority," in *Indonesia*, ed. Ruth T. McVey (New Haven: Human Relations Area Files, 1963), pp. 97–117; idem, "Java's Chinese Minority: Continuity and Change," *Journal of Asian Studies*, 20 (May 1961): 353–62; Donald E. Willmott, *The Chinese of Semarang: A Changing Minority Community in Indonesia* (Ithaca, N. Y.: Cornell University Press, 1960); Lea Williams, *Overseas Chinese Nationalism: The Genesis of the Pan-Chinese Movement in Indonesia, 1900–1916* (Glencoe, Ill.: Free Press, 1960); Leo Suryadinata, *The Chinese Minority in Indonesia* (Singapore: Chopmen Enterprises, 1978). Other recent works, like those by Peter Carey, have addressed earlier periods; see Peter Carey, "Changing Javanese Perceptions of the Chinese Communities in Central Java, 1755–1825," *Indonesia*, 37 (April 1984), pp. 1–47.

[3] See Claudine Salmon, *Literature in Malay by the Chinese of Indonesia. A Provisional Annotated Bibliography* (Paris: Éditions de la Maison des Sciences de l'Homme, 1981) and other works by Salmon, including her article in this issue.

[4] Liem Thian Joe, *Riwajat Semarang (Dari Djamannja Sam Poo Sampe Terhapoesnja Kongkoan)* (Semarang: Boekhandel Ho Kim Yoe, 1933). Liem died in 1963.

genealogies, and where bankruptcies and contested inheritances have long since divided kin from kin and story from story. (To avoid being embroiled in such controversies, Liem Thian Joe expurgated the *Riwajat*, as he frankly admits.) Lore about the Chinese in Indonesia has an importance all its own, but in reconstructing the last century, it must obviously be weighed against facts and observations retrieved directly from the times. Where can facts be found?

One unequipped to use Javanese sources directly unavoidably turns to the Dutch. As Java's industrious colonial masters, they were busy keeping track of things—certain things. For example, year by year, their *Regeerings Almanak* listed by name all of Java's Chinese officers, residency by residency, district by district. Java's Dutch-appointed Chinese majors, captains, and lieutenants were truly influential men who stood between the colonial state and its Chinese subjects, and who also dominated the Chinese economy. Therefore, the *Almanak* provides something akin to a demography of power among the Javan Chinese, permitting one to *place* the leading families and, where auxiliary genealogical information is available, to trace the rise of some, the demise of others. (The Bes and the Oeis, both based in Semarang, are dramatic examples.)

The *Koloniale Verslagen*—the colonial ministers' voluminous annual reports to parliament—periodically give population figures for Chinese, although the figures are somewhat impressionistic. (It is not clear, for example, who was counted as a Chinese woman.) Nevertheless, its figures permit one, roughly, to place the Chinese population spatially in Java, mapping its concentrations and dispersements across the island. After 1875, these population figures are given by *afdeling* (more or less coterminous with a regency) and after 1895, by district. The same report gives yearly accounts of the government's revenue farms, and, thus, vast amounts of information about regionally based Chinese enterprise—for virtually all revenue farms were Chinese-run. Colonial officials in Java generally made it a point to keep politicians at home in the dark about certain realities in the colony, the enormous economic influence of the Chinese among them. This is probably why the *Koloniale Verslagen* rarely identify the revenue farmers by name. Only occasionally do they acknowledge in print that they were Chinese at all. (When they do, however, the facts are telling: the *Koloniaal Verslag* for 1875 reveals, for example, that of 922 licensed pawnshops in the East Indian possessions in 1874, all but nine were held by Chinese!)[5] Knowing the connection between government revenue farms and the Chinese, however, makes the *Verslagen* rich sources for charting the health of the Chinese economy region by region. In fact, if one looks carefully, the Chinese appear often in the *Verslagen*. (For example, in appendix A of the *Verslag* for 1889 one learns inter alia that there were then twenty-two Chinese furniture makers in Kediri, and that in all Java, only fifty-five Chinese were Christian!)

The Chinese can also be found in other official documents. Between 1866 and 1886, for example, the colonial government at Batavia published twenty-one or so statutes designating and expanding Java's authorized Chinatowns; these statutes can now be found in bound volumes entitled *Staatsbladen van Nederlandsch-Indië*. Another example is the massive *Onderzoek naar de Mindere Welvaart der Inlandsche bevolking op Java en Madoera* (10 vol., 1905–1914), in which Chinese economic activities late in the century are examined in the context of a perceived decline in the welfare of Java's indigenous population.[6]

---

[5]Dutch East Indies, *Koloniaal Verslag*, 1875, pp. 164–65.

[6]Dutch East Indies, *Onderzoek naar de Mindere Welvaart der Inlandsche bevolking op Java en Madoera*, 10 vols. (Batavia: 1905-1914) [hereafter cited as *Mindere Welvaart Report*].

The Chinese appear in even greater profusion and sharper focus in the archives of the former Dutch Ministry of Colonies. Here rest file upon file of raw materials unedited for public consumption, although, it is true, carefully selected for internal perusal. Those unfamiliar with archives and perhaps imagining shelves full of dull reports far removed from the nitty-gritty of Java will be surprised to discover the richness and intimacy of these sources—the result of bureaucratic procedure. When reporting administrative actions to his minister at home, the governor general in Batavia ordinarily appended to his official letter a bundle of supporting documents—the advice of his secretariat, of his advisory council (the *Raad van Indië*) and, often, of his administrative subordinates in the field. Thus, alongside routine reports from Batavia—reports used to fill the various chapters of the annual *Verslagen*—came supporting documents for administrative decisions, among them revisions to regulations governing Chinese residence and the revenue farms. Many of these documents have remained unread until now and are filed permanently with the *mailrapport* (equivalent to a diplomatic pouch) in which they were originally shipped to the Netherlands. Others were taken for study and deliberation, then deposited in separate files, by subject, as the minister or his staff finished with them. The same thing happened to additional materials drawn from the colony at the request of parliament.

Appended to deliberations concerning revenue farms, for example, one finds court documents and colonial intelligence reports detailing the business operations of wealthy Chinese merchants, audits of their plantations and mills, lists of their real estate holdings, notarial acts giving the names of their *kongsi* partners (and their respective shares in, say, an opium farm), and, now and then, descriptions of their private wealth—such as the gems and betel boxes treasured by reclusive peranakan women. Although to the modern researcher the archive yields its data unsystematically, it does so abundantly.

Even so, Dutch preoccupation with fiscal matters leaves vast areas unexplored. Some of these areas may be approached in unofficial Dutch sources, colonial newspapers and magazines, plus books offering sketches, memoirs, fiction, and polemics—although here, too, economic matters often prevail. The Chinese appear regularly, for example, in the *Indisch Weekblad voor het Recht*, the Indies lawyers' trade paper that reported precedent-setting cases. Indeed, this is a unique source of published information about the inner workings of Chinese business partnerships—those that had dissolved, that is.[7] From newspapers, too, the fragments one gathers are more often than not economic—advertisements for this *toko* or that, and announcements like this one from the *Javansch Courant*, December 10, 1872: "Ho Tjienio, wife of Tan Tjong Toen, declared bankruptcy on December 6, 1872." But newspapers sometimes reported other news: marriages, deaths, grand events, and crimes involving the leading Chinese. From two stray notices in 1864 one learns, for example, that Be Biauw Tjoan contributed 55 guilders to a school for Chinese orphan boys in Semarang and that he owned rice warehouses in Surabaya. (The latter had been robbed.)[8]

Dutch novels, sketches, and "investigative reports" provide glimpses into aspects of Chinese social life and behavior unrecorded elsewhere. But because they were written either for the amusement of their fellow Dutch or for their edification—more often than not the latter—they tend to emphasize the extravagant or the scandalous. Some, like M.T.H. Perelaer's *Baboe Dalima* (1886) and Isaac Groneman's *Uit en over Midden Java* (1891) are frankly polemical and reflect sinophobia among the Dutch and fears about the Yellow Peril. Yet it is

---

[7]In issue no. 1331 of 1888, for example, the *Indisch Weekblad van het Recht* took up a civil suit involving ten members of a kongsi that had been formed to manage the opium farm in Batavia, Krawang, and the Lampongs.

[8]*De Locomotief*, November 25, 1864; February 29, 1864.

writers like these who also tell you what people are wearing; take you along to a wedding; or walk you down the main street of Chinatown in a provincial capital, as does Louis Couperus in *The Hidden Force (De stille kracht)* (1900). And it is often from them, as well as from peranakan sources directly, that one can learn something about those in Java's Chinese community who are hardest to find, the women. But keep in mind that Therese Hoven's comment about peranakan ladies more or less says it all, "We rarely see them."[9]

In fact, this is true of most *individuals*. Many appear in my notes only once: Tan Ing Tjan, a convert to Christianity who did not (the news clipping makes a point of remarking) Europeanize his name, died in October 1889.[10] I know nothing more about him. In the same way, the best description of an opium farm auction comes from Semarang; of an opium farm's internal structure, from Madiun; and of the private wealth of a Chinese officer, from Kediri. The fit is never perfect. Yet, building from sources such as these, one can begin to place the Chinese in late nineteenth-century Java.

As far as the Dutch knew, 198,233 Chinese lived in Java in 1878, a little more than half of them men. They were massed heavily in Batavia and its immediate environs and in the north coast cities of Cirebon, Rembang, Surabaya, and Semarang. With a Chinese population of some thirteen thousand, Semarang hosted the second largest community after Batavia and was the commercial gateway opening to Central and East Java. Virtually all residency capitals contained Chinese populations of a few thousand, with communities ranging from several hundred to one or two thousand souls scattered in the district towns and beyond. The exception was the Priangan, whose population of Chinese numbered less than one thousand. In general, the Chinese were more densely concentrated closer to the north coast and the older centers of trade. But by the late 1870s, outside the Priangan, every regency in Java had at least a few hundred, including the eastern frontier residencies of Probolinggo and Besuki.[11]

Altogether the Chinese accounted for only one percent or so of the entire population, a very small minority indeed. Yet no one living in, say, Rembang at the time would have had any trouble finding them or identifying them as Chinese. Chinese men especially were completely conspicuous. Every one of them wore a long braid down his back, the mark of the Manchus that the Dutch also required of their Chinese subjects. (Men and boys shaved the front part of their heads; boys rolled their braids into buns.) Chinese were also required to "dress" like a Chinese. Photographs and paintings show Chinese officers in Mandarin-style gowns and otherwise depict men wearing pajama like garments of loose shirts and robes over wide pants. Thick-soled shoes were also distinctively Chinese.[12] Although some men living in villages with local wives no doubt assimilated to Javanese ways—and a tiny handful, by decree, were made "Dutch" *gelijkgestelden*—generally speaking, there was no mistaking a Chinese male.[13] Although officially lumped together with other Foreign

---

[9]Therese Hoven, *In sarong en kabaai* (Amsterdam: L. J. Veen, 1892), p. 93.

[10]*De Indische Tolk van het Nieuws van den Dag*, October 15, 1889, p. 1.

[11]*Koloniaal Verslag*, 1875, app. A, 1879.

[12]See the photographs and illustrations in Rob Nieuwenhuys (Breton de Nijs), *Tempo Doeloe; Fotografische documenten uit het oude Indië* (Amsterdam: E. Querido, 1973); James Rush, *Opium to Java* ; and Liem, *Riwajat*.

[13]The Dutch were extremely reluctant to give Dutch status to Asians. As one member of the *Raad van Indië* noted, "For the cunning Chinese here, Dutch nationality would be a 'cover' [*dekmantel*], just as Christianity is in the Philippines." Memorandum and Advice, *Raad van Indië*, April 17, 1857, filed in the colonial archives in Verbaal no. 22, March 1, 1888.

Orientals—a category that embraced "Arabs," "Moors" and "Bengalis"—in practice, Chinese were treated as a special group. They lived under the authority of their own officers and enjoyed a mixed legal status: in criminal and civil matters they were subject to codes and procedures for Natives; in commercial ones, those for Europeans. At court, Chinese officers sat prominently by to advise the Dutch judge.

Every city or town of consequence had its own Chinese quarter *(patjinan)* and the Chinese were generally required to reside there. These neighborhoods were often set off with ornamental gates and were characterized by crowded streets of shop-houses, temples, and the family compounds of the better off. (As an observer of Semarang's patjinan remarked in 1850, "The tasteful home and pretty gardens of the Chinese Captain are worth a look.")[14] Although a few Chinese were exempted from living in them, and others took advantage of lax vigilance here and there, these official ghettos gave the community a clear spatial focus in each city and town. They were places apart to Javanese and Dutch alike, where sounds and smells, the shape of buildings, and the pace and habits of daily life were strange. In smaller towns, too, the Chinese tended to live in clusters, probably in or near a clutch of buildings just off the *alun-alun*, including a few provision shops and the local opium store, pawnhouse, and bordello. These city neighborhoods and small-town clusters were the centers of Chinese life and commerce on Java, and to the Javanese they must have seemed something like beehives: busy and dangerous havens, full of honey, from which swarms of menacing but useful intruders fanned out daily in a relentless, apparently instinctual, quest for livelihood.

It was the intensity and variety of this quest for livelihood that most thoroughly marked the Chinese, for they were everywhere "material man." As people of commerce in Java they were not unique, of course; Javanese, Dutch, Eurasians, and others, to one degree or another, also had a hand in the economy. The Dutch dominated large-scale importing and exporting, the heights of the European banking sector, and other activities where industrial acumen or privileged access to government concessions gave them an edge, as in railroad building. Although already losing their traditional hold, Javanese merchants still carried on in the tobacco and textile industries and, on a small scale, in many others. Village men and women who provided commodities for market and engaged in petty trade were legion.[15] But where the economy was concerned, the Chinese were ubiquitous and essential. Sooner or later everyone doing business in Java had to do business with a Chinese—from the Dutch planter needing wagons and tools to the Javanese villager with fruits and eggs to sell. So dependent were Europeans and other urbanites on Chinese-provided goods and services that daily life itself—as they came to know and enjoy it—was impossible without them. Moreover, except for a few schoolmasters, Java's Chinese men—and an untold number of the peranakan and indigenous women to whom they were married or related—were almost all active in the money economy.

From top to bottom, commerce marked the Chinese. They were shippers, warehousemen, and labor contractors; builders and repairmen; and suppliers of *all things* to town and country. They were tinsmiths, leather tanners, and furniture makers. They bought and sold real estate, worked timber concessions, and speculated in the plantation economy. They organized the manufacture of batik and tobacco products. (In 1877, villagers in Wonosobo

---

[14]P. Bleeker, "Fragmenten eener Reis over Java: Reis langs de Noordkust van Midden-Java," *Tijdschrift van Nederlandsch-Indië* 1 (1850): 18.

[15]On batik, see Christine Dobbin, "From Revenue Farmers to Entrepreneurs: The Chinese in the Javanese Textile Industry, 1870–1939." Author's collection. Typescript, n. d.

still remembered the names of the Chinese who some seventy years before had taught them how to cultivate tobacco.)[16] The Chinese brought the products of village farmers to market—rice, sugar, indigo, cotton, pepper, coconuts, cacao, and soybeans, fruits, ducks, chickens, and eggs. They milled rice, tapioca, cotton and sugar; processed *kapok* and copra and castor oil; and manufactured *tahu* and soy sauce. (Investigators for the *Welvaart Onderzoek* found fifty Chinese-run *kecap* "factories" in Surabaya.)[17] And, aside from their own wares, they supplied indigenous vendors with goods like gambir, salt, *trasi*, and cooking oil for the village trade. As opium farmers they brought opium to everyone; and as, for instance, "water buffalo farmers" they took in fees for slaughtering animals and, on the side, did a brisk business in hides. Those Chinese who acted as officials were not only merchants but Java's biggest and richest entrepreneurs.

Chinese merchants, shopkeepers, and petty traders were also often the first source for loans and credit and certainly the last. Most of Java's day-to-day banking was in their hands. Most of this activity occurred *within* the Chinese community, but Dutch and *priyayi* officials also borrowed heavily from them—loans were provided on easy terms in return for privileges and favors. In the rural economy, Chinese loans to village farmers and petty hawkers fueled the trade of village commodities for store-bought things: threads and yarns, knives, scissors, mirrors. These debts compromised the Dutch: they bent the priyayi to Chinese interest; and they bound the peasant to the Chinese peddler (and his patrons elsewhere), who offered cash and goods on credit secured by the upcoming harvest. Debt, in fact, was fundamental to the Chinese economy, inside and out. Alongside employment giving and the official status of Chinese officers, debt was a decisive variable in placing each individual on his or her step in the pyramidlike formations of patrons and clients that formed the invisible skeleton of the community.[18]

This skeleton took the shape it did in part because of certain distinctive features of the Chinese community: first, the prominent role of trade in the Chinese economy, which facilitated a division into a chain of credit-giving/debt-paying patrons and clients; second, the place within it of economically rooted peranakan Chinese families, on the one hand, and a steady flow of newcomers from China on the other. (Chinese *singkeh*, as the newcomers were known, naturally sought jobs among their own people, gravitating first to those with similar surnames and home districts. In any case, upon arrival, singkeh would immediately have been steered to the Chinese quarter and the office of the Chinese officers, where connections could be made. They needed a patron quickly; without a job they could be sent home.)[19] But some elements of its structure were uniquely tied to the Dutch colonial household on Java and the *official* role of the Chinese within it, namely, as revenue farmers.

---

[16] *Mindere Welvaart Report: Landbouw* 1: 152.

[17] *Mindere Welvaart Report: Inlandsch Handel en Nijverheid* 4: 130.

[18] The role of credit in the Javan Chinese economy is discussed extensively in contemporary documents. The relationships connecting petty traders to "big men" are also described. Moreover, some detailed information about the dynamics of these debt relationships as they related to the Chinese pecking order comes from Dutch accounts of opium farmers who, in crisis, attempted to cover debts to the state by calling in *their* debts. However, as I have remarked elsewhere, it was T'ien Ju-k'ang's study of the Chinese in Sarawak that showed me how debt (and not simply monetary debt) disciplined relationships of this kind, that is, through Chinese officer-dominated chains of patrons and clients. T'ien Ju-k'ang, *The Chinese of Sarawak: A Study of Social Structure*, London School of Economics and Political Science, Monographs on Social Anthropology (London: 1953).

[19] J. E. Albrecht, *Soerat Ketrangan dari pada hal kaadaan Bangsa Tjina di Negri Hindia Olandia* (Batavia: Albrecht en Rusche, 1890), p. 5.

As revenue farmers, Chinese merchants were a critical part of the state apparatus. They had been so since the earliest days of Dutch East India Company (VOC) enterprise on Java. Over the centuries, the Chinese had delivered vast sums to the colonial treasury through an array of franchised or "farmed out" monopolies. By the late nineteenth century, some of these had fallen by the wayside, notably the market farm, abolished in 1851 in an attempt to weaken the hold of the Chinese on the rural economy. Of those that remained, the opium farm was paramount. In most of Java, the others—such as the pig- and cattle-slaughtering farms—were invariably subordinate to it, not by official design but as a logical byproduct of the way the Chinese economy was shaped by Holland's revenue-farming policies.

As noted, Holland required most of its Chinese subjects to live in ghettos. To move beyond them, traders needed passes approved by Chinese officers and invigilated locally by priyayi officials. Because of their large and apparently irreplaceable contributions to the colonial treasury, however, revenue farms were accorded privileged access to Java's rural markets. Farm employees were exempt from the pass and residency rules. They were also permitted, with a wink and a nod from local officials, to use coercive techniques to protect the farmer's tax-gathering monopolies. In a typical residency, an opium farmer's formal organization included several dozen official stores and a small army of Chinese salesmen, clerks, and chemists; their work was augmented informally by hundreds of Chinese and indigenous vendors who bore opium (and other products) into the villages. Moreover, teams of spies and toughs hired by the farm stood by everywhere to muscle aside black-market dealers and otherwise to foster the opium farmer's interests.

These interests were legion. Under the protective umbrella of the opium farm, members of the farm organization and other clients of the farmers and their kongsi partners traded comprehensively throughout the farm territory. Whenever possible, opium farmers gained control of the minor revenue farms as well. In the hands of their (Chinese) competitors they could be conduits for opium smuggling and other unwelcome commercial competition. In such a system, opium farmers' positions within the commercial life of a residency could be quite domineering, all the more so when the opium farmers and/or his kongsi partners were Chinese officers. And they nearly always were. For these reasons, in much of Java the pyramids of patrons and clients that provided the internal structure of the Chinese economy (and that also established the pecking order of social position in the community) were either linked to the opium farm itself and headed by the farmer and his partners—the dominant constellation—or represented *competing* pyramids (or fragments thereof) headed by the farmers' competitors, that is, alternative or potential opium farmers.[20]

Liem Thian Joe tells us that the peranakan Chinese called the opium farm auctions "the battle of the kings." It was not being an opium farmer per se that made men like Be Biauw Tjoan and Ho Yam Lo "kings," however, or for that matter, being named Chinese captain or major. What really made them big men was their position as paramount patrons of central Java's great Chinese commercial networks.

But this power was based, in part, on the colonial system itself. Holland's revenue-farming policies limited the number of key players and made it possible for a *few* men to achieve great wealth and influence. Enjoying it meant *to be part* of the system, to accept the basic premise of power on which it was based—Dutch preeminence. And it also meant, wherever possible, manipulating the state's institutions and its agents to personal advantage. This was important because, officially speaking, many farm activities were in violation

---

[20]There were no opium farms per se in the Priangan or Bantam, although the farmer for Batavia was permitted to operate a few stores in Bantam.

of the state's laws and policies. Almost no real revenue farm adhered strictly to the rules and regulations the Dutch set for it; a farmer's agents in the countryside often went beyond the powers allotted them by the state, for example, in collecting debts and fending off competitors roughly. And, to speak of more flagrant illegalities, opium farmers routinely imported opium to Java independently of the state; that is, they smuggled. To protect these activities the Chinese placed themselves as close as possible to local Dutch officials and to the priyayi administrators of the countryside. The most advantageous place to be, and the safest, was *close to power*.

And so one witnesses a pattern of behavior among the peranakan "kings" characteristic of a dependent elite, constantly and conspicuously currying the favor of other elites: the Dutch, who were more powerful than themselves and the Javanese, who were more numerous and permanent. The friendly loans mentioned were but a small aspect of this behavior. There were also overt gifts, covert bribes, and a variety of subtler subsidies for officials and their establishments. For regents *(bupati), wedana*, and other priyayi officials, there was free opium, plus bonuses for good work done on behalf of the farm or other Chinese interests—money to shore up an official's own small retinue of client subordinates and to meet obligations to the official's many needy relatives. Chinese obsequiousness to Dutch officials was the subject of caricature by the Dutch themselves, and the lavish entertainments at which Dutch guests were feted are a matter of record. (In 1866, a senior official from Batavia issued this warning to residents, "I have pointed out elsewhere how cautious it behooves one to be in regard to the goodwill and obligingness of Chinese Officers or wealthy Chinese, who in Java . . . are everywhere involved in the opium farm.")[21]

Aside from strategies of this kind—part of the dance of collaboration in which the relationship between official rules and actual behavior was negotiated among local elites—it is worth emphasizing that the Chinese were also *physically* close to power. They were concentrated in the provincial capitals, which were the centers of Dutch administration, and in the regional towns, where only a few Dutch were posted and where the priyayi prevailed. The seats of bupati, wedana, and assistant wedana were also the sites of opium stores and other Chinese-run enterprises—the smaller the town, the more obvious the connection. Moreover, court cases related to violations of the revenue farms reveal that collaboration between opium farm spies and police agents of local priyayi was commonplace in village Java. From top to bottom, the Chinese were close to power and nested within the power structure.

At the same time, however, Chinese activities intersected broadly and regularly with Java's criminal world. Interdicting competitors in the countryside required working with specialists, as, of course, did opium smuggling. Moreover, certain shadowy realms on the fringes of polite society—those of prostitutes, itinerant entertainers, and other denizens of the "opium world"—were also part of the Chinese place in nineteenth-century Java. Other groups entered these realms selectively and only episodically, but the Chinese moved pragmatically within them day by day. Connections like these made Chinese friends useful as conspirators—Dutch novels of the times depict both Dutch and Javanese going to them for secret undertakings[22]—but connections also tainted the Chinese and lent an aura of corruption to their all-too-conspicuous wealth.

---

[21]Circular to Residents, December 31, 1866, no. 5081, filed in Verbaal Kabinets Geheim, no. 17/C, January 27, 1869, colonial archives.

[22]See P. A. Daum (Maurits), *Ups and Downs of Life in the Indies* [1892], trans. Elsje Qualm Sturtevant and Donald W. Sturtevant (Amherst: University of Massachusetts Press, 1987); and Isaac Groneman, *Een Ketjoe-geschiedenis, Vorstenlanden Toestanden II* (Dordrecht: J. P. Revers, 1887).

Aside from the penniless newcomer, ever present, there were plenty of small-scale vendors and tradespeople among the Chinese whose incomes were modest. Some never rose above menial occupations; others toiled all their lives in small shops for small profits. Only a few achieved the affluence of the peranakan upper class, the *cabang atas*. Those who did, however, lived ostentatiously in grand "villas" with specially designed gardens, as did the Chinese captain mentioned above. They showed off their wealth in lavish parties and in largesse to the community. They were borne from place to place in fine horse-drawn carriages; and when they walked about at night, attendants bearing lamps and torches walked with them. Among the Dutch this wealth was a subject of wonder and notoriety. How much more so it must have been to the Javanese, to whom the local Chinese shopkeeper, standing amidst his myriad wares, seemed to possess so many things. Even the lowly peddler always had money.

A Javanese of the late nineteenth century might well have said, "The Chinese are everywhere *with* us, but they are not *of* us"—all the more so because the distinctions born of legal status, dress, residence, occupation, and wealth were reinforced by those of culture itself. Peranakan culture was by its very nature one of constant blending and change: formed on the one side by a steady flow of men from China and on the other by indigenous or peranakan wives and concubines. By the nineteenth century, the pattern of its formation seems to have stabilized: Chinese men adhered self-consciously to a sense of Chineseness as manifested in custom, dress, and language and, in the upper reaches, paired in marriage their peranakan sons to peranakan daughters of suitable status. Although few peranakan really spoke Chinese, their Malay was evidently interlaced with Hokkien words and spoken with a "Chinese" accent.[23] Merchants, kongsi, and Chinese officers identified themselves by special Chinese names and ideographs, and shopkeepers hung from the front of their shops cloth banners decorated with lucky Chinese characters. New arrivals from Amoy kept the Hokkien dialect alive at a certain rudimentary level among the men. Indeed, the fact that until later in the century most singkeh were of Hokkien origin gave the Chineseness of peranakan culture a certain homogeneity and facilitated taking in newcomers. For singkeh, the vitality of the peranakan-dominated economy and its internal structure based on a patronage hierarchy—offering upward mobility to the talented and enterprising—made assimilation to peranakan society attractive and in many parts of Java the only practical course.

The peranakan "big men," opium farmer-Chinese officers, set a tone of Chineseness for the community at large. At the lunar New Year they sponsored great celebrations and distributed alms. They endowed and maintained temples. (Tan Hong Yan and Be Ing Tjioe, for example, together refurbished the temple Tay Kak Sie in Semarang; a few years later when their sons Tan Tjong Hoay and Be Biauw Tjoan were named Chinese captains, the ceremonies of investiture were held there.)[24] They also patronized Chinese arts. Some brought architects and master craftsmen from China to build their homes and gardens and hired Chinese musicians to perform, alongside Javanese gamelan players, for their private pleasure. Some of them sent sons to live in the ancestral homeland and otherwise fostered a connection with China by acts of charity. China's leaders were aware of this and rewarded generous donations with Mandarin titles and honorific robes and hats. In 1873, for example, Be Biauw Tjoan was named Mandarin Fourth Class by the emperor of China for his contri-

---

[23]The peranakan accent is commented on in the Javanese short story "Tjandoe Peteng Toewin Panjegahipoen," which, from the context, was written no later than 1903. In G. W. J. Drewes, *Eenvoudig Hedendaagsch Javaansch Proza* (Leiden: E. J. Brill, 1946), pp. 61–71.

[24]Liem, *Riwajat*, pp. 104–7, 109, 116.

butions of money and goods to war-ravaged Fukien [Hok Yan] province.[25] No less than Li Hung-chang approached the Indies government in 1891 asking it to confer special status upon its overseas "Mandarins."[26]

Private education was another link to things Chinese. Dutch officials counted 190 Chinese schools in Java in 1887. In them, some 3,452 pupils learned Chinese bookkeeping and memorized "the most important" ideographs. Among Semarang's schoolmasters were degree holders from China—or, more likely, failed degree candidates. But observers noted that such rote learning provided little understanding of the language; moreover, girls rarely attended such schools.[27]

Indeed, in this show of peranakan Chineseness the role of women was largely ornamental. Liem complains that peranakan men of the times paid little attention to their daughters, so the girls were influenced exclusively by the female side of the family, that is, by their peranakan or indigenous mothers and grandmothers and by indigenous servants. That these women spoke no Chinese meant that both daughters and sons spoke Javanese or Malay as their mother tongue—one reason that command of Chinese atrophied so quickly from one generation to the next. Indigenous wives of Chinese men wore local clothing; so, too, did peranakan women, who preferred *sarong* and *kebaya*. (Ladies of the cabang atas, however, complemented their finery with silks and other adornments from China, one reason, as Skinner has remarked, that "no one could mistake the Peranakan ensemble for the Javanese.")[28] In other ways as well, Liem tells us, women of the Chinese community adopted local custom, as in filing their teeth and chewing betel. It should be noted that outside the cabang atas, where women seem to have lived in seclusion, women very likely worked alongside their men in shops and stalls, providing them with critical links to their customers. (This is especially interesting in light of the prominent role of Javanese and Sundanese women in rural marketing generally.)

Thus did the Chinese community form, and re-form, itself in each generation between the self-conscious Chineseness of its men and the Java-ness of its women. By the late nineteenth century, this complex social chemistry had long since yielded a distinct culture. Like the society itself—poised between Dutch and native, city and countryside, legality and illegality—its place in Java was also one in between, to the Javanese and other indigenes at once familiar and strange.

The evolving peranakan culture was an important source of cohesion among the Chinese of Java, reinforcing other ties of presumed kinship among Hokkien, of special legal status, and of the mechanisms of social control built into the Chinese economy and exaggerated by the Chinese officer system and government revenue farming. But Java was changing rapidly in the late nineteenth century, subjecting the cohesion of the community to new strains. Ironically, rising prosperity was one of these. The opening of Java to private enterprise in 1870, the year after the Suez Canal opened, set off a fresh round of development on the island. European planters opened new lands to commercial agriculture for sugar, tobacco, and coffee. This expansion was accompanied by government-sponsored schemes to build roads and railroads, bridges, dikes, irrigation channels, and harbor works. The Chinese moved quickly to take up new opportunities, penetrating regions of the interior now

---

[25] *De Indier*, December 6, 1873, p. 1039.

[26] Minister of colonies to the governor general, January 7, 1892, no. 24/43, filed in Verbaal Kabinets Geheim, no. 24/43, January 7, 1892, colonial archives.

[27] *Koloniaal Verslag*, 1889, p. 120.

[28] Skinner, "Java's Chinese Minority," p. 257.

awakening to enterprise and moving in larger numbers to frontier territories in the East Hook.[29] Many of the richest became planters themselves; Chinese outnumbered Europeans in acquiring long-term land leases from the Javanese.[30] Otherwise, Chinese merchants supplied the nuts and bolts to carry out infrastructure projects and contracted with the Dutch to build warehouses, haul produce, and provision construction crews and plantation laborers. The vast numbers of people now abandoning villages to provide the raw muscle for all this expansion—and who earned wages in money to do so—swelled the ranks of opium smokers and profits to opium farmers. As word of this boon spread to south China, increasing numbers of men made their way to Java, raising the number of singkeh seeking places within the peranakan-dominated economy. Of these new arrivals, a growing number were Hakka and other non-Hokkien.

The massive rural depression of the mid-1880s knocked the wind out of this boom and strained the Chinese community. Losses to Chinese-run revenue farms were catastrophic to the peranakan elite, many of whom lost their farms and their fortunes; this in turn provoked a partial breakdown along Java's Chinese patron-client chains. Very likely, competition among them for the spoils of the countryside also became rougher because the same years were accompanied by a rising tide of complaints by Dutch observers of Chinese cheating, usury, and racketeering. For newcomers there were no patrons, and as singkeh now scrambled to wrest a living from money-scarce Java they found the peranakan authority structure—so close to power—an impediment to survival. In Yogyakarta, in 1889, they rebelled against it.[31] Such behavior made the "singkeh flood" visible to the Dutch. Seeing it amidst other evidence of Chinese danger to the colony, a few of them raised the flag of Yellow Peril and led an anti-Chinese campaign that resulted, a few years later, in dismantling the government revenue farms.

The full impact of all this on the Chinese community was not immediate. Java's economy recovered in the wake of the mid-1880s crisis and so did that of the peranakan. Many of the major opium farmers did not recover. The losers were replaced by competitors from within the cabang atas, the most astute and successful of whom was Oei Tiong Ham. Java's Chinese-run opium farms were dismantled gradually, beginning in 1894; by 1905 there were none on Java. The minor revenue farms were replaced more or less at the same time. These changes comported with the Ethical perception that Chinese business practices were a cause of poverty among the Javanese. In tune with this, the enforcement of residence and pass regulations was especially harsh in those years.

Java's Chinese community was, therefore, under duress as it entered the twentieth century and was deprived of an institution essential to the structure of its economy and to its social cohesion. As noted, the real power of Chinese officers rested upon their position as senior patrons of the peranakan economy. As the huge farm-based patronage pyramids headed by them fragmented and broke down in the late 1890s and early 1900s, the authority of the officers could not be sustained by Dutch-conferred titles alone. (Soon, bedecked in Dutch military-style costumes with ribbons and braids, they would became symbols of unquestioning deference.) These changes undermined the authority of the peranakan elite as cultural arbiters as well, all the more so as new waves of non-Hokkien singkeh arrived in the colony and formed local communities independent of the peranakan, communities with

---

[29] See C. Baks, "De Chinezen in Oostelijk Java, een demografisch onderzoek naar de penetratie over de periode 1815–1930," Sterling Memorial Library, Yale University, Typescript, 1962.

[30] See *Koloniaal Verslag*, 1885, p. 77.

[31] See Isaac Groneman, *Uit en over Midden-Java* (Zutphen: W. J. Thieme en Cie., 1891), pp. 297–306.

wholly different standards for Chineseness. For almost the first time, Chinese women joined Chinese men in Java to form "pure" Chinese families. (A similar "pure" community was now forming among the Dutch as well. Both were called *totok*.)

In the 1880s, the peranakan had begun exploring new standards of Chineseness themselves—judged at least by the sudden popularity of Confucian primers and popular Chinese novels published in Malay. Alienated from and unattracted to the low-class Chineseness of the totok, many peranakan looked instead to China for models. Some joined the Confucian revival and helped to form the Tiong Hoa Hwe Koan in 1900 and other "modern" Chinese organizations. At the same time, peranakan were becoming attuned to winds of modernity blowing from the West. They began learning Dutch in earnest (and English). They cut off their braids and began to wear Western-style clothing, some of them even before it was permitted. And many of them began to gravitate to the more genteel professions, abandoning the hurly-burly of commerce, a realm that was gradually overtaken by the totok. Oei Tiong Ham's legendary success was an exception among the peranakan.

In short, as the new century begins, we find Java's Chinese making a new place for themselves. It was a more fragmented place, because the community itself was becoming very rapidly diverse. And it was a more ambiguous place, especially for peranakan now torn between the attractions of Western modernity, to be learned from the Dutch, and their self-conscious identity as Chinese. Most of all, it was a more vulnerable place, for the Chinese were no longer close to power. Even though the Chinese officer system survived officially until the early 1930s, long before then—indeed, from the turn of the century—peranakan and totok alike needed to mobilize themselves in new ways. They did so successfully. New Chinese organizations provoked important reforms—the residence and pass regulations went out; Dutch-Chinese schools came in. But the institutional context in which this transition was accomplished was wholly changed.

The Chinese now faced the state as outsiders. Even after the Dutch departed, half a century later, it remained so. The most calamitous event of the period for Java's Chinese was not their altered status within the colonial state. It was, instead, the coincidence of a powerful wave of sinophobia—prompting the Dutch to dismantle the revenue farms and, in part, to launch the "Ethical Policy"—with the embryonic stages of the Indonesian nationalist movement, a movement whose heirs would build the *new* state and decide who, exactly, was truly Indonesian. And who was not.

A Critical View of the Opium Farmers as Reflected in a *Syair* by Boen Sing Hoo (Semarang, 1889)

Claudine Salmon

Indonesianists are well aware that the opium farm failures of the 1880s were accompanied by an increasingly violent attack upon the farm system by Dutch missionaries, journalists, politicians, and even writers.[1] Among the latter, the most important were M. Th. H. Perelaer, a retired military man who served for some twenty-five years in the Indies and Dr. Isaac Groneman, who spent several years in Yogya as permanent physician to the sultan and was well known for his anti-Chinese feelings. Perelaer wrote a political novel called *Baboe Dalima* (Dalima the nanny, 1886).[2] It criticized the opium farm, which Perelaer regarded as a scandalous source of income for Hollanders. Although it has never been regarded as a masterpiece of literature, the novel made a considerable impact and was translated into English in 1888. Groneman wrote a novel entitled *Een Ketjoegeschiedenis* (A bandit's tale 1887). It was less ambitious than *Baboe Dalima* and was based on the author's intimate knowledge of Javanese society. The villains were, of course, the Chinese farmers and their agents.

Historians have done very little to investigate the literature in Malay that emanated from the Indonesian Chinese of the time to know whether writers among them may have reflected upon the problem. A very attractive *syair*, which at first glance may be regarded as a symbolic poem for the characters are represented by animals, is about the auction of the shares of the opium farms held by the Hoo (usually written Ho) family in Semarang, which

---

I would like to thank Henri Chambert Loir and Denys Lombard for their comments and James Siegel who polished the English of the text.

[1] See James R. Rush, "Opium Farms in Nineteenth-century Java: Institutional Continuity and Change in Colonial Society, 1860–1910," (Ph.D. diss., Yale University, 1977), chap. 9. An edited version has just been published under the title: *Opium to Java, Revenue Farming and Chinese Enterprise in Colonial Indonesia 1860–1910* (Ithaca N.Y.: Cornell University Press, 1990). For a different view about opium among French writers, see Chantal Descours-Gatin, in "L'opium dans la société coloniale: Thème littéraire et réalité sociale,"*Opium et finances coloniales: La formation de la Régie Générale de l'Opium en Indochine 1860–1914* (Thèse de 3ème cycle, Université de Paris 7, 1987), chap. 3.

[2] See Karin Evers, "De opiumroman *Baboe Dalima* (1886) van M.T.H. Peralaer" Indische Letteren jrg 1, no. 2 (June 1986): pp. 53-65.

took place on July 23, 1889, soon after the Ho partnership declared bankruptcy. The poem was written soon after and was published in Semarang on August 28, 1889. The author, who signed with the chop of his firm, Boen Sing Hoo, or "Literary Flourishing," in effect wanted to criticize the world of the opium farmers, of which he had intimate knowledge. It is, apparently, the first critical poem of its kind ever published in book form in Java. This piece of *littérature engagée* reveals what a peranakan writer could say in spite of the political pressure emanating from the opium farmers, on the one hand, and the limits imparted by the censorship of the time, on the other.

Boen Sing Hoo: Real Name, Tan Tjien Hwa

Little is known about Tan Tjien Hwa. He was the owner of a bookshop in Tjapkauwking (off Gang Pinggir) in the Chinese district of Semarang and was an agent for books published in Batavia—especially those printed by Albrecht and Rusche—and eventually in other cities of the Dutch Indies.[3] His profits must have been very limited because his name never appeared among the donors who contributed to the construction or repair of temples in Semarang.[4] He had a good knowledge of Chinese and Malay for he was among the first translators of Chinese novels into Malay. His first renditions in book form appeared in 1885. He translated no less than eight novels, which appeared between 1885 and 1891. Some of these have been reprinted up to six times, such as his *Tjerita dahoeloe kala di negri Tjina terpoengoet dari tjerita-an boekoe menjanji-an, Sam Pik—Ing Taij* (An ancient story set in China and adapted from a ballad called (Liang) Shanbo yu (Zhu) Yingtai), which was printed for the last time in 1922.[5] He apparently received better schooling in Chinese than in Malay. When he translated this story of Liang Shanbo and Zhu Yingtai, he made some attempts to retell it in verse, but after a few stanzas he admitted that the task was beyond him.

Apart from his writing in verse, *Boekoe Sair Binatang*, (Poem of the animals), which will be discussed here, it seems that at least one other work may be attributed to him—an anonymous poem entitled *Boekoe Sjairnja jang maha moelia Sri Padoeka Kandjeng Toewan Soesoehoenan di Solo dateng ka Semarang pada tanggal 10 Juni 1903*, which is about the visit to Semarang of the Susuhunan of Solo, Paku Buwono X, from June 10 to June 16, 1903. The poem was published in Semarang by Hap Sing Kong Sie in the same year. The last lines read: "Who the writer of this *syair* is is not said clearly/He works for the newspaper *Warna Warta*/And lives in Gang Pinggir in the city of Semarang."[6] Tan Tjien Hwa worked as a

---

[3] At the end of his translation of a short story taken from the *Jin gu qiguan* (Wonders new and old), which appeared in 1887, Tan Tjien Hwa (also written Tan Tjin Hwa and Tan Tjin Hoa) in an advertisement for his bookshop states that he will provide a list of already completed translations from the Chinese, free of charge: "Ini boekoe, bole dapet beli di Toko-Boekoe Tan Tjien Hwa, Tjapkauwking-Semarang. Begitoe djoegak ada sedia lain-lainnja boekoe tjerita Tjina njang telah tamat. Daftar boekoe kaloek di mintak boleh dapet pertjoema."

[4] Two of his relatives (cousins or brothers) were Tan Tjien Teng, who in 1805 was among the chief donors who contributed money to the repair of the pavilion in front of the Sam Po Tong or San Bao Cave, giving eight "old cash" and Tan Tjien Goan, who in 1890 gave ten guilders, a very moderate amount, for the repair of the main temple in town, the Tay Kak Sie, or Dajuesi. See Wolfgang Franke, Claudine Salmon, and Anthony Siu, *Chinese Epigraphic Materials in Indonesia*, vol. 2, *Java* (Singapore: South Seas Society, in press).

[5] For a complete list of Boen Sing Hoo's translations, see Claudine Salmon, *Literature in Malay by the Chinese of Indonesia: A Provisional Annotated Bibliography* (Paris: Éditions de la Maison des Sciences de l'Homme, études insulindiennes-archipel 3, 1981), pp. 155–57.

[6] Soeda tamat Sjairnja Soesoehoenan Soerakarta,
Siapa pengarangnja tida terseboet njata,
Pembantoenja soerat kabar *Warna-Warta*,
Tinggal Gang Pinggir Semarang kota. (p. 96)

journalist for the daily *Warna Warta*,[7] launched in Semarang ca. 1902 by Kwa Wan Hong (b. 1861), the manager of the N. V. Drukkerij en Handel in Shrijfbehoeften Hap Sing Kong Sie,[8] and edited by J. C. Doppert. Although meant to be a paper for all the *bangsa*, or "nations," of the Indies and commercially oriented with eight pages of advertisements to only two of news and articles, it nonetheless proclaimed itself the "unofficial organ of the Tiong Hoa Hwe Koan (Chinese Association)."[9]

Tan Tjien Hwa, as well as Kwa Wan Hong, were among the people who initiated the Tiong Hoa Hwe Koan in Semarang.[10] In 1904, the year it was founded, Kwa Wan Hong had the position of first secretary, whereas Tan Tjien Hwa had that of commissaris, and Lieutenant Ho Sie Tik, a grandson of Ho Ijam Lo, was its president.[11] After this date, no information about Tan Tjien Hwa remains. These data, limited though they are, still provide some insight into the preoccupations of the author. It is obvious that he was concerned with the education of peranakan children as well as with reforms that he felt had to be implemented to improve the morality of his community. In view of this, one may better understand why he was so critical of the opium farmers.

The Boekoe Sair Binatang

The complete title of the first edition of this poem in book form reads *Boekoe Sair Binatang: Landak, Koeda dan Sapi, terkarang dalem bahasa Melajoe rendah* (Poem about animals: Porcupine, horse and ox, written in Low Malay); it was published in Semarang by the firm of P. A. van Asperen van der Velde and is thirty-five pages long. A second printing was published in Batavia in 1895 by the translator and publisher (*yang poenja*) Tjiong Hok Long (1847–1917) on the press of Albrecht and Rusche. According to a note on the cover, this reprint was, at the request of the author, dated December 16, 1893, which means that the book had continued to be in demand.[12] But it is not clear why the reprint did not appear until 1895.

The edition used in this study is forty-four pages. The cover bears a new title that further clarifies the intention of the author: "*Sair Sindiran*" *tatkala lelang restantnja pacht madat tahon 1889 diantara meninggalnja Pachter "Hoo Ijam Lo" di Semarang. Tjerita "Gadjah poetih Radja di Oetan*" (Satirical poem about the auction of the remnants of the opium farms after the death of the farmer Hoo Ijam Lo in Semarang. Story of the white elephant, king of the forest). The original poem consisted of 230 stanzas (pp. 3–41). Two addenda of 7 stanzas each were

---

[7] Liok An Tjoe, "Drukkerij Tionghoa jang paling toea di Semarang," *Sin Po* (weekly), p. 19; no. 963, Sept. 13, 1941, p. 18.

[8] The N. V. Hap Sing Kong Sie, which had its headquarters in Gang Pinggir, had been founded in 1901. This newspaper was to compete with the *Slompret Melajoe*, which was published by the firm of Van Dorp. Kwa Wan Hong, whose father was a physician born in China, became a big entrepreneur in Central Java. See Liok An Tjoe, "Drukkerij Tionghoa," pp. 18–19; Claudine Salmon, "L'édition chinoise dans le monde insulindien," *Archipel* 32 (1986): 130.

[9] See *Warna Warta*, no. 335, June 6, 1904, and no. 137, June 21, 1910; quoted from Achmad Adam, "The Vernacular Press and the Emergence of Modern Indonesian Conciousness 1855–1913" (Ph.D. diss., London, School of Oriental and African Studies, 1984), p. 151.

[10] According to Nio Joe Lan, *Riwajat 40 taon dari Tiong Hoa Hwe Koan Batavia, 1900–1939* (Batavia: Tiong Hoa Hwe Koan, 1940), p. 50, in June 1903, Kwa Wan Hong himself wrote a letter to the committee running the THHK in Jakarta to inquire about the functioning of the association.

[11] Cf. Liem Thian Joe, *Riwajat Semarang 1416–1931* (Semarang: Ho Kim Yoe, ca. 1933), p. 174.

[12] "Atas permintaän: 'Boen Sing Hoo di Semarang' dengan soerat ddo 16 December 1893 minta akan di tjitak njang kadoewa kali ja itoe: Sair Binatang."

composed later; one entitled *Ankatan Betawi datang kombali* (The group of Batawi came again) (pp. 42–43) is, in fact, a sequel added after another auction held on September 6 of the same year, whereas the other, entitled *Sam Kok* (The Three Kingdoms), is a kind of epilogue (pp. 43–44). The main poem is divided into four parts: the introduction, the presentation of the animals, the auction itself, and a rather stereotyped conclusion.

The Introduction

In the introduction, Boen Sing Hoo provides two interesting comments: the first about the language he uses, which is the unrefined Malay mixed with Javanese spoken in the market in Semarang and the second, about the symbolism of his poem.

Toewan pembatja djangan lah goesar,	Honorable reader, don't be angry,
Sair ini, bahasanja kasar,	The language of this poem is rude,
Melajoe Semarang di dalem pasar,	It is the Malay as spoken in the market in Semarang,
Serta lagi banjak kasasar. (p. 3)	And quite often goes astray.

Then he explains how he will proceed: he does not want to express his thoughts directly, he says, but will represent the characters, "the wealthy people" (*orang berharta*), by animals (*Di oepamaken binatang poenja tjerita*). According to Boen Sing Hoo, the reader will have no difficulty in identifying them because they are all well known in Semarang:

Maski begitoe nanti djadi lah terang,	As it is, it will nevertheless become clear
Sebab namanja, terkenal banjak lah orang,	For many names are well known,
Njang kenal dia, tida lah koerang,	Those who know them are plenty,
Soedah kasoehoer dalem Semarang (p. 3)	They are famous in Semarang.

He even presents his syair like a game, saying that the reader "just has to rack his brain,/Then the jesting will become clear" (*Misti lah tjari dalem pikiran/Baroe lah njata, ini sindiran*, [p. 4]). But at the same time, he is a bit apprehensive of the eventual response of the readers to his satire and he further states:

Djangan Toewan bersakit lah hati,	Please, Sir, don't worry,
Kaloe ada famili terseboet nanti,	If some relatives of yours are mentioned,
Soedah takdirnja *Allah* dan *Goesti*,	This has been decreed by the Almighty,
Djahat dan baik, terkarang misti. (p. 4)	Evil and good must be recorded.

He carefully advises those who may be infuriated or grow sad by discovering some of their relatives' names in the syair not to read it. No doubt, Boen Sing Hoo was a bit afraid of the eventual reprisals of the opium farmers.

Then he invites the reader to proceed to the *Kebupaten*, or regent's residence, to become acquainted with all the fierce animals (*chewan njang garang*) who are seated in a line facing the authorities:

Doedoek berderek kiri dan kanan,	They are seated in a line on the left and right,
Pangkat *Majoor Kapitan* dan *Luitenan*,	Those with the rank of major, captain, and lieutenant,
Orang kaja asal toeroenan,	The wealthy whose ancestors belonged to the elite
Dan orang dagang dalem Petjinan. (p.16)	And the merchants from the Chinese quarter.[13]

---

[13] Boen Sing Hoo does not allude to the fact that the bidders were given alcohol; cf. William Barrington d'Almeida, *Life in Java with Sketches of the Javanese* (London: Hurst and Blackett, 1864), 2: 16–17: "Shortly after our arrival, a carriage drove up, bringing the two assistant Residents of Ngawie and Ponorogo. After kirsch-wasser had been handed round in small glasses, the secretary, as representing the Resident, who was still an invalid, took his seat near the middle of the upper end of the table, the two assistant residents placing themselves on each side of him"; see also, Rush, *Opium Farms*, pp. 31–32: "They (the Dutch authorities) provided legitimate farm

They are waiting for the big business of the day: the sale of this marvelous fruit called "antidote" (*boewah "Penawar"*) which is imported from abroad and enjoyed by many people in Java—for "When you smoke it, the vapor comes out,/Filling your entire body flesh and skin with ease."[14] This auction is for the sale of the "rice fields" (*sawah*) of Semarang, Surakarta, Yogya, and Kedu.

The Animals Face to Face

About forty animals are involved in the auction.[15] Athough Boen Sing Hoo mentions their names one by one, it is clear that what interests him are the various relationships that link the animals into several partnerships, or *koempoelan*. This kind of presentation is particularly instructive because it provides insight into the social life of the peranakan Chinese elite, especially in Central Java. Indeed, several descriptions exist of auctions held in different cities of Java in the 1880s and 1870s[16] and even one from the 1860s,[17] but their European authors were not familiar enough with Chinese society to perceive its social structure and the links that were interwoven at social and economic levels. Perhaps they were also more interested in the auction procedure.[18]

Boen Sing Hoo now presents the animals and, to appraise his portraits more clearly; their real identities will be unveiled simultaneously and comments will be added to allow the twentieth-century reader to perceive the context of the time. Altogether seven partnerships took part in the auction: two from Semarang, Batavia, and Kedu, respectively, and one from Yogyakarta. Of these, only the two from Semarang were really powerful. But before scrutinizing these new rivals, Boen Sing Hoo lingers over the rise and fall of the *Landak*, or "Porcupine," family.

The Defunct Ho Partnership

The defunct partnership run by the "Porcupines" who symbolize the Ho family, was one of the most powerful in Central Java until the death of its founder, Landak Toewa, or Ho Ijam Lo, on June 22, 1888. Unlike the other big opium farmers of the time, Ho Ijam Lo was a self-made entrepreneur: "He did not belong to the aristocracy" (*Landak itoe soewatoe lah chewan/Asalnja lagi boekan bangsawan*, [p. 10]). According to a Dutch report published in the press when he died, Ho Ijam Lo's father owned a small *toko*, or shop, in the Chinese quarter, and Ijam Lo himself started as a cashier for the Dutch firm of Dorrepaal before opening his own shop, presumably in Gang Warung where he then resided. His activities were quite successful, and he easily obtained credit from Dutch firms.[19] His rise may be traced to ca.

---

candidates with free transportation to auction, and at preauction festivities served champagne to loosen the inhibitions of prospective bidders."

[14] "Kaloe di isep, koekoesnja kaloewar/Enakken badan, dalem dan loewar." (p. 6)

[15] See the list in app. 2.

[16] See Rush, *Opium Farms*, p. 31, n. 4, who mentions three descriptions in Dutch, two of which were published in 1872 and the third in 1889.

[17] Barrington d'Almeida, *Life in Java*, 2: 13–22, provides a vivid description of an auction held in Madiun in the early 1860s.

[18] See, for instance, Barrington d'Almeida, *Life in Java*, 2: 22. At the end of his description, he merely says, "I was informed, on good authority, that the Government on that day made as much as a million of rupees."

[19] *De Locomotief*, June 23, 1888. Liem Thian Joe, *Riwajat Semarang*, p. 141. According to the epigraphic material kept in the temples of Semarang, the Ho family was already established in Semarang at the beginning of the nineteenth century. Ho Ijam Lo had a brother or cousin named Ho Hok Lo, who in 1845 contributed 200 guilders to the repair of the Houfu miao and in 1854, 60 guilders for a restoration of the Tay Kak Sie (Dajue si). Ijam Lo made his first and only (?) contribution to the Houfu miao in 1870, giving 80 guilders.

1874 when he started to purchase opium farm leases: "He had been rich for about 15 years,/Until his position became uncertain" (*Ampir 15 tahoen doedoek hartawan,/Kemoedian djadi tida karoewan*, [p. 10]).

Ho Ijam Lo invested the profits earned from his revenue farms in other activities. He had purchased from a Dutchman named Pietermaat the sugar mill of Maron in Probolinggo and held long-term leases on indigo and coffee lands in the district of Pekalongan and rice lands in Semarang.[20] As early as 1876, he built a Western-style residence[21] next to a garden designed by Chinese artists at Gergaji, south of Semarang, and had the idea of developing the hilly area of Candi (further south) into a holiday resort.[22] For this purpose, in 1887 he first constructed a hotel, which was run by a Dutch manager, and decided to pay for the water supply of the whole area of Candi. Boen Sing Hoo only alludes to this last project when he speaks of the flood (of June 17, 1889) that ruptured a dam,[23] a cataclysm that, according to him, was the sign of the fall of the Ho family.[24] Ho Ijam Lo wanted to be considered a philanthropist. As early as 1878, he created a fund to defray the costs of decent funerals for those who could not afford them.[25] Although Boen Sing Hoo does not allude to this fund, he mentions another charitable foundation initiated by Ho Ijam Lo that was inaugurated after his death. It was a kind of dispensary (*roemah obat*) located in Jalan Krangang, opposite his own dwelling, where a Chinese physician, a pharmacist, and their assistants treated the indigent patients without ethnic distinction.[26] A touch of criticism toward Ho Ijam Lo is evident here, when Boen Sing Hoo writes:

---

[20] *De Locomotief*, July 7, 1888; Rush, *Opium Farms*, p. 110.

[21] After the bankruptcy of Ho Tjiauw Ing, the mansion and the garden were purchased by Oei Tiong Ham, who repaired them. His daughter Hui-lan Koo (Madame Wellington Koo, b. 1889), in her memoirs, *An Autobiography, as Told to Mary van Reusselaar Thayer* (New York: Dial Press, 1943) pp. 30–1, provides an interesting description of them: "My father's house in the European quarter was Dutch Colonial in style. . . . A long entrance-drive wound through an ornamented garden filled with quaint rockeries, pergolas, and other fanciful Chinese conceits. The house itself, dazling [sic] silhouette against a background of extravagant tropical trees, spread regardless of space. Its single story, high roofed with moss-gray tiles, was surrounded by a broad verandah. Inside, the huge, high-ceilinged rooms opened onto corridors made wide to coax any errant breeze.

Behind the house was an informal garden shaded by tall trees. . . . Beyond this shady spot stretched a miniature park with a plump little hill in its exact center. Stuck to the top of its grassy slopes, like a candle on a cake was a lone, exceedingly dignified tree.

The park had been laid out by a remarkable Chinese gardener whom my father had discovered on the neighboring island of Sumatra. . . . There were exciting artificial caves and rockeries dotted with dwarf shrubs. Canals threaded through the lawns and were spanned with steep camelbacked bridges, while pools, shallow as saucers, were crowded with goldfish that nibbled lazily at lotus roots." See plates.

[22] According to Liem Thian Joe, *Riwajat Semarang*, p. 150, Ho Ijam Lo was the first Chinese who was permitted to reside in Gergaji. *De Locomotief*, May 5, 1887.

[23] *De Locomotief*, June 25, 1889.

[24]
Landak ini, *Landak* Prawira,	As for Porcupine, Porcupine the Warrior,
Banjak orang tiada lah kira,	Contrary to all expectations,
Alamat datang dengan lah gara,	A sign arrived with a cataclysm,
Aer di sungei bagi segara.	In the river, the water was like a sea.
Lantaran djatoehnja, *Landak* sa'orang,	Because of the fall of the Porcupine,
Bandjir besar dalem *Semarang*,	There was a big flood in Semarang,
Hari "Pektjoen" Langitlah terang,	The day of the Pecun, the sky was clear,
Tida kira aer menjerang," (p. 11)	There was no prospect that the water should flow over.

[25] *De Locomotief*, July 11, 1888, "Een philanthropische Instelling."

[26]
| Pesenan *Landak* njang soeda mati, | According to the late Porcupine's will, |
| *Roemah obat* terboeka misti, | The dispensary had to be opened |

Djoewal obat moerah sekali,	The medicines were sold very cheap,
Separo ter'amal separo di beli,	A part given for free, the other sold,
Hendak perbaik nama kembali,	He wanted a good name in return,
Soepaija tertoeloeng Dewa dan Wali. (p. 13)	So as to be assisted by Gods and Saints.

After the death of Ijam Lo, his son, *Landak moeda*, "Porcupine Junior," or Ho Tjiauw Ing, who had been appointed lieutenant on December 20, 1886, was his sole heir and inherited the farms of Semarang, Yogya, and Kedu. Tjiauw Ing also acquired the farms of Surakarta (on June 29, 1888) and Madiun (on February 3, 1889) after the previous licencees had gone bankrupt, so that he held five farms.[27] He had three main partners. Tikoes, "Rat," or Goei Som Han, was a wealthy merchant, landowner, and entrepreneur in Pandean at Semarang[28] who had worked for Koeda Toewa, "Horse Senior" or Be Biauw Tjoan (an enemy of the Ho as we will see below), before joining Ho Ijam Lo. Gangsa Yogya, "the Goose from Yogya," or Liem Kie Djwan, who since 1883 had been captain and Landak Yogya, "the Porcupine from Yogya," Ho Tjiauw Ing's elder brother Ho Tjiauw Soen,[29] who also resided in Yogya where he had been appointed lieutenant in 1884. For a time, Tjiauw Ing also hired his cousin Ho Tiang Goan to administer his opium farm in Madiun.[30] But for years he had two enemies: one called Lintah, "Leech," who was lieutenant in Semarang, presumably Tjoa Sien Tjing (appointed lieutenant in Sept. 1883 and captain in Dec. 1889), because he was married to a daughter of Koeda Toewa, or Be Biauw Tjoan,[31] the principal enemy of the Ho. When he comes to the fall of Ho Tjiauw Ing and consequently that of his partners,[32] Boen Sing Hoo does not provide a clear explanation.

Boewat toeloeng orang njang tida seperti,	In order to help the indigent,
Tandanja berdjalan baik lah hati." (p. 13)	As a lasting sign of his generosity.

Cf. also *De Locomotief*, July 11, 1888, "Een philanthropische Instelling" and "In die apotheek zullen alle behoeftigen, Chinezen, Europeanen, Arabieren, inlanders, Afrikanen enz. die zulks verlangen, gratis geneeskundige hulp en medicijnen kunnen bekomen." For a comparison with similar private medical institutions in China, see Leung Ki Che, "Organized Medicine in Ming-Qing China: State and Private Medical Institutions in the Lower Yang Zi Region," in *Late Imperial China* 8 (1) (1987): 134–66 (Taipei: Institute of the Three Principles of the People, Academia Sinica).

[27] *De Locomotief*, Nov. 26, 1891.

[28] The tomb of Goei Som Han (Wei Senhan) and his wife, Chen Quanniang, erected by their three sons and eight grandsons, was still in situ in the early 1980s. As for Be Biauw Tjoan (see n. 44), his was erected during the lifetime of Goei Som Han, for it is dated 1885. One of his sons, Goei Keh Pien, was appointed lieutenant in Semarang in November 1884. From another tombstone inscription still in situ in Semarang, it appears that the Goei and the Ho were related by marriage; Wei (Goei) Jingtai, an uncle of Goei Som Han, married a certain He Lanniang (Ho Lan Nio); their tomb is dated 1867. Goei Som Han was at least a third-generation peranakan. His grandfather, Wei Bingyao, was buried in Semarang, and his tomb is dated 1853; cf. Franke, Salmon, Siu, *Chinese Epigraphic Materials*. According to Arnold Wright, ed., *Twentieth Century Impressions of the Dutch Indies*, (London: Lloyd's Greater Britain Publishing Company, 1909), pp. 511–12, the Goei family of Semarang came to Java in the late 1770s.

[29] It seems they were three brothers; the third was possibly Ho Tjiauw Hai, whose name appears among the donors who in 1870 contributed for the repair of the Houfu miao. He only gave four guilders; Ho Ijam Lo gave 80.

[30] Cf. *De Locomotief*, November 26, 1891. Ho Tiang Goan was apparently based in Semarang, for in 1890 he contributed 15 guilders to the repair of the Tay Kak Sie (Da Juesi) and in 1900, 100 guilders for the construction of the Ganfu miao.

[31] Cf. unpublished genealogy of the Be (Ma) family. This source is from Myra Sidharta.

[32] According to the *Bintang Soerabaia*, June 22, 1889, one of his two guarantors, Liem Kie Djwan, even tried to poison himself.

Landak djatoeh di itoe hari,	Porcupine fell that day,
Lantaran *patah*, dia poenja doeri,	His prickles being broken,
Bikin gojangnja lima negeri,	Shaking five lands,
Orang njang kaget di kanan kiri.	The people were afraid all around.
Lima negeri, seloeroeh Dessa,	Five lands including all the villages,
Tanah *Madioen* djoega berasa,	The territory of Madiun also felt it.
Sehandei *Landak*, tida binasa,	Had Porcupine not been exterminated
Terlebieh koewat, dari Raksasa. (p. 12)	He would have been stronger than a giant.

He, nevertheless, gives the impression that the ruin of the Ho had been partly caused by their enemy, the Be family.

Landak bermoesoeh sama si' *Koeda*	Porcupine and Horse have been enemies,
Dari njang Toewa sampe njang moeda,	From the old to the young generation,
Sahingga sekarang, masih lah ada,	Up to now it is still so,
Simpan dendem di dalem dada. (p. 11)	Their hearts are filled with grudges.[33]

This impression is even more clearly expressed in the epilogue, where it is said that for three years Bapanja Saboe (presumably Be Ik Sam)[34] had been smuggling opium into their territory.[35] It is known from Dutch sources that Ho Ijam Lo did support the policy initiated by TeMechelen to control opium smugglers along the northern coast.[36] But elsewhere, Boen Sing Hoo also alludes to the fact that after the death of Ho Ijam Lo, "The management was not satisfying,/The commissioners were not committed enough,/and as a result the name of Ho fell."[37]

---

[33] *Locomotief*, July 26, 1888, in a note entitled "Eene ongepaste aardigheid," reports that because of the bad relations between these two families, Be Biauw Tjoan had decided to organize a nautical race that would start just the day of Ho Ijam Lo's funeral, but the Dutch authorities opposed it. Eventually, Be Biauw Tjoan contented himself by entertaining in his residence the poor of the place, to whom he gave half a guilder each. The reporter comments, "De toeloop bij de begrafenis is er evenwel niet minder groot om gewest." According to Boen Sing Hoo, it seems that Lintah, "Leech," or Tjoa Sien Tjing, was among the initiators of this race (p. 15).

Soenggoeh *Lintah* bersakit lah hati,	For sure Leech was hurt,
Gemesnja *Landak* setengah mati,	Porcupine [junior] was infuriated,
Lantaran koeboeran di tjegati,	Because the funerals were obstructed,
Tjilaka datang lantas berganti.	Misfortunes succeeded each other.

[34] Be Ik Sam was captain of the Chinese in Bagelen from 1862 to 1864. In the 1860s, he and his brother Be Biauw Tjoan had formed a kongsi. They not only controlled the opium farms in their own districts, but together with the local captain also managed the farm in Banyumas. In 1864, they were found guilty of malpractice and were stripped of office, heavily fined, and for a time forbidden to participate in opium farms as farmers, guarantors, subfarmers, or employees. They were rehabilitated in the early 1870s. In the early 1880s, Be Ik Sam was established in Semarang as a trader, owned lands in the area of Japara, and held the opium farms of Bagelen and Kedu. He became famous as the author of an open letter to the king in which he gave insight into the shortcomings of the opium farm system and offered his recommendations for reform. Be Ik Sam, *Vijftien millioen vermeerdering der staatsinkomsten zonder belasting verhooging, Open Brief aan Z. M. den Koning der Nederlanden* (Djokjakarta: Buning, 1886).

[35] See app. 1.

[36] Cf. Rush, *Opium Farms*, pp. 189–90, 197.

[37] Tatkala mati si *Landak Toewa*,
Djalankan prentah banjak katjiwa,
Koerang setia sekalian Poenggawa,
Maka namanja, djatoeh di bawa (p. 10). Cf. also Rush, *Opium Farms*, pp. 220–23.

The Be/Lim Partnership

This group was the most prestigious, for it was headed by the two most powerful Chinese in Semarang: Oelar Naga, "Dragon," or Liem Liong Hien, major since 1885, and Koeda Toewa "Horse Senior," or Be Biauw Tjoan, honorary major since 1873.[38] Liem Liong Hien was a native of Gresik *(Poetra di Gresiek, lah soedah terang)*. He was the son of Liem Khee Soen (1810–1896), who in the 1860s was lieutenant in the same city and an opium farmer in Surabaya in 1871.[39] He married Be Biauw Tjoan's daughter Tiong King Nio (b. 1844).[40] Liem Liong Hien was a refined and competent person:

Oeler Naga sebagi (M)erpati,	Dragon is like a dove,
Orangnja haloes, moerah lah hati,	He is refined and generous,
Kaloe bekerdja, amat lah titi,	And strict while working,
Memegang Sawah, dan Oetan Djati." (p. 7)	He holds rice fields[41] and teakwood forests.

Liem Liong Hien became an opium farmer in association with his father-in-law. During the farm term 1887–1889, he was party to the Bagelen, Batavia, Krawang, and Banten opium farms. In the late 1880s, he was a license holder, as were Ho Tjiauw Ing and Be Kwat Kong, for the exploitation of forests in the district of Semarang.[42]

Boen Sing Hoo gives the following portrait of Be Biauw Tjoan (1826–1904).

Koeda Toewa, asal di Birma,	Horse Senior is native to Bima,[43]
Soedah kesoehoer dia poenja nama,	Famous is his name,
Maski Toewa, masieh oetama,	In spite of his old age he is still prominent,
Dari kajanja tiada njang sama. (p. 7)	And his wealth is incomparable.[44]

---

[38] Be, or Ma in Mandarin, also means "horse."

[39] According to the late Basuki Soejatmiko, *Etnis Tionghoa di awal Kemerdekaan Indonesia* (Surabaya: P. T. Surya Chandra Kencana Press, 1982), pp. 314–15, Liem Khee Soen's grandfather arrived in Tuban from Fujian province in 1750. Rush, *Opium Farms*, pp. 40–41: "Liem Kee Soen kept a district around Gresik—where he was Chinese lieutenant—for himself and subfarmed the Surabaya, Sidoarjo, and Mojokerto districts to others."

[40] "Djadi mantoenja, si 'Koeda Gerang,'" p. 7 (He became the son-in-law of Horse the Fierce). We assume here that *gerang* stands for *garang*.

[41] Here, opium farms.

[42] Rush, Opium Farms, p. 101. Regeerings Almanak, 1880s.

[43] This verse raises a problem. According to Liem Thian Joe, *Riwajat Semarang*, p. 91 and the genealogy of the Be family, Be Ing Tjioe (1803–1857) had been brought from China as a child by a successful peranakan dealer in tobacco and later, interisland shipping. He eventually married the dealer's daughter, Tan Tjiauw Nio (b. 1808). He served as manager of the opium farm in Bagelen under Tan Tiang Tjhing and was appointed lieutenant in 1833 and captain in 1835. Later he returned to Semarang where he worked in partnership with Major Tan Hong Yan (Tan Tiang Tjhing's son) and became the richest businessman in the city. In 1841, he was appointed honorary major. He had three sons who were born in Java: Biauw Tjoan (1826–1904), Soe Ie (1833–1888), and Ik Sam (1838–1891), and three others who were born in China. When Be Ing Tjioe died, Biauw Tjoan succeeded him. The Be were allied to Tan Hong Yan through the marriage of Biauw Tjoan to the daughter of the former Djiang Nio (1825–1870). Consequently Birma, which probably stands for Bima, should be interpreted as the horses' place of origin as well as Sawu and Roti (see app. 1).

[44] Be Biauw Tjoan, like his children, was a big landowner. He also owned several ships (cf. *Regeerings Almanak* 1870) and for a time had been involved in the opium farm in Singapore (cf. Rush, *Opium Farms*, 100, 110). Some years ago, one could still see his sumptuous tomb to the south of Semarang, on the western side of Jalan Haryono (see plate). Like many wealthy, influential persons, he had it constructed during his lifetime. The stone inscription bears the date 1882. It is worth noting that Goei Som Han (see n. 28) did the same.

He adds further, "But he had the temperament of a woman" *(Tjoema tebijatnja sebagi prampoewan)*. A ballad in Chinese from the midnineteenth century states that Be Biauw Tjoan's father was a homosexual.[45] The Be and the Liem families formed a partnership:

Naga dan *Koeda*, ada disitoe,	Dragon and Horse are present,
Anak *Koeda* sedia, boewat bantoe,	Horse Junior is ready to help,
Tiga berkoempoel, djadi lah satoe,	The three of them are united,
Aken toeroet tawar, soedah tentoe. (p. 8)	No doubt they will take part in the bargain.

"Horse Senior," or Be Kwat Kong (b. 1843), was also quite successful: Major Liem Liong Hin's son, Tjoe Tiang, had married his daughter, Pien Nio (b. 1867) (*Anak Naga djadi lah Mantoe, Mantoenja Koeda, njang Ka'satoe,* [p. 8]).[46] He himself had been appointed lieutenant in 1878 (*Memangkoe Pangkat, di dahoeloe hari*, p. 8). Moreover, through other children he was related to Banteng or "Wild Buffalo" from Kediri, very likely Han Liong Ing (*Besannja tinggal, Tanah Kediri, Banteng besar memegang negeri,* [p. 8]), who held the farms in Cirebon, Tegal, Pekalongan, Rembang, and Japara.[47]

The Oei Partnership

The second group from Semarang was rather new to managing opium farms, but it was very promising. It was composed of Sapi, "Ox," or Oei Tjie Sien (1835–1900), and Anak Sapi, "Ox Junior," or Oei Tiong Ham (1866–1924), who had been appointed lieutenant in 1886, and Sapi Soerakarta, "the Ox from Surakarta," or Oei Tjo Pie, who was the guarantor. Only the latter two attended the auction:

Anak *Sapi* doedoek sebelah kanan,	Ox Junior is seated on the right side,
Masih moeda berpankat *Luitenan*,	Still very young but named lieutenant,
Asal Sapi Tjina poenja toeroenan,	His father is a totok from China,
Berdagang gereh ikan ikanan. (p. 16)	A trader in salted fish.[48]

The business of Oei Tjie Sien prospered, and in 1863, with some partners, he launched the firm of Kian Gwan, "Source of All Welfare," which traded in Chinese commodities and exported some sugar and tobacco:

---

[45] Cf. Gustave Schlegel, "Philippica des Chinesen Tan Iok Po gegen den Kapitän des Chinesen Li-Ki-Thai," *T'oung Pao*, ser. 1, 1 (1890): 32, who translated it into German: "Erst diente er (a certain Li Ki Thai) Sun-bi (Be Ing Tjioe's style) mit der grössten Speichelleckerei:/Er schlachtete, kochte und bereitete die Speisen, um seine Kunst zu zeigen,/Liess sich von ihm prügeln und befehlen, ohne etwas zu erwidern,/Und war verächtlich wie ein Sklave oder eine Sklavin."

[46] Liem Tjoe Tiang was educated in Dutch and in Chinese. In 1888, he launched a Western-style shop called Bazaar Insulinde. It was the first attempt of a Chinese to open a Western-style department store, especially in the European district, but after two or three years he was compelled to close it, perhaps because of the competition of the Dutch-owned firms. Cf. Liem Thian Joe, *Riwajat Semarang*, pp. 150–51, 153.

[47] Rush, *Opium Farms*, p. 102. In 1870, he was appointed lieutenant in Berbek (Kediri district).

[48] According to Liem Thian Joe (quoted by Charles Coppel, "Liem Thian Joe's Unpublished History of Kian Gwan," in *Oei Tiong Ham Concern: The First Business Empire of Southeast Asia*, ed. Yoshihara Kunio (Kyoto University: Center for Southeast Asian Studies, 1989) p. 127 and Liem Tjwan Ling, *Raja Gula Oei Tiong Ham*, (Surabaya: Liem Tjwan Ling, 1979) p. 8. Oei Tjie Sien left China because he was involved in the Taiping rebellion (1850–1864). He is supposed to have landed in Semarang in 1858 accompanied by his brother Oei Sien Tjo (about whom little is known except that he settled in Parakan and was buried in Semarang) and his nephew, Oei Tjo Pie, who resided in Surakarta and who remained an associate of Oei Tjie Sien and Oei Tiong Ham until he died around 1904. According to Boen Sing Hoo, Oei Tjoe Pie was also wealthy and was the guarantor of the Be from Semarang (*Sapi ini djoega berharta, Boewat borgnja, lah soedah njata*). According to the Oei's genealogies (in Chinese and in Malay) provided by Charles Coppel, Tjie Sien married Tjan Biet Nio (1839–1896), the fourth daughter of Zeng (Tjan) Kanshui, a merchant based in Semarang.

Ho Ijam Lo's house at Gergaji as it stood in the 1970s

Main building

Gate leading to the Chinese garden

Portrait of Be Biauw Tjoan by an unknown western painter

Overview of Be Biauw Tjoan's tomb as it stood in the early 1970s

Sapi berdagang oentoeng njata,	Ox's business has been successful,
Lantaran tertoeloeng oleh Dewata,	Because he is assisted by the Gods,
Toewan tanah dan banjak harta,	He is a landowner and a wealthy man.[49]
Gedongnja berderek sa'dalam kota.(p. 16)	He has rows of buildings in the city.

The Oei were allied through marriage to the big families of Semarang and Rembang, says Boen Sing Hoo: Oei Tiong Ham first married a daughter of "Rat," Goei Bing Nio. The granddaughter of "Porcupine," Ho Kiem Hoa (1901–1965), and a daughter of "Garudas," Tan Sien Nio, were his seventh and eighth wives.[50] A sister of Tiong Ham had been given in marriage to the wealthy Mendjangan, or "Deer," from Rembang (*Tjoetjoe Landak dan anaknja Garoeda Semarang, Ketarik famili lah soedah terang*, [p. 17]).[51] Ajam, "Chicken," or The Tik Goan, who had been appointed lieutenant, also became Oei Tjie Sien's son-in-law:

Ajam garang *Ajam* kabiri,	Chicken the fierce, Chicken the capon,
Tiga mantoenja moeda bastari	The third son-in-law, is bright,
Mampoe memegang pekerdja'an negeri,	He assumes his office with talent,
Oentoengnja *Ajam* soekar tertjari. (p. 17)	Profits similar to his are difficult to obtain.[52]

Formerly, The Tik Goan and his brothers were also partners in the opium farms run by Ho Ijam Lo.[53]

The External Partnerships

Boen Sing Hoo insists that since the disappearance of Ho Ijam Lo, the animals from other countries have dared to cross the sea to take part in the battle, especially those from Batavia (*Binatang Betawi, brani menjerang, Langkah laoetan dateng Semarang*, [p. 14]). They were not united and constituted two different partnerships (*Dari Betawi doewa koempoelan, Tida sama dan lain djalan*, [p. 23]). The most impressive was headed by two captains: Boeaja Emas, "Gold Crocodile," or Loa Tiang Hoei, who had been appointed in the capital in 1879[54] and the opium farmer and honorary captain, Oei Hok Tiang, who was granted his title in September 1883.

---

[49] In 1878, he purchased the land of Simongan, where the Sanbao Cave is located, (the stone inscription of 1879 commemorating the event is still in situ) and that of Penggiling next to it, where Oei Tjie Sien had his *Landhuis* or "cottage."

[50] According to Yoshihara, *Oei Tiong Ham Concern*, pp. 148, 184, who interviewed the two sons of Hoo Kiem Hoa (or Lucy Hoo, 1901–1965), Oei Tjong Ie and Oei Tong Tjay, Oei Tiong Ham had nine wives. In a brief portrait of his mother Tjong Ie says: "My mother was an overseas Chinese born in the Netherlands Indies, and compared with my father's other wives, she was well educated—Western educated. I know for instance, in the later years of his life, my mother helped him a lot in his business, especially in dealing with Dutch-speaking people. I think she was also useful to my father in Singapore" (p. 150).

[51] Oei Tjie Sien had four daughters, but the genealogy of the family does not mention their names. According to Song Ong Siang, *One Hundred Years' History of the Chinese in Singapore* (Singapore: University of Malaya Press, 1967), p. 353, another sister of Tiong Ham married Mr Lim E. Ging, at one time a well-known merchant in Singapore, who owned large brickworks at Pasir Panjang. According to Liem Tjwan Ling, *Raja Gula*, p. 12, Liem Ie Khing's (Liem E. Ging) father, Liem Liat Boen, was in charge of the Kian Gwan office in Singapore.

[52] According to Arnold Wright, ed., *Twentieth Century Impressions*, p. 546, The Tik Goan's father, The Siok Lian from Surabaya, "carried on business as a merchant and was the owner of a large sugar factory." Cf. also Liem Thian Joe, *Riwajat Semarang*, 152.

[53] "*Ajam* Djago, Ajam kabiri, bersama Ajam poenja soedara sendiri, Bertjampoer *Landak* di dahoeloe hari, Pegang sawah di ini negeri" (p. 18).

[54] The *Bintang Barat* of July 20, 1889, states that Captain Loa Tiang Hoei, Lieutenant Liem Goan Tjing, Tan Djien Soei, Kan Tjeng Sie, and other wealthy persons from Batavia went to Semarang to take part in the auction to be held on July 23.

Boeaja Emas sebagi Pendita,	Gold Crocodile looks like a clergyman,
Toeroenan berdagang lah soedah njata,	He belongs to a merchant's family,
Kesoehoer amat di *Betawi* kota,	He is quite famous in Batavia,
Moerah hati dan banjak harta.	He is generous and wealthy.

...

Kawannja njang satoe terlaloe pinter,	"One of his companions is very clever,
Sapi katee, *Sapi* di Meester,	That is dwarfish Ox from Meester,
Akalnja sampe bisa tepoeter	He is tricky,
Dalem negeri berpankat *Pachter*. (p. 20)	An opium farmer in his country.[55]

They were accompanied by two merchants: Koetjing di oetan, "Wild Cat," presumably Kan Tjeng Sie,[56] and Boeloes Lautan, "Sea Tortoise," possibly Tan Djien Soei, of whom Boen Sing Hoo gives the following portraits.

Koetjing di hoetan, boekannja kata	Cat from the forest, not from the mud,[57]
Pegang Tambak, dan banjak harta,	Owns fishponds and is very rich,
Orangnja koeroes, tadjem lah mata,	He is thin and his eyes are sharp,
Pinternja lagi, soedah lah njata.	Obviously, he is cunning.
Boeloes laoetan, boekannja kali,	Sea Tortoise, not Land Tortoise,
Orangnja tinggi, tjakep sekali,	Is tall and capable,
Omongnja manis, dengan lah geli,	His talk is pleasant and humorous,
Pandei berdagang, berdjoewal beli. (p. 20)	He is good at business."

Tan Djien Soei was related to the "Garuda" or the Tan, who joined the partnership together with other animals from Semarang such as Ayam Kabiri or The Tik Goan, Boeroeng Noeri, "Lory," a merchant born in China, who had quarreled with Oei Tjie Sien (*sama Sapi koening, ada stori*, [p. 22]), and another bird named Dandang Emas "Gold Cormorant" (?).

The second group from Batavia was represented by Kidang Bogor, the "Deer from Bogor," or Captain Tan Goan Pauw, who had been appointed in June 1883, and his two companions: Oelar sawa, "Python," a funny merchant who was not native to Java (*Langkah laoetan dateng di Djawa, Loetjoenja lagi, tida lah doewa*, [p. 24]) and Seetan, "Satan,"[58] well respected in Batavia and whose brother was captain (*Dalem Betawi banjak kahormatan, Soedaranja lagi, berpangkat Kapitan*, [p. 24]). Boen Sing Hoo obviously does not know much about them:

Menoeroet kabar orang poenja tjerita,	According to the rumor,
Betoel tidanja beloen lah njata,	Which has not yet been confirmed,
Koempoelan ini hendak memegang kota,	This group wants to hold a city,
Njang di ingin, sawah *Soerakarta*.(p. 24)	They longed for the rice fields of Surakarta.

---

[55] According to the *Regerings Almanak* (1879, 1885), Oei Hok Tiang was also the president of a Chinese association called "Batavia," which was founded in 1876. He owned property in Batavia and in 1877 had been appointed lieutenant.

[56] The name of Kan Tjeng Sie appears among the donors who in 1890 contributed to the repair of the Jinde yuan in Jakarta, along with the name of a relative (brother or cousin), Kan Tjeng (Soen).

[57] The meaning of this verse is not clear. I have supposed here that *kata* stands for *gatak*, which in Javanese means "mud."

[58] Or Shé Tan, "a certain Tan." If that were the case, he would be the brother of Captain Tan Boen Kwi, who had been appointed in 1883.

The two partnerships that came from the district of Kedu were rivals; the one from Magelang was headed by the Bébék or "Ducks," who were on friendly terms with Be Biauw Tjoan (*Bébék Magelang Bébék bangsawan, Koeda toewa poenja lah kawan,* [p. 25]) because they were related through marriage (*Bébék dan Koeda maka berkawan, Ketarik dari famili prampoewan,* [p. 25]). One was "Duck Senior," or Kwee An Ki, who had been appointed captain in Magelang in 1878; the other was his son, Anak Bébék, "Duck Junior," or Kwee Siang Ging, who had held the position of lieutenant in Ambarawa since 1878:

Berpangkat Kapitan Si '*Bébék* itoe,	That Duck has the rank of captain,
Tinggal *Magelang* sebelah itoe,	He resides in the neighborhood of Magelang,
Sama *Koeldi* termoesoeh tentoe,	Duck and Donkey are enemies,
Tapi si' *Koeda* tida membantoe.	But in that Horse does not interfere:
Anak *Bébék* di bilang Meri,	Duck Junior is said to be envious,[59]
Tinggal di *Ambarawa* dalem Negeri,	He resides in the country of Ambarawa,
Berpangkat *Lieutenan* di ini hari,	And currently has the position of lieutenant,
Adilnja terpoedji di kanan kiri. (p. 25)	Everywhere, people praise his fairness.

The rival group from Kedu was headed by Koeldi, "Donkey," a dealer in tobacco whose father had the position of captain. His two guarantors Loetoeng, "Monkey," and "Bamboedoeri" (a sort of bamboo) were regarded as insufficiently strong by his enemies the "Ducks" (*Borg Koeldi kena di sawat, Loetoeng terbilang koerang lah koewat,* [p. 25]), who were quite arrogant because "Duck Senior" had been decorated by the Dutch authorities.[60]

The last group, which came from Yogya, was also very fragile. It was represented only by Kambing, "Goat," or Njo Gai Sing, a young man without title and with little capital, but who was ready to act as manager for Be Biauw Tjoan:

Dateng djoega Si'*Kambing* Djockdja,	The Goat from Yogya also came,
Kambing njang pinter, ber'akal Kodja,	Keen and shrewd like a Khoja,
Angkatan Goela, dia poenja kerdja,	Conveyor of sugar is his job,
Toeroenan ketjil, boekan lah Radja.	A man of low extraction, not a king.

...

Kambing beloen ada kekoewattan sendiri,	The Goat does not yet have power of his own,
Boewat pegang sawahnja Negeri,	To hold his own rice fields,
Koeda Toewa sigra di tjari,	He immediately approached Horse Senior,
Maka berkoempoel lah itoe hari. (pp. 26–27)	At the auction they gathered together.

The Battle of the Animals

Boeroeng Peking, "Pekingese Bird," or Tan King Gie, secretary since 1881, announced the terms for the competition, which was held under the presidency of Gadjah Poetih, "White Elephant," or the Resident of Semarang, symbol of Dutch authority:

Boeroeng Peking boeloenja serat,	Pekingese Bird has his feathers well stuck,
Pangkat Secretaris di dalam Rat,	He has the rank of secretary in the council,
Lantas berdiri, membatja lah soerat,	He stands while reading the text,
Soewara njaring, tida lah sarat. (p. 27)	His voice is loud and clear.

---

[59] *Meri* in Javanese means "envious" and in Malay, *anak itik,* or "duckling," so this verse may also be rendered as "Duck Junior is a duckling."

[60] *Bébék* terbilang di taboer Perada,   Duck is said to be coated with gold,
    Dapet nama baik, pada Baginda,   He was granted a title by His Majesty,
    Dateng soerat kapoedji'an dari Ollanda, He received a letter of praise from Holland,
    Ber'bintang Emas, di atas dada.(p. 26) He bears a gold decoration on his chest.

When this preliminary proceeding was terminated, the announcement of the name Semarang caused great excitement:

| Orang njang tawar ganti sa'oetan, | The bargainers one by one made an offer, |
| Sama braninja, soedah keliattan (p. 28) | Obviously equally daring. |

...

| Orang njang nonton, bersoeka hati, | The spectators were delighted, |
| Siapa njang dapet, belonnja misti.(p. 28) | It was too early to assign the license. |

"Dragon," or Liem Liong Hien, stopped his bid, but the contest continued between "Gold Crocodile," or Loa Tiang Hoei, and "Ox Junior," or Oei Tiong Ham. The onlookers enjoyed themselves, wanting to laugh at the competition between the two rivals:

Boeaja menawar, lagi sekali,	Crocodile made another offer,
Anak *Sapi* tambah kembali,	Ox Junior raised the bid,
Soedah poetoes, tiga lah kali,	The final "thrice" was decisive,
Sawah *Semarang, Sapi* njang beli. (p. 29)	It was Ox who purchased the ricefields of Semarang.

The value of the license was no less than 125,300 guilders. According to rumor, "Ox Junior" had been too audacious. He had exceeded the calculations of his father and the latter was infuriated:

Orang di loewar pada berkata,	The people outside all said,
Anak *Sapi*, berani sendjata,	Ox Junior dared to fight,
Melanggar Bapanja poenja kata,	He transgressed his father's words,
Liwatin taksiran, lah soeda njata. (p. 30)	And exceeded his estimation.

But the license had been assigned, and "Ox Junior" had to look for his guarantors: one was Oei Tjie Sien himself and the second, his son-in-law from Rembang, named "Deer." Against all expectations, *Landak di Djocdja*, the "Porcupine of Yogya," or Ho Tjiauw Soen, who was formerly associated with his brother Ho Tjiauw Ing, was also a party:

Djalanken kerdja, pegang koewasa,	To run a farm, to act as manager,
Landak di *Djocdja* memang biasa,	These tasks are familiar to the Porcupine in Yogya,
Maski namanja soedah binasa,	Although his reputation has been ruined,
Tapi doerinja masieh berbisa. (p. 31)	His spines are still poisonous.

In effect, Ho Tjiauw Soen was also a shareholder, and it was he who could show the Oei how to run the opium farm (*Bikin persero satoe koempoelan, Pekerdja'an Landak njang kasi djalan*, [p. 31]). In the same way, Andjing, "Dog," another partner of the Ho, was also hired by the Oei:

Andjing item djadi Poenggawa besar	Black Dog has become high commissioner,
Boeloenja haloes, tida lah kasar,	His hair is soft, not coarse,
Andjing tertjinta oleh Pembesar,	He is loved by the great ones,
Maka Toewannja, takoet lah goesar. (p. 32)	So his masters are afraid to anger him.

Further, Boen Sing Hoo states that "Dog" had already worked for several masters and that they were all afraid of him, although they liked him (*Toewannja lagi, berganti-ganti, Semoea takoet dan tjinta hati*, [p. 32]). When the name of Surakarta was announced, Anak Koeda, "Horse Junior," or Be Kwat Kong, bid first; he was immediately followed by Boeroeng Noeri, "Lory," and Oeler Sawa, "Python," who raised the bid to 54,000 and 60,000 successively; but Koeda Saboe, Koeda pingittan, "Horse from Sawu, Horse the secluded," or Be Kwat Koen, who was captain in Solo,[61] offered 60,010, and he got it:

Di karang pèndèk, ini lah tjerita,	In short, the story is this,
Soedah poetoes sawah di *Soerakarta*,	The rice fields of Surakarta have been assigned,

...

Koeda Saboe, Pachter di Djawa,	Horse from Sawu became farmer in Java,
Borgnja lagi famili berdoewa,	His guarantors, two relatives of his,
Koeda Moeda dan *Koeda* Toewa. (p. 34)	Horse Junior and Horse Senior.

The same process was repeated for the farm of Yogya. Kambing Moeda, "Goat Junior," or Njo Gai Sing, vied with Boeroeng Noeri, who was a supporter of the Batavia-based partnership. The bargaining was rapid and soon reached 30, 630 (*Tjepatnja lagi, sebagi sikatan, 30,630, soedah kelihattan,* [p. 36]). And the winners were again the Be:

Soedah poetoes, sawah *Djocdjakarta*,	The ricefields of Yogya have been assigned,
Kena si' *Kambing*, lah soedah njata,	The winner is that Goat,
Doewa Borgnja, *Koeda-kareta*,	The cart horses are his two guarantors,
Koeda Semarang, njang banjak harta. (p. 36)	The wealthy Horses from Semarang.

The last territory to be sold on that day was that of Kedu, which had been managed by Bébék istri, "Duck's wife," or the wife of Captain Kwee An Ki (*Hendak terdjoewal, sawah di Kedoe Negeri, Njang terpegang, oleh Bébék istri,* [p. 36]). Further, Boen Sing Hoo makes clear that "she was a woman" (*Bébék istri, Bébék prampoewan,* [p. 37]). It is the only reference to a woman administrator of an opium farm found so far. This time, the contest between the Bébék, or "Ducks," and their rival Koeldi, "Donkey," was sharp. Because Koeda Toewa or Be Biauw Tjoan finally refused to support Bébék istri, she had to give way to Koeldi who bid 25,000, although he still had to find a guarantor (*Borg Koeldi masieh lah koerang, sebab njang koewat tjoema sa'orang,* [p. 39]).

This was the end of the auction, which was marked by the sound of a gamelan orchestra:

Lantas moendoer, samoea Pembesar,	Then all the officials left,
Gamelan berboenji, lagoe njang kasar,	The gamelan started a vulgar melody,
Orang njang nonton pada bergingsar,	All the spectators disappeared,
Soedah habis, dan boebar pasar. (p.39)	It was the end, the market was dispersed.

The two groups from Batavia did not obtain any farm:

Tida beroentoeng ini lah hari,	Today they were unlucky,
Angkatan *Betawi* tida pegang negeri,	The groups from Betawi do not hold lands,
Tetapi ada ingetan, di dalem diri,	But in their hearts they cherish the hope,
Lain lelang, hendak kemari. (p. 35)	To the next auction they will come again.

Indeed, they came again to Semarang at the beginning of September to take part in an auction, but Boen Sing Hoo neither mentions the name of the territory nor that of the purchaser.

---

[61] According to Tan Hong Boen, *Orang-orang Tionghoa jang terkemoeka di Java* (Solo: Biographical Publishing Centre, ca. 1935), p. 128, Be Kwat Koen was born in Purworejo (Bagelen) in 1863. As Be Ik Sam (see nn. 34, 43) was then in that city, where he was promoted to the position of captain in 1864, one may assume that Kwat Koen was his son.

The *Syair Sindiran* as a Literary Genre

The peranakan certainly appear to have had a pronounced taste for Malay classical literature at this time and to have been familiar with the fashionable genres. Many nineteenth-century syair about animals or plants, which, as Overbeck has shown,[62] were symbols for real people, generally nobles whom the poet did not dare mention by name, were known to the peranakan. In Batavia at the end of the nineteenth century, an image of the *Burung Nuri* and the *Burung Bayan* (two kinds of parrots) were even carried in procession during the Capgomeh festival.[63] Some peranakan also wrote poems in this vein. To the best of our knowledge, the first to appear in book form, entitled *Saier mengimpie dan Saier boeroeng* was written by Tan Kit Tjoan.[64] Toward the end of the nineteenth century, a peranakan assisted by a Malay published a version of *Syair ikan* (poem about a fish) in romanised Malay.[65] Fables such as the well-known story of Kancil (mouse deer) were found in many Chinese lending libraries in Java. It may be that the peranakan borrowed the satirical syair in which people are represented by animals from the Malays as well.

Unfortunately, little is known about the rise of the *syair sindiran*. In the peranakan world, one may assume that the genre was already popular in the midnineteenth century. The *Bintang Barat* of November 5, 1872, alludes to a *Sair Satoe Kidang* (Poem about a deer) written by a certain Tan Giok Laij from Bogor to criticize a woman who had run away to follow her lover.[66] Certainly Boen Sing Hoo was neither the first and nor the only poet to ridicule the opium farmers. In 1865, a certain Kiai Kong Bing[67] had already published a brief syair without title in the *Bintang Timoer* (Nov. 25), which makes fun of an opium farmer from Besuki who was called by his initials "K. B." He is depicted as being tricked by three brothers, who are referred to as three heroes from the *Romance of the Three Kingdoms*. It is quite likely that such satirical poems also appeared in the press in the 1870s and 1880s. So far, two other syair aimed at making fun of the farmers have been traced: one supposedly appeared in Batavia 1891, and the second was definitely published in Batavia in 1897. The first is only known from a poem that appeared in the *Bintang Soerabaia* of March 31, 1891. Therein the author, Babah K.T. (assisted by K. S. H.), asks his relatives residing in Besuki (East Java) for permission to circulate in Semarang a poem about contests between opium farmers *(Dari perkara pachter lah tjandoe, Siapa jang pegang siapa jang ganggoe)* that he wants to

---

[62] Hans Overbeck, "Malay Animals and Flowers Shaers," *Journal of the Malayan Branch of the Royal Asiatic Society*, 12 (2) (1934): 108–48.

[63] Cf "Boeroeng noeri djenge" (Burung nuri's procession), *Bintang Soerabaija*, March 1, 1894.

[64] Tan Kiet Tjoan was a knowledgeable landowner established in Batavia, where he had purchased several plots of lands in Pekojan, Pangkalan, and Klenteng. (cf. *Bintang Barat*, July 19, 1872). In the 1860s, he enjoyed reading Malay newspapers and even published articles and poems in *Bintang Barat* (Batavia) and *Bintang Timoer* (Surabaya). He was versed in classical Malay literature for he quoted the *Bustanus Salatin* (cf. *Bintang Timoer*, April 6, 1867). The first surviving edition of his poem dates back to 1882. However, an earlier edition is known by an advertisement in the *Bintang Barat* of January 7, 1871.

[65] See Salmon, *Literature in Malay by the Chinese of Indonesia*, p. 31.

[66] The editor refused to publish it because, he said, this woman had already rejoined her first master: "Tan Giok Laij di Bogor! Baba poenja tjerita dan sair satoe kidang, tapi mengertinja satoe prampoean dari kampoeng Patjebokan njang bekas di piara oleh satoe Kapitan dan kerna di pikat oleh satoe orang Bogor nama Tj. S. sampe dapet, abis terlepas kombali, kita fikir tiada baik boeat di masoekin didalem soerat kabar. Sobat djangan ambil pergoesar."

[67] Kong Bing or Kong Ming is, in effect, the style of Zhuge Liang (A.D. 181–234), another hero of the Three Kingdoms period (A.D. 220–65).

print in book form in Batavia the following month. He states that the aim is not to be insulting:

Tapi familikoe djanganlah soesah,	But my relatives, do not worry,
Tida kira koe bikin lah hina,	According to me it is not offensive,
Tjoema di bikin sedikit tjerita,	It is just a short account
Keada'annja segala perkara.	Of events as they are.

He apparently received a favorable reply, for the author published in the same newspaper (May 19, 1891) a second syair ("Soerat kiriman sairan") to express his gratitude and his hope that they would not be sued:

Djika soenggoe soeka noeloengi,	If you really want to help,
Saja trima bersenang hati,	I will be pleased,
Tapi misti jang hati-hati,	But you should be cautious,
Djangan sampe naik Raad Justitie.	Not to take legal action.

The second poem, which was published by Albrecht and Co., is anonymous. Its title is *Sair Binatang, Soewatoe dongeng jang betoel soedah kedjadian di Betawi, berikoet Sair Madat,* (Poem about animals, A true story about an opium farm case that occurred in Betawi [pp. 3–20]), followed by a poem about opium [pp. 21–33]). This *Sair Binatang*, like the one by Boen Sing Hoo, is a poem *à clés*, but its interpretation is much more difficult for at least two reasons. First, the story is not precisely set in space or time—the writer only says that he composed it a long time ago *(Sair hewan terkarang lama)*. Second, the portrayal of the characters is not sufficently detailed to allow a noncontemporaneous reader to identify them. One only knows that some of them were native to Bogor, whereas another one was based in Deli. The author's aim is nevertheless clear: he intends to show the malpractices of opium farmers and their victims. The appended syair about opium (pp. 21–33) describes the suffering of the opium addicts and is intended to discourage people from taking up opium smoking.[68]

The Exemplarity of Boen Sing Hoo's Syair

To twentieth-century readers, the poem by Boen Sing Hoo is undoubtedly the most attractive. It allows one to perceive how educated peranakan of the middle class looked at the *cabang atas* and shows that the author had an intimate knowledge of social networks, economic connections, and stratagems. Especially well described is the part played by women in the making of new alliances by means of intermarriages. One can see, for instance, that the Oei, who were just at the beginning of their social climb, could rely on their *bésan* (children's in-laws) to obtain the required capital and competent assistants to help them run their newly purchased farm. One can also see the mobility of this elite. Boen Sing Hoo never forgets to mention the successful newcomers who entered the battlefield. Apart from Oei Tjie Sien, he also alludes to Boeroeng Noeri, who was also born in China *(Asalnja di Tjina, boekan di Semarang,* [p. 35]), and Oeler sawa, or "Python," who also came from abroad *(Langkah laoetan dateng di Djawa,* [p. 24]), probably from China or from Singapore. These newcomers, who were extremely keen to acquire farm leases, quite often raised their bids in an inconsiderate manner. This is stressed by Boen Sing Hoo when he relates how Oei Tiong Ham bargained to obtain the opium license for Semarang, thereby arousing the fury of Boeaja Emas, or Loa Tiang Hoei:

---

[68] Judging from the language of this poem, which contains numerous Hokkien terms, one may assume that its author was a peranakan Chinese.

Boeaja Emas, boeaja laoettan,	Gold Crocodile or Sea Crocodile,
Sapi moeda, *Sapi* di hoetan,	Ox Junior or Ox from the forest,
Sama-sama ada kakoewatan,	Have the same strength,
Bertaroeng sampe loepa ingettan. (p. 29)	They fight until they forget all.

He continues:

Hendak bertaroeng, njang sampe mati,	They want to fight to the death,
Tida lah inget, di hari nanti,	Not even thinking of the future,
Soedah melangkah, taksiran njang mesti. (p. 29)	They have already exceeded decent limits.

A similar attitude of a totok was remarked upon in the 1860s for Probolinggo.[69] Whereas in Probolinggo the totok was defeated, here, on the contrary, the peranakan farmer from Batavia is beaten:

Boeaja Emas, berhati lah marah,	Gold Crocodile is furious in his heart,
Warna moekanja, sampe lah merah,	His face is flushed with anger,
Hatinja panas, sebagi barah,	His heart is as hot as live coals,
Blakang kali, *Boeja* menjerah. (p. 29)	Next time he will give up.

It is interesting to see how Boen Sing Hoo proceeds to ridicule the peranakan elite. Reduced to the position of fierce animals who spend their time contending for territory, the opium farmers are just good enough to entertain the populace. Thus, the auction becomes a way to derive amusement The spectators apparently attended the auction as if it were a show, as if they were watching a cockfight or a bullfight. They looked at the opium farmers as if they were simply figures in a contest; their social status was no longer visible. The author does not state who was permitted to attend the auction, but we know from other sources that many people crowded around the pendopo. He merely says, "The onlookers were numerous" (*Njang nonton, banjak lah orang*, [p. 28]). He describes the beginning of the auction with the sale of Semarang:

Njang nonton, pada madjoe menjerang,	All the spectators advance offensively,
Maoe dengerken, njang sampe terang, (p. 28)	They want to hear clearly.

He even provides insight into the enjoyment of the spectators:

Orang njang nonton soeka semoewa,	The spectators enjoyed everything,
Rasanja hati, hendak tertawa. (p. 29)	In their hearts, they feel like laughing.

In his portraits of the opium farmers, Boen Sing Hoo takes liberties. He alternates reverential portraits—as in Oelar Naga (prior mention)—with caricatures of real creatures like Tikoes or Goei Som Han:

Idoengnja *Tikoes*, seperti gerdoe,	Rat's nose is like a sentry box,
Matanja lagi, sebagi gandoe,	His eyes are like black rounded pips,
Bitjaranja manis, terlebih madoe,	His speech is sweeter than honey,
Sebagi *Advocaat*, bisa mengadoe. (p. 15)	He is able to argue as a lawyer does.

In his epilogue, which is in a different vein, Boen Sing Hoo exhibits even more satirical wit. Probably to avoid censorship, or perhaps just because the allegories came

---

[69] The *Bintang Timoer* (February 13, 1867), in an interesting report about the sale of opium farms in Probolinggo (*Kabar di residentie Probolinggo tempo lelang pacht apion di dalem boelan Dec. tahoen 1866 poor tahoen 1867*), noticed that the former opium farmer Oen Tik Gowan (or Wen Baochang), who also held the position of captain (from 1860 to 1869), was compelled to purchase the license at a prohibitive price because he would not give way to an adventurous totok. The totok, here called *China Gendeng* or "Crazy Chinese," dressed extravagantly (*berpake bagoes, tjelana Loktjan, badjoe kinsin, laken hitam*) and successively dared to raise his bid higher than Oen Tik Gowan.

spontaneously to his mind, he draws a scathing comparison between the opium farmers and characters from the Three Kingdoms period (in China, A.D. 220–265). Whereas he guarantees that his *Sair Binatang* is clear, here he states that his "Semarang Three Kingdoms Story" will remain obscure. However, one may assume that for his contemporaneous peranakan readers, who were still quite familiar with the *Romance of the Three Kingdoms*, this was just another game, perhaps slightly more sophisticated than the first one. The heroes of the *Three Kingdoms* were so well known among the Chinese that they were used as qualifiers in daily speech.

For Boen Sing Hoo, the story of the fall of the Ho is as follows: Ho Ijam Lo, represented by Tjoo Tjhoo (Cao Cao), a famous cunning rebel, is attacked by Be Biauw Tjoan, or Soen Kwan (Sun Quan), a talented military man. On the advice of the clever Bang Tong (Pang Tong), another strategist, (here, Be Biauw Tjoan's brother, Ik Sam), the Be manage to trick him for three years and finally succeed in burning down his fleet. The defeat of Tjoo Tjhoo, that is, Ho Lam Ijo, delights Bang Tong, or Be Ik Sam, and at the same time allows Soe Ma Jam (Sima Yan), here Oei Tiong Ham, to start his own life.[70] As one may see in this epilogue, the author shows very little sympathy toward the big farmers of the time.

Considering the wealth of information about the mental attitudes of the peranakan found in the works by writers such as Boen Sing Hoo, Tan Teng Kie, and Na Tian Piet,[71] one wonders whether it would not be worth studying the literature that appeared in the press in Malay of the nineteenth century. Such in-depth research would enable a better appraisal of how the peranakan perceived the surrounding world, how they reacted to the impact of Western culture, and how they reflected on China and upon themselves.

In so doing, one would have to reappraise the reformist movement of the Tiong Hoa Hwe Koan, which was preceded by a phase during which educated peranakan merchants began to express their views and to exchange ideas through the press.

---

[70] See the Malay text and its English translation given in app. 1.

[71] Cf. Claudine Salmon, "The Batavian Eastern Railway Co. and the Making of a New 'Daerah' as Reflected in a Commemorative Syair by Tan Teng Kie (1890)," *Indonesia*, 45 (1988): 49–62, and idem, "Na Tian Piet et sa vision du monde malais dans les années 1890," *Archipel* 42 (in press).

Appendix 1

| SAM KOK | THE THREE KINGDOMS |

Samkok tiroean dalem *Semarang*,
Terkarang pendek, tida lah terang,
Tjerita *Binatang*; boekan lah orang,
Angkat sendjata sama lah perang.

Perang ini di *"Kang Lam"* negara
Tjoo Tjhoo dan *Soen Kwan* poenja perkara,
83 laksa, banjaknja tentara,
Djadi binasa tida lah kira.

Bapanja Saboe, di bilang *Rotti*,
Sebagi *Bang Thong*, poenja mengarti,
Djalanken tipoe, amat lah titi,
Gemesnja *Tjoo Tjhoo*, setengah lah mati.

Lantaran *Bang Thong* poenja akallan,
Pake tipoe dari *Bangkalan*
3 Tahon tipoenja berdjalan,
Bikin *Tjoo Tjhoo* djadi seselan.

Tipoeanja *Bang Thong* sebegi boekit,
Tjoo Tjhoo kena lah sampe sakit,
Roeginja lagi, boekan sedikit,
Rasanja tida bisa berbangkit.

Perang *"Kang Lam,"* perang di kali,
Praoe teriket sama lah tali,
Terbakar abis sama sekali,
Bang Thong liat, hatinja geli.

Praoe terbakar, kanan dan kiri,
Tjoo Tjhoo kepaksa misti lah lari,
Soen Kwan menang perang negri,
Soe Ma Jam djoega, bakal berdiri.

The San Guo Story of Semarang,
Is made concise and abstruse,
It is not a story of men, but of animals
Taking up arms, as if they were at war.

The war in the "Southern Countries,"
Was between Cao Cao and Sun Quan.[72]
The armies amounted to 830,000,
Inconceivable was the number of the victims."

Horse Senior from Sawu, also named Roti,
Was as clever as Pang Tong,[73]
So tricky were his stratagems
That Cao Cao was most infuriated.

Pang Tong, thanks to his cunning mind,
From Bangkalan had been playing tricks,[74]
Which lasted for three years,
Making Cao Cao repent in vain.

Pang Tong's tricks had piled up as high as a hill,
Making Cao Cao fall ill,
Inflicting great loss on him,
Causing him to feel that he could not rise again.

The Jiangnan War occurred on the river.
The boats bound together with ropes
Were completely burnt down,
At this sight, Pang Tong was amused.[75]

The boats on the left and right being destroyed,
Cao Cao was compelled to run away,
Sun Quan won the war,
But Suma Yan was about to rise.[76]

---

[72] Cao Cao (155–220) obviously stands for Ho Ijam Lo. This figure from the San Guo period is rather complicated. He is popularly regarded by the Chinese as a type of bold minister and cunning, unscrupulous rebel. His large armies are proverbial. Sun Quan (181–252) symbolizes Be Biauw Tjoan. After a long and successful resistance against Cao Cao, he finally recognized him as his suzerain; when Cao Cao died and was replaced by his son, Sun Quan threw off his allegiance.

[73] Pang Tong (185–221) was not successful as an administrator, but he was an excellent strategist. Pang symbolizes Be Kwat Koen's father, presumably Be Ik Sam (see nn. 34, 43).

[74] Here Boen Sing Hoo probably alludes to the smuggling of opium from Madura into Ho Ijam Lo's territories.

[75] This passage, which refers to the famous Chibi, or Red Wall, Battle (on the Yangzi River) during which Sun Quan inflicted a severe blow to Cao Cao by destroying his fleet, possibly alludes to the unsuccessful attempts of Ho Ijam Lo to control the smuggling along the coast.

[76] Sima Yan (236–290) was the eldest son of Sima Zhao, who had been made prince of Jin. In 265 his father died, and at the end of the year he deposed the emperor Yuandi and founded the Jin dynasty, placing his capital at Luoyang in Henan. Here in the poem, Sima Yan is the symbol of Oei Tiong Ham, who has replaced Ho Ijam Lo in Semarang.

Appendix 2
Identification of the Names of Opium Farmers and Partners Appearing in the Poem

The Defunct Partnership of the Ho family (bankrupt on June 12, 1889)

Landak Toewa, "Porcupine Senior" — Ho Ijam Lo (d. June 22, 1888).

Landak Moeda, "Porcupine Junior" — Ho Tjiauw Ing (b. 1845), who inherited the three farms held by his father (in Semarang, Yogya, and Kedu). In June 1888, the same month in which Ho Ijam Lo died, Ho Tjiauw Ing acquired the Solo farm; the following February, he took over Djie Bok Hien's farm in Madiun as well. Appointed lieutenant in Semarang on December 20, 1885.

Landak Djocdja, the "Porcupine from Yogya" — Ho Tjiauw Soen, eldest son of Ho Ijam Lo, appointed lieutenant in Yogya on August 9, 1884.

Gangsa Djocdja, the "Goose from Yogya" — Liem Kie Djwan, appointed captain in Yogya in 1883.

Tikoes, "Rat" — Goei Som Han, merchant, landowner, and entrepreneur in Semarang, former partner of Be Biauw Tjoan.

The Auction of July 23, 1889, and the Seven Competing Partnerships

Gadjah Poetih, Radjah di hoetan, "The White Elephant, King of the Forest" — The Resident of Semarang.

Boeroeng Peking, "Pekingese Bird" — Tan King Gie, secretary of the Kongkoan, or Chinese Council, appointed on September 17, 1881.

Partnership 1 (The Be/Lim from Semarang)

Oelar Naga, "Dragon" — Liem Liong Hien, son of Liem Khee Soen (b. 1810, lieutenant in Gresik), married Be Biauw Tjoan's daughter, Tiong King Nio (b. 1844). Appointed lieutenant in 1866, captain in 1877, and major in 1885.

Anak Naga, "Dragon's Son" — Liem Tjoe Tiang, married Be Kwat Kong's daughter, Pien Nio (b. 1867). Appointed lieutenant on December 20, 1889.

Koeda Toewa, "Horse Senior" — Be Biauw Tjoan (1826–1904). First wife was Major Tan Hong Yan's daughter, Djiang Nio (1825–1870). Appointed honorary major in 1873.

Koeda Moeda, "Horse Junior" — Be Kwat Kong (b. 1843), eldest son of Be Biauw Tjoan; married Tan Bola Nio, a granddaughter of Tan Goan Sing, captain in Kudus. Appointed lieutenant in 1878.

Koeda Saboe, the "Horse from Sawu" — Be Kwat Koen (b. 1863), Be Biauw Tjoan's nephew (presumably a son of Be Ik Sam, 1838–1891). Appointed captain in Surakarta in 1888.

48 *Claudine Salmon*

Banteng, "Wild Buffalo"	Han Liong Ing?, *besan* of Be Kwat Kong, appointed lieutenant in Berbek (Kediri) in 1870 and opium farmer.

Partnership 2 (The Oei father and Son from Semarang)

Sapi Toewa, "Ox Senior"	Oei Tjie Sien (1835–1900) founder of the firm Kian Gwan (1863). Married Zeng (Tjan) Kanshui's daughter, Tjan Biet Nio (1839–96).
Sapi Moeda, "Ox Junior"	Oei Tiong Ham (1866–1924), appointed lieutenant 1886; related to the Goei by his first wife, Goei Bing Nio, to the Ho by his seventh wife, Ho Kiem Hoa, and to the Garudas of Semarang by his eighth wife, Tan Sien Nio.
Mendjangan, "Deer"	Merchant in Rembang married to a daughter of Oei Tjie Sien (unidentified).
Ajam, "Chicken"	The Tik Goan, Oei Tjie Sien's son-in-law, appointed lieutenant.
Djalak Oeren, "Black Mynah Bird"(?)	Oei Tjie Sien's son-in-law.
Sapi Soerakarta, the "Ox from Surakarta"	Oei Tjo Pie (d. ca. 1904): Oei Tjie Sien's nephew.
Landak Djocdja, the "Porcupine from Yogya"	Ho Tjiauw Soen, appointed lieutenant in Yogya in 1884.
Andjing, "Dog"	Unidentified former partner of the Ho.

Partnership 3 (from Batavia)

Boeaja Emas, "Gold Crocodile"	Loa Tiang Hoei, appointed captain in Batavia in 1879.
Sapi di Meester, the "Ox from Meester Cornelis"	The opium farmer Oei Hok Tiang, appointed honorary captain in 1883.
Koetjing di Hoetan, "Wild Cat"	The merchant Kan Tjeng Sie from Batavia(?)
Boeloes Laoetan, "Sea Tortoise"	Tan Djien Soei from Batavia(?)
Boeroeng Garoeda, "Garuda Birds"	the descendants of major and opium farmer Tan Hong Yan from Semarang, whose daughter, Tan Djiang Nio (1825–1870), married Be Biauw Tjoan.
Ajam, "Chicken"	The Tik Goan, Oei Tjie Sien's son-in-law.
Boeroeng Noeri, "Lory"	A totok merchant from Semarang.
Dandang Emas "Gold Cormorant"(?)	Unidentified.

Partnership 4 (from Batavia)

Kidang Bogor, the "Deer from Bogor"	Tan Goan Pauw, appointed captain in Bogor in 1883.
Oelar Sawa, "Python"	(?)
Seetan, "Satan" or "a certain Tan"	(?)

Partnership 5 (from Kedu)

Koeldi "Donkey"	Son of a captain, and tobacco dealer.

Loetoeng "Monkey"   (?)

Bamboe-doeri (a kind of bamboo)   (?)

Partnership 6 (Magelang)

Bébék "Duck Senior"   Kwee An Ki, appointed captain in Magelang in 1878, friend of Be Biauw Tjoan but rival of *Koeldi*.

Anak Bébék "Duck Junior"   Kwee Siang Ging, appointed lieutenant in Ambarawa in 1878.

Partnership 7 (Yogyakarta)

Kambing "Goat"   Njo Gai Sing, sugar conveyor based in Yogya, accomplice of Be Biauw Tjoan.

LIST OF CHINESE CHARACTERS

Bang Thong (Pang Tong) 龐統
Be Ing Tjioe 馬瀛洲
Be (Ma) Biauw Tjoan 馬淼泉
Be Ik Sam 馬益三
Be Kwat Koen 馬厥昆
Be Kwat Kong 馬厥功
Be Pien Nio 馬彬娘
Be Soe Ie 馬思怡
Be Tiong King Nio 馬忠敬娘
Boen Sing Hoo 文興號
Cao Cao 曹操
Chen Quanniang 陳全娘
Chi bi 赤壁
Ganfu miao 感福廟
Goei Bing Nio 魏明娘
Goei Keh Pien 魏嘉賓
Goei Som Han (Wei Senhan) 魏森漢
Han Liong Ing 韓隆口
Hap Sing Kong Sie 合興公司
He Lanniang 何蘭娘
Ho Hok Lo 何福老
Ho Ijam Lo 何炎老

Ho Kiem Hoa 何金花
Ho Sie Tik 何世德
Ho Tiang Goan 何長[源]
Ho Tjiauw Hai 何朝海
Ho Tjiauw Ing 何朝[熒]
Ho Tjiauw Soen 何朝順
Houfu miao 厚福廟
Jinde yuan 金德院
Jin gu qiguan 今古奇觀
Kan Tjeng Sie 簡增泗
Kan Tjeng (Soen) 簡增純
Kian Gwan 建源
Kong Bing (Kong Ming) 孔明
Kwa Wan Hong 柯遠芳
(Liang) Shanbo yu (Zhu) Yingtai
梁山伯與祝英台
Liem Goan Tjing 林元貞
Liem Liong Hien 林隆興
Liem Tjoe Tiang 林梓樟
Loa Tiang Hoei 賴長輝
Oei Hok Tiang 黃福長
Oei Sien Tjo 黃神助
Oei Tjie Sien 黃志信

Oei Tiong Ham 黃忠涵
Oei Tjo Pie 黃祖庇
Oei Tjong Ie 黃宗詒
Oei Tjong Tjay 黃宗才
Pektjoen 爬船
Penggiling 楓宜嶺
Sam Pik - Ing Taij 山伯英台
Sam Po Tong (Sanbao dong) 三保洞
Shé Tan 氏陳
Sima Yan 司馬炎
Simongan 時望安
Soe Ma Jam (Sima Yan) 司馬炎
Soen Kwan (Sun Quan) 孫權
Sun-bi 順美　(Be Biauw Tjoan's style)
Sun Quan 孫權
Tay Kak Sie (Dajue si) 大覺寺
Tan Boen Kwi 陳文貴
Tan Djiang Nio 陳讓娘
Tan Hong Yan 陳烽烟
Tan Sien Nio 陳莘娘
Tan Tiang Tjhing 陳長菁
Tan Tjiauw Nio 陳招娘
Tan Tjin Goan 陳振源

Tan Tjien Hwa (Tan Tjin Hoa) 陳振華
Tan Tjin Teng 陳振廷
Tay Kak Sie (Dajue si) 大覺寺
The Tik Goan 鄭德源
Tiong Hoa Hwe Koan 中華會館
Tjan Biet Nio 曾蜜娘
Tjapkauwking 十九間
Tjiong Hok Long 鍾福隆
Tjoa Sien Tjing 蔡承貞
Tjoo Tjhoo (Cao Cao) 曹操
Wei (Goei) Bingyao 魏炳耀
Wei (Goei) Jingtai 魏景泰
Wen Baochang 溫寶昌
Zeng (Tjan) Kanshui 曾坎水
Zhuge Liang 諸葛亮

THE CHINESE OF INDONESIA AND THE DEVELOPMENT OF THE INDONESIAN LANGUAGE

Dédé Oetomo

Introduction: Malay, Indonesian and the Chinese of Indonesia[1]

Since early in the formation of their communities, the *peranakan* or *baba* Chinese[2] of the Malay Archipelago have communicated among themselves in local languages and in various dialects of the Malay language.[3] They have also produced literature in local languages

---

This article was written while I was a Fulbright scholar-in-residence attached to the 1990 Southeast Asian Studies Summer Institute at Cornell. I would like to thank the institute, particularly its director, John Wolff, for inviting me to present the paper at the symposium and, more generally, to attend the institute. Thanks are also owed the United States Information Agency, the Council for International Exchange of Scholars, and the American-Indonesian Exchange Foundation for providing the Fulbright grant. Claudine Salmon and Jim Collins helped me shape many of the ideas in this paper, and John Wolff gave extensive and incisive comments on the first draft; to them goes my sincere gratitude. Of course, I alone am responsible for what I have written.

[1] The term *Malay* here refers to all dialects of Malay before the rise of the nationalist movement in Indonesia, whereas *Indonesian* refers to varieties that developed thereafter.

[2] The term peranakan, or baba, Chinese, is used here to refer to descendants of unions between male Chinese immigrants who came to the Indies before the end of the nineteenth century and local women or women born from such relationships. Culturally, the peranakan or baba have adopted numerous local elements. The other subcategory of Indonesian Chinese, the *totok*, consists of immigrants who came after the turn of the century and their descendants. Totok culture shows its Chinese roots more prominently. Cf. G. William Skinner, "The Chinese Minority," in *Indonesia*, ed. Ruth T. McVey (New Haven: HRAF Press, 1963), pp. 103–10. Although the peranakan use Malay and/or a local language, most totok use a Chinese dialect or, until very recently, a local language. See Dédé Oetomo, "Multilingualism and Chinese Identities in Indonesia," in *Changing Identities of the Southeast Asian Chinese since World War II*, ed. Jennifer Cushman and Wang Gungwu (Hong Kong: Hong Kong Univ. Press, 1988), pp. 97–106.

[3] Claudine Salmon, *Literature in Malay by the Chinese of Indonesia: A Provisional Annotated Bibliography* (Paris: Éditions de la Maison des Sciences de l'Homme, 1981), p. 15, for example, cites the seventeenth-century Chinese text *Dongxi yangkao* as mentioning the existence of Chinese who "acted as secretaries and interpreters for the Sultan of Banten (West Java), which suggests that some of them, at least, learned the local language fairly quickly" (*Dongxi yangkao* [Kyoto: Chubun shuppan sha, 1969], 3: 29). Furthermore, she quotes Ong Tae Hae (Wang Dahai), who in his *Haidao yizhi* mentions that "when the Chinese remain abroad for several generations, without return-

and starting in the second half of the nineteenth century, have published even more literature in Malay.[4]

Malay, renamed Indonesian, was declared the national language of Indonesia in 1928 and has, since the rise of the nationalist movement, the Japanese occupation, and Indonesian independence, acquired an increasingly larger number of speakers among indigenous Indonesians in non-Malay-speaking areas.[5] Many people, however—historians, linguists, and other social scientists, as well as average Indonesians—have failed to recognize that before Malay became a code in the daily speech of the majority of non-Malay-speaking Indonesians in the postindependence era, it had already been used extensively by an immigrant minority.[6]

The discourse on the Chinese of Indonesia is often marked by the designation of an "ethnically separate" dialect of Malay, "Chinese Malay" (*Melayu Tionghoa, Melayu Cina*). Most present-day Indonesians, including ethnic Chinese, believe that there is indeed a so-called Chinese Malay dialect.[7] What they have in mind is usually two quite different things. First, they are thinking of the language used in works in Malay by Chinese authors from the second half of the nineteenth century to the early 1960s[8] and, perhaps more familiar to them, the language used in kungfu (*silat*) stories translated from Chinese or originally written in Malay/Indonesian.[9] Second, in Javanese-speaking areas, they have in mind the mixture of Javanese and Malay/Indonesian that they perceive to be spoken exclusively by ethnic Chinese but that actually is also spoken by other ethnic Asians, Eurasians, and indigenous Indonesians connected in some way with the Chinese.[10]

The term "Chinese Malay" is really a misnomer. There may be a continuity between "Chinese Malay" and modern Indonesian, especially because the former was also used in

---

ing to their native land, they frequently cut themselves off from the instructions of the sages; in language, food and dress they imitate the natives and studying foreign books, they do not scruple to become Javanese, when they call themselves Islam (*Sit-lam*)." Salmon, *Literature in Malay*, pp. 15-16; Ong Tae Hae, *The Chinaman Abroad: A Desultory Account of the Malay Archipelago Particularly of Java*, trans. W. H. Medhurst (Shanghai: Mission Press, 1849).

[4] Regarding literature in local languages, see Gilbert Hamonic and Claudine Salmon, "La vie littéraire et artistique des Chinois Peranakan de Makassar (1930–1950)," *Archipel* 26 (1983): 143–78; Claudine Salmon, "A Note on Javanese Works Derived from Chinese Fiction," in *Literary Migrations: Traditional Chinese Fiction in Asia (17–20th Centuries)*, ed. Claudine Salmon (Beijing: International Culture Publishing Corporation, 1987), pp. 375–94; Liang Liji, "Sastra Peranakan Tionghoa dan Kehadirannya dalam Sastra Sunda," *Archipel* 34 (1987): 165–79. For studies on literature in Malay, cf. Nio Joe Lan, *Sastera Indonesia-Tionghoa* (Djakarta: Gunung Agung, 1962); Salmon, *Literature in Malay*; Leo Suryadinata, "Sastra Peranakan di Indonesia," in *Kebudayaan Minoritas Tionghoa di Indonesia*, ed. Leo Suryadinata, trans. Dédé Oetomo (Jakarta: Gramedia, 1988), pp. 100–118.

[5] See, for example, Sutan Takdir Alisjahbana, "Bahasa Indonesia," in *Dari Perjuangan dan Pertumbuhan Bahasa Indonesia: Kumpulan Esai 1932-1957*, (Jakarta: Dian Rakyat, 1978), pp. 20–53.

[6] It should be pointed out that the Chinese were not the only immigrant community to speak Malay among themselves; the Dutch and Eurasians and other so-called Foreign Orientals spoke it too.

[7] Some Indonesians even call it "Chinese language" (*bahasa Tionghoa, bahasa Cina*).

[8] Cf. n. 5.

[9] See Salmon, *Literature in Malay*, 1981, passim; and Leo Suryadinata, "Postwar Kungfu Novels in Indonesia: A Preliminary Survey," in Salmon, *Literary Migrations*, pp. 623–55.

[10] In Javanese-speaking areas, one can perceive a speech continuum from pure Javanese all the way to standard Indonesian, with different varieties of Javanese and Malay/Indonesian mixtures in between. In general, the more formal and polite the situation is, the more Malay/Indonesian forms and the fewer Javanese forms are employed. In fact, in formal situations, the Malay variety used resembles very closely written "Chinese Malay."

the written discourse of members of ethnic groups besides the Chinese in the colonial period and well into the postindependence era.

Although no one refers in the literature to spoken, mixed Javanese-Malay, in some literature that can rectify the myth of a "Chinese Malay," two facts are pointed out:[11] (1) the daily language of Malay-speaking Chinese varies dialectally from region to region, so that one cannot speak of one dialect of Malay used by ethnic Chinese everywhere in the archipelago; and (2) there is little difference between the local dialect of the Malay-speaking Chinese and other local Malay speakers (although this fact needs empirical investigation).

Here the goal is, first, to reinforce the argument for a general urban pre-Indonesian Malay[12] used by all ethnic groups in the Netherlands Indies by examining samples of written language found in periodicals and monographs produced by both indigenous and Chinese authors from the turn of the century up to the 1950s (see app. 1).[13] While arguing for a general urban Malay, I will attempt to explain the differences, some subtle and others not so subtle, that exist at a subdialectal level between the various varieties of the regions and those of different authors.

Second, I will point out the dynamics of the development of different varieties of Malay/Indonesian, by looking at the written language used by indigenous Indonesians and ethnic Chinese in different periods. By looking at the different contexts of language use, one can better appreciate the apparent differences between the variety used by indigenous Indonesians and that used by ethnic Chinese. More recent developments in Indonesian show that the use of Malay/Indonesian has always gone hand in hand with the development of a modern, cosmopolitan, bourgeois culture.

A Grammatical Sketch of Pre-Indonesian Malay

An examination of the grammar of written pre-Indonesian Malay (PIM), paying careful attention to the possible variations in language usage found in the samples, will illustrate how different the dialect is from standard Malay/Indonesian. The latter is the product of language engineering by the colonial linguistic establishment and, later, by similar agencies, which are often continuations of the former, set up by the Republic. The phonology, inasmuch as it can be gathered from the orthography and from older speakers' pronunciations, and an examination of the morphology and syntax as well as some vocabulary items will

---

[11] See Sutan Takdir Alisjahbana, "Kedudukan Bahasa Melayu-Tionghoa," in *Dari Perjuangan*, pp. 57–63; Armijn Pané, "Het Chineesch-Maleisch en het Indonesisch," *Sin Po wekelijksche editie*, 13: 661, (30 xi 1935), 25–26; Pramoedya Ananta Toer, ed., *Tempo Doeloe: Antologi Sastra Pra-Indonesia* (Jakarta: Hasta Mitra, 1982), pp. 1–16; Claudine Salmon, "La notion de sino-malais est-elle pertinente d'un point de vue linguistique?" *Archipel* 20 (1980): 177–86 (an English translation may be found in Salmon, *Literature in Malay*, pp. 115–22).

[12] I am grateful to Ben Anderson for pointing out the designation "urban" for the variety of Malay discussed here. The term *pre-Indonesian* was first used by Pramoedya Ananta Toer (see, for example, his introduction to *Tempo Doeloe*, pp. 1–16, where he also uses the term *lingua franca Malay*).

[13] See the list of the materials scanned at the end of this article. The samples were selected according to their availability in my personal collection as well as that of the Cornell University library Echols Collection on Southeast Asia. They were further selected according to place of publication (Java or the Outer Islands) and for historical moments when one might expect to see a major change in language use, such as the establishment of the Balai Poestaka/Commissie voor de Volkslectuur colonial state publishing house (1908), the Japanese occupation (1942–1945), the proclamation of independence and independence war (1945–1949), and the transfer of sovereignty from the Dutch (1949). I ended the scan in the 1950s because the decade saw the start of the development of a distinct variety of Indonesian in which one can no longer discern any differences between the styles of indigenous Indonesians and ethnic Chinese in the formal written language.

show that (1) in general, a Malay of urban centers is used by different ethnic groups, especially when one compares it to other varieties of Malay used elsewhere; (2) one can also discern subdialectal differences, especially through loanwords from the languages originally used by each ethnic group; and (3) the influence of language standardization was felt in the written language of indigenous authors and of Chinese authors writing for indigenous or general publications after the establishment of a standardized system of spelling (1901) and the Balai Pustaka (1908) but was not apparent in the writings of most Chinese authors until after Indonesian independence (1949). However, even a cursory glance at the spoken language shows that old habits die hard; one still finds older speakers of Indonesian speaking with the grammar of PIM, although their vocabulary has come to include modern items.

The Phonology and Orthography of Pre-Indonesian Malay

Although audio recordings of pre-Indonesian Malay are not available, the dialect can be deduced from the orthography and the pronunciation of most speakers of modern Indonesian in Java. All of the authors use quite consistent spelling systems, although these may differ slightly from author to author or from publication to publication. If one compares the pronunciation of the large majority of speakers of modern Indonesian in Java, for example, to the orthography, one realizes that not much has changed, especially in the language of older speakers or in the informal variety spoken by younger speakers.

Some peculiarities of different varieties of PIM are apparent. Although the sounds themselves are shared by the different varieties, the way they are arranged in syllables (the phonotactics) shows interesting differences from standard Indonesian.

The earliest printed materials do not evidence major differences in the orthography among those written by Eurasians, Chinese, or other Foreign Orientals and indigenous Indonesians. An 1845 Malay primer,[14] for example, contains samples of letters written in different Indonesian regions from the late eighteenth century to the middle of the nineteenth century. One was written in Yogyakarta on February 22, 1828, apparently by an Arab, and addressed to the Resident of Surakarta, Colonel Naguijs.[15] The following features, also found in later specimens of PIM are immediately apparent:

1. Where standard Malay (SM) has an *h* at the end, PIM does not, for example, *soeda* (SM *soedah*), "already";[16] *kasie* (SM *kasih*) "give"; *bolee* (SM *boléh*), "be allowed to"; *Roepiea* (SM *Roepiah*), "name of currency"; *lebeenja* (SM *lebihnja*), "the rest"; *tana* (SM *tanah*), "land." Interestingly, in one instance, the writer does use a form ending in *h*, namely, *itoelah*, "that." Similarly, where SM has an initial *h*, PIM does not in some forms, for example, *ati* (SM *hati*), "liver, heart, feelings."

2. Where SM has a final *au*, PIM has *oe*, at least in some words, for example, *kaloe* (SM *kalau*), "if, when."

3. Where SM has a syllable ending in *aC*, where *C* is a consonant, PIM has a syllable ending in *eC* in many forms, for example, the suffix *-ken* (SM *-kan*), "transitivitizing/causative-benefactive suffix"; *dalem* (SM *dalam*), "inside"; *dengen* (SM *dengan*), "with"; *patjek* (SM *padjak*), "tax"; *dapet* (SM *dapat*), "obtain, gain"; *dateng* (SM *datang*), "come"; *harep* (SM

---

[14]A. Meursinge, *Maleisch leesboek voor eerstbeginnenden en meergevorderden*, pt. 2 (Leiden: S. en J. Luchtmans, 1845).

[15]Meursinge, *Maleisch leesboek*, pp. xxviii–xxx.

[16]The spelling of standard Malay/Indonesian follows that of Van Ophuijsen (1901); cf. Ch. A. van Ophuijsen, *Kitab Logat Melajoe: Woordenlijst voor de Spelling der Maleische Taal met Latinsche Karakter* (Batavia: Landsdrukkerij, 1903).

harap), "hope." However, some forms are spelled in the same way as in SM, for example, *saban*, "each, every."

4. On the other hand, where SM has *e*, especially in prefixes, PIM has *a* in some forms, for example, *kapada* (SM *kepada*), "to"; *barnama* (SM *bernama*), "be named"; *bartemoe* (SM *bertemoe*), "meet"; *ampat* (SM *empat*), "four"; *katiega* (SM *ketiga*), "third"; *kaampat* (SM *keëmpat*), "fourth"; *sarta* (SM *serta*), "as well as"; *salama lamanja* (SM *selama-lamanja*), "as long as possible"; *maningalken* (SM *meninggalkan*), "abandon"; *manariema* (SM *menerima*), "accept"; *kaloear* (SM *keloear*), "go out," *mengartie* (SM *mengerti*), "understand."

5. Where SM has *oea*, PIM has *oewa*, such as in *oewang* (SM *oeang*), "money"; *soewatoe* (SM *soeatoe*), "some kind of."

6. Many forms containing the sequence *-CerV-* in SM, where C is a consonant and V a vowel, appear with the sequence *-CrV* in PIM, such as in *priksa* (SM *periksa*), "examine"; *negrie* (SM *negeri*), "country."

7. The glottal stop is not indicated in the spelling of some authors, such as in *tida* (SM *tida'*), "not," or is represented by the letters *h* or *k*, such as in *perkatahan* (SM *perkataän*), "word, phrase," or *tjoetjoek* (SM *tjoetjoe*), "grandchild."

8. Some forms are spelled in ways that are peculiar to PIM, such as *njang* (SM *jang*),[17] "that, who, which"; *koetika* (SM *ketika*), "when (as conjunction)."

The 1828 specimen also contains many peculiar spellings not found in later specimens. When one compares it with other specimens in the primer written in Java, one finds that the previously mentioned spelling conventions are consistently followed. One exception is a letter from Bandung dated August 8, 1829, in which *dateng* and *harep* are spelled *datang* and *harap*, respectively; however, the orthography is otherwise basically the same as in the letters from Central and East Java and Madura.[18] It is when one compares these specimens from Java to those from Kupang and Arau Wukan in eastern Indonesia dated 1797 to 1804[19] that one notices some orthographical differences, such as the sound [u][20] inconsistently represented by *u* such as in *tuwan*, "sir, lord" and *mulija*, "noble"; and *oe*, such as in *satoe*, "one," and *doea*, "two"; or SM final *n* appearing as *ng*, such as in *kapang* (SM *kapan*), "when," and *laing* (SM *lain*), "other."

The same features of PIM can still be found in an announcement for the Surabaya-based *Soerat Kabar bahasa Melaijoe* (January 12, 1856), published by the Eurasian E. Fuhri and aimed at a Chinese audience,[21] and in excerpts from two Batavian newspapers of 1879: *Bintang Barat*, April 1 and *Pembrita Betawi*, February 7.[22] Both of the latter were published by Eurasians employing Eurasian, Chinese, and indigenous journalists. However, another announcement from *Soerat Chabar Betawie* (April 3, 1858) does show one orthographic feature closer to the SM spelling introduced more than forty years later, namely, words such as

---

[17] After the turn of the century, it seems that this spelling was completely replaced by *jang*, although in spoken language one can hear older speakers pronounce it as *njang*.

[18] Meursinge, *Maleisch leesboek*, p. xxxi.

[19] Ibid., pp. xv–xxviii.

[20] I am here using symbols of the International Phonetic Association.

[21] Sudarjo Tjokrosisworo, ed., *Kenangan Sekilas Sedjarah Perdjuangan Pers Sebangsa* (Jakarta: Serikat Perusahaan Suratkabar, 1958), pp. 139–40.

[22] These excerpts are reprinted in issues dated June 11 and June 6, 1990, of the Jakarta-based newspaper *Jayakarta*; the orthography seems to have been faithfully preserved.

dalam (PIM *dalem*), "inside"; *dengan* (PIM *dengen*), "with"; and *menjatakan* (PIM *menjataken*), "declare."[23]

This was, then, the situation of Malay orthography toward the turn of the century. The orthographic features of works by the Chinese, despite inconsistencies between authors and over time, were generally similar to those of the system just described. Thus, up to the 1900s, except for a few unusual cases like the letter from Bandung and the announcement from *Soerat Chabar Betawie*, the orthography of PIM does not show differences based on the ethnicity of the authors.

In 1901, the colonial government introduced the spelling devised by Van Ophuijsen.[24] Most nongovernmental, indigenous publications, such as the nationalist periodical *Kaoem Moeda* based in Bandung, complied with the new orthography. In its January 2, 1915, issue, for example, one can read the following:

> Soerat kabar "Preanger Bode" soedah membikin pertanjaan demikian [Sanggoepkah Duitschland menjerang ketanah Inggris?], laloe memberi poela djawabannja dengan pandjang lebar bahwa diwaktoe ini beloem boleh diharap jang Duitschland akan bisa menoeroenkan lasjkarnja dengan hasil ditanah Inggris.[25]

The first chief editor of this publication was Abdoel Moeis, some of whose works were published by the state-owned Balai Poestaka, so it is not surprising that *Kaoem Moeda* complied with the new orthography. But one also cannot help correlating the spelling of words like *dengan*, "with," *diharap*, "be expected," *akan*, "will," and *menoeroenkan*, "land" with the fact that the publication came out of Bandung (cf. the letter from Bandung).

Nevertheless, from time to time one does find inconsistencies, such as in the annual report of the nationalist organization Boedi Oetomo for 1917–1918[26] in which on the same page one can find the words *mengoeraikan*, "expound," and *dengen* (SM *dengan*), "with." One interesting case can be found in Mas Marco Kartodikromo's *Sair rempah-rempah*.[27] The Semarang-based publisher included an errata sheet (*rectificatie*) in which the erroneous *membitjarakenja*, "speak about it," is corrected as *membitjarakannja*. However, whoever corrected it apparently did not read the Van Ophuijsen manual carefully because he or she also corrected SM *karena*, "because," and *berani*, "brave," to PIM *krena* and *brani*, respectively.

Moreover, it seems that people's compliance became lax in advertising materials, such as those found in Semaoen's *Hikajat Kadiroen*.[28] Although the contents are at least orthographically consistent with the standardized spelling, an advertisement on the last page of the book reads as follows: "Soedara-soedara jang maoe membikin barang-barang tjitakan, oepamanja: soerat-soerat OELEM, STAAT-STAAT, BRIEFKAART, VISITE KAARTJES dan lain-lainnja, hareplah memesen pada Drukkerij V.S.T.P. KARANGBIDARA atau SINAR-

---

[23]Tjokrosisworo, *Kenangan*, pp. 140–41. This feature in Lie Kimhok's grammar (*Malajoe Batawie: Kitab deri hal perkataän Malajoe, hal memetjah oedjar-oedjar Malajoe dan hal pernahkan tanda-tanda batja dan hoeroef-hoeroef besar* [Batavia: W. Bruining, 1884]) differs from the common practice of his day. Otherwise, he consistently spells in the same way as the system described.

[24]Van Ophuijsen, *Kitab Logat Melajoe*.

[25]"The newspaper *Preanger Bode* has posed the following question [Does Germany have the capability to invade England?], then has also given the answer at length that at the moment one cannot expect that Germany will be able to land its troops successfully in England" (my translation).

[26]*Verslag Boedi Oetomo*, Tahoen Kesepoeloeh 1917–1918 (Solo: Albert Rusche, 1919).

[27]Mas Marco Kartodikromo, *Sair rempah-rempah*, vols. 1, 2 (Semarang: Sinar Djawa, 1918).

[28]Semaoen, *Hikajat Kadiroen* (Semarang: Kantoor P.K.I., 1920).

DJAWA KAOEMAN-SEMARANG."[29] Notice the spelling of *soedara* (SM *saudara*), "brother, second person pronoun"; *tjitakan* (SM *tjétakan*), "printed"; *hareplah* (SM *haraplah*), "please"; and *memesen* (SM *memesan*), "order." A similar example from somewhat later can be found in an advertisement for a hair oil produced by the Chinese drugstore Jo Tek Tjoe in Batavia published in the monthly women's magazine *Doenia Kita* (Batavia-Centrum, March 1938):

> "Membikin kepala djadi enteng,
> tida koreng
> matiken koetoe
> ilangken ketombe."[30]

And if people think the ad is spelled that way because it was written by a Chinese, one notes the following advertisement for "Het Djamoehuis uit de Vorstenlanden" (The Herbal Medicine House from the Principalities), presumably owned by a Javanese merchant, which starts off with "Soepaja U tida kesalahan beli djamoe bikinan BETAWI, datenglah pada."[31] Many other advertisements use similar nonstandardized orthography, which probably indicates that the business world did not pay too much attention to the standardized orthography.

One indigenous newspaper that almost consistently "flouted" the standardized orthography was *Medan Prijaji*,[32] in which one can read passages such as the following:

> Itoe semoea orang dapet taoe dengan membatja soerat kabar Pembrita Tjoeng Wa sebab ini soerat kabar ada pake bahasa Melajoe rendah, soeatoe bahasa jang gampang orang mengerti dan jang djadi bahasanja sebagian besar pendoedoek di Hindia Nederland (1909).[33]

> Barang kali kebanjakan Bopati tida dapet taoe jang Sripadoeka jang di pertoean Besar Gouverneur Generaal Idenburg ada di poedji dan di pertjajai oleh Santri-santri kita. (May 21, 1910).[34]

The fact that the standardized version of Malay was based on "Riau Malay" meant that Sumatran publications exhibited little of this nonstandardized orthography, at least in formal writing. However, one does find an interesting case in cartoons in the periodical *Soeara*

---

[29] "Those of you who would like to make printed materials, for example: INVITATIONS, FORMS, POSTCARDS, VISITING CARDS and others, please order them at the V.S.T.P. KARANGBIDARA or SINAR-DJAWA Printing Press, KAOEMAN-SEMARANG" (my translation).

[30] "Makes your head feel light/prevents scabs/kills lice/gets rid of dandruff" (my translation). In standardized spelling, it would read: "Membikin kepala djadi enteng/tida' koreng/matikan koetoe/hilangkan ketombe." Note, however, the use of typically PIM vocabulary: *membikin* (SM *memboeat*) "make, cause" and *enteng* (SM *ringan*) "light."

[31] "Lest you make a mistake buying herbal medicine made in BATAVIA, come to" (my translation). In standardized spelling, it would read: "*Soepaja U tida' kesalahan beli djamoe bikinan BETAWI, datanglah pada.*"

[32] At least in the issues available to me.

[33] (Cited in Salmon, *Literature in Malay*, p. 115) "Everyone can understand by reading the newspaper *Pembrita Tjoeng Wa* because it uses Low Malay, a language easily understood and the language of a majority of the population in the Netherlands Indies" (my translation). In standardized Malay orthography, it would read, "*itoe semoea orang dapat tahoe dengan membatja soerat kabar Pembrita Tjoeng Wa sebab ini soerat kabar ada pakai bahasa Melajoe rendah, soeatoe bahasa jang gampang orang mengerti dan jang djadi bahasanja sebagian besar pendoedoek di Hindia Nederland.*"

[34] "Perhaps most Regents cannot understand that His Excellency the Great Lord Governor General Idenburg has been praised and trusted by our Followers" (my translation). In standardized orthography, it would read "*Barangkali kebanjakan Boepati tida' dapat tahoe jang Sripadoeka jang dipertoean Besar Gouverneur Generaal Idenburg ada dipoedji dan dipertajai oléh Santri-santri kita.*"

berkala "Alhambra" (Roman jang modern), published in Belawan-Deli in the 1930s. The informal dialog in the cartoons includes sentences such as *"Sobar2 adjélah ngobrol sampe"* (SM *Sabar2[?] adjalah ngobrol sampai)*,[35] which reminds one of Batavian/Jakarta Malay pronunciation.

It is somewhat ironic that whereas most indigenous nationalists quickly complied with the spelling introduced by the colonial government, it was actually the Chinese periodicals and books that remained in the nonstandardized orthography. Many examples can be cited, but to select at random, consider this excerpt from the Batavia-based *Sin Po* of July 1, 1914: "Dalem taon 1912 dalem soerat kabar N. Soer. Crt. ada dimoeat satoe protest atas hal kasi balik kombali ka Soemba itoe tiga radja Lowa jang diboewang."[36]

A similar orthography was used by a Chinese newspaper, *Han Po*, published in Palembang, South Sumatra. This example from its first issue was dated November 8, 1926: "Dalem proefnummer kita soeda tida menerangken, kenapa kita poenja soerat kabar soeda dapetken itoe nama 'Han Po'? Disini kita rasa baek djoega kaloe pembatja bisa taoe."[37] Apparently, even in a place like Palembang in Sumatra, the nonstandardized spelling was also used by Chinese publishers.

During the Japanese occupation (1942–1945), when the regime encouraged the further cultivation of what was by then called Indonesian, the Chinese newspaper *Kung Yung Pao* continued to use the nonstandardized orthography, as in the following excerpt: "Berhoeboeng dengen diboekanja permoesjawaratan Kesoesastra'an Asia Timoer Raya jang ke II di Tokio pada tg. 25–26 Agoestoes 2603, Poesat Keboedajaan (Keimin Bunka Shidosjo) di Djakarta soedah mengirimken kawat oetjapan slamet salinannja dari bahasa Nippon."[38]

Chinese-published newspapers during the independence war era (1945–1949) also used nonstandardized orthography. In the first issue of the Semarang-based *Sin Min* (February 1, 1947), one can read the following introductory remark: "Djikaloe satoe soerat-kabar baroe sebagi *Sin Min* sampe boeat pertama kali di tangan pembatja, soeda samoestinja di antara berbagi-bagi pertanja'an jang timboel dalem hati pembatja adalah jang teroetama: Begimana haloeannja."[39]

---

[35]But this is definitely a moot point because the language is clearly so informal. However, this is brought up here to show that even in Sumatra one does come across nonstandardized orthography.

[36]"In the year 1912, in the newspaper *N. Soer. Crt.*, a protest was published on the matter of the return to Soemba of the three exiled kings of Lowa" (my translation). In standardized orthography, it would read *"Dalam tahoen 1912 dalam soerat kabar N. Soer. Crt. ada dimoeat satoe protest atas hal kasih balik kembali ke Soemba itoe tiga radja Lowa jang diboeang."*

[37]"In our trial issue, we have not explained why our newspaper has acquired the name 'Han Po.' Here we think it is good if the readers can know" (my translation). In standardized orthography, it would read *"Dalam proefnummer kita soedah tida' menerangkan, kenapa kita poenja soerat kabar soedah dapatkan itoe nama 'Han Po'? Disini kita rasa baik djoega pembatja bisa tahoe."*

[38]"In connection with the opening of the second assembly on Greater East Asian Literature in Tokyo on 25–26 August 2603, the Cultural Center (Keimin Bunka Shidosjo) in Djakarta has sent a congratulatory cable, whose translation from Japanese . . ." (my translation). *Kung Yung Pao*, August 23, 1943. Note the spelling of *dengen* (SM *dengan*), "with"; *mengirimken* (SM *mengirimkan*), "send"; *slamet* (SM *selamat*), "congratulations."

[39]"When a new newspaper like *Sin Min* reaches the readers for the first time, it is only natural that among the different questions that crop up in their minds, the foremost question will be What is its ideology like?" (my translation). In standardized orthography, it would read, *"Djikalau satoe soerat-kabar baroe sebagai Sin Min sampai boeat pertama kali ditangan pembatja, soedah semestinja diantara berbagai-bagai pertanja'an jang timboel dalam hati pembatja adalah jang teroetama: Bagaimana haloeannja."*

Apparently, Chinese-published newspapers gradually standardized their orthography to conform to the 1947 Suwandi spelling system only after the transfer of sovereignty from the Netherlands to the Republic of Indonesia. Thus, in the February 24, 1950, issue of *Keng Po*, one can read the following: "Dalam pertemuan tanja djawab istimewa jang pertama diadakan sesudah penjerahannja surat-surat kepertjajaan kepada presiden Truman, duta besar Indonesia di Washington, Mr. Ali Sastroamidjojo, menerangkan kepada koresponden politik Aneta, bahwa ia tidak berpendapat kemadjuan komunisme di Asia akan mendjadi bahaja jang langsung bagi Indonesia."[40] However, another look at the advertising page again reveals nonstandardized spelling of words such as *tida* (standard Indonesian [SI] *tidak*), "not"; *sampe* (SI *sampai*), "arrive, until"; *djato* (SI *djatuh*), "fall"; and many others.

Thus, it is safe to conclude that in Java authors writing in romanized Malay orthography had initially used the same spelling system. After the establishment of the 1901 Van Ophuijsen spelling, however, most indigenous authors complied with this standardized spelling, at least in formal writing, whereas most ethnic Chinese authors only adapted their spelling system to the 1947 Suwandi Republican spelling after the transfer of sovereignty in 1949.

Despite this difference in orthography, the pronunciation of Indonesian has remained undifferentiated by speaker ethnicity to this day. Granted, some speakers of present-day Indonesian of Javanese language background, for example, do attempt to standardize or de-Javanize their pronunciation, but the majority still speak Indonesian with a fairly strong Javanese accent. It is interesting to note that even some present-day Indonesian speakers from other regional language backgrounds are starting to pronounce the transitivizing/causative-benefactive suffix *-kan* as [kən]. The author hypothesizes that this shift has been caused by the Javanese-accented pronunciation of national leaders of Javanese language background, such as Presidents Sukarno and Suharto, who pronounce forms ending in [-aC] as [-əC], such as in [daləm] and [datəŋ] instead of the standard forms [dalam] "inside" and [dataŋ] "come." One might speculate that these non-Javanese are in a position to benefit most from loyalty to the regime.

With the increasing inclination of national leaders to speak off the cuff on the radio and television, one can hear the way they actually pronounce Indonesian. It is not uncommon for leaders who are in their fifties and sixties to show peculiarities often thought to be the sole property of PIM, as in words like [misɨh] (SI [masih] or [masɨh] "still, yet") and [kalɔʔ] (SI [kalaʔ] or [kalɔʔ] "if, when"). Thus, the early PIM authors, whatever their ethnic background might have been, were spelling their Malay in a phonetically faithful way. It was, in fact, the new standardized spelling of Van Ophuijsen and later the Suwandi and 1972 spellings that did not represent PIM faithfully.

The Morphology of Pre-Indonesian Malay

One feature of PIM morphology is the dropping of the verb prefixes *ber-* 'stative' and *meN-* "active." Thus, in the reprint from the February 7, 1879, issue of *Pembrita Betawi* referred to previously, one finds phrases like *orang njang maoe rampas aerlodjinja itoe toewan*[41] (a man who wanted to take the gentleman's watch by force), *soepaja itoe toewan kaloewarin aerlo-*

---

[40]"In a special press conference held after he handed over his credentials to President Truman, Indonesia's ambassador in Washington, Mr. Ali Sastroamidjojo, explained to Aneta's political correspondent that he did not think the progress of communism in Asia would become a direct danger to Indonesia" (my translation). By this time, no comment can be made on the orthography except that it complies fully with the Suwandi spelling.

[41]The SM equivalent would be *orang jang maoe merampas arlodji toean itoe*.

djinja,[42] (so that the gentleman took his watch out), *Si rampok pegi tanja*,[43] (the robber went and asked). However, in the same excerpt one also finds full forms such as *menampar*, "slap." No certain way of generalizing is apparent to ascertain when the prefix *ber-* and *meN-* may be dropped.

One also sees a tendency to use prefixes interchangeably, even in the work of the same author, such as *berdjawab* and *mendjawab* "answer," or *bernama* and *ternama*, "be called, named." At times, one also finds *hypercorrect* forms such as *berdoedoek* (SM *doedoek*), "sit," and *memakan* (SM *makan*), "eat." The passive verb prefix *di-*, however, seems to be used properly, most likely because it carries a clearly different meaning in a sentence.

Another feature of PIM morphology is the use of the all-purpose transitive suffix *-in*, originally from Batavian Malay (e.g., *kaloewarin*, "take out" [SM *keloearkan*]). The fact that Batavian Malay has collapsed the two Malay suffixes *-i* "locative" and *-kan* "causative-benefactive"[44] has meant that many authors tend to use them interchangeably, such as in *segala orang boleh masoki di soerat chabar inie segala pemberitaan* (all kinds of people may publish all kinds of news in this newspaper) and *barang kali kita masoq-kan soerat pengadjaran* (perhaps we shall publish educational writings).[45]

But certainly every author—Dutch, Eurasian, Foreign Oriental, and indigenous—wrote this kind of Malay. After prescriptive grammars became available, those who were sensitive to language engineering tended to comply with them, but others seemed to ignore them almost altogether. Generally speaking, Chinese authors again tended to lag behind in complying with standardized Malay, and only after 1949 did they seem to standardize their morphology considerably.

Thus, as with phonology, one sees here a case wherein the colonial government, and later also the Republican government, prescribed a grammar that really did not represent the language used in everyday life.

The Syntax of Pre-Indonesian Malay

It is in the syntax of PIM that one finds agreement among many indigenous and most Chinese authors even after independence, in that both differed from the prescribed standard.

Both in Chinese and nationalist indigenous publications written by authors of Javanese language background, one finds syntactic constructions such as *itu*, "that," or *ini*, "this" + noun: for example, *itoe toewan (SM toean itoe)*; "that gentleman"; the possessive constructions $noun_2$ + *-nja* + pronoun/$noun_2$ or $noun_2$ + *dari(pada)* + $noun_2$ or $noun_2$ + *(em)poenja* + $noun_2$ where $noun_2$ is the possessed and $noun_2$ is the possessor, for example, *toean-toean empoenja Comité* (SM *Comité toean-toean*), "your committee," and *roemahnja toean Assistent-Wedono dari onderdistrict Semongan djoego* (SM *roemah toean Assistent-Wedono onderdistrict Semongan djoego*) "the house of the assistant district head of the subdistrict Semongan Djoego." It should be mentioned here that authors even in nongovernment publications in Medan, North Sumatra, used this kind of syntax.

---

[42]The SM equivalent would be *soepaja toean itoe mengeloearkan arlodjinja*.

[43]The SM equivalent would be *Si rampok pergi bertanja*.

[44]Of course, spelled *-ken* by many authors.

[45]*Soerat Chabar Batawie*, April 3, 1858, reprinted in Tjokrosisworo, *Kenangan*, pp. 140–41. The SM equivalent would be *segala orang boleh memasoekkan segala pemberitaan di soerat chabar ini* and *barangkali kita masoekkan soerat pengadjaran*, respectively.

One also finds the use in PIM of certain function words or conjunctions that differs from standard usage, such as the different use of *ada* in sentences like *ini soerat kabar ada pake bahasa Melajoe rendah* (this newspaper uses Low Malay) (SM *soerat kabar ini memakai bahasa Melajoe rendah*), and the different use of *jang* or *njang* in phrases like "*boléé diharep jang Duitschland aken bisa menoeroenken*" ([it] may be expected that Germany will be able to deploy) (SM *boléh diharap[kan] bahwa Duitschland akan bisa menoeroenkan*)

One should mention also the extensive use in PIM of a semipassive construction, such as in *pekara [n]jang orang mengartie* (issues that people understand) (SM *perkara jang dimengerti orang*). The "full" passive using the *di-* prefix is also used, however.

It is true that some Balai Poestaka-oriented publications, mostly written by indigenous authors but also by a few Chinese, did comply with the syntactic rules of standardized Malay. But this usage was perhaps indicative of the colonial establishment wanting to "purify" PIM by employing Sumatran editors, who were, supposedly, the real and pure speakers of Malay. *Soeara Timoer*, the magazine of the *Perikatan Perkoempoelan Radio Ketimoeran* (Association of Oriental Radio Organizations), a multiethnic association active in the early 1940s, was an interesting case in point. The editors and contributors of this periodical consisted of indigenous Indonesians and ethnic Chinese and Arabs. In its first issue (December 28, 1940–January 11, 1941), in the middle of articles written in standardized Malay, was an article by the Chinese Mrs. Tjoa Hien Hoeij; it is clear that the editors were trying to standardize her language, but apparently they found the job overwhelming and gave up after the first paragraph or so.

It is probably safe to conclude that more indigenous authors flouted the rules of standardized Malay in syntax than in orthography and morphology. With education in standardized Indonesian after independence, syntactic constructions peculiar to PIM tended to disappear in formal discourse.

However, a cursory look at the colloquial language of modern Indonesia reveals that many people still use the syntax of PIM. In fact, as late as the mid-1960s one could still find someone like Sukarno speaking off the cuff and using PIM syntax. The same can be said about the unrehearsed language of President Suharto and other officials today. It is interesting that now some people complain about the so-called *bahasa pejabat*, "officialese," with features like the excessive use of *daripada*, "of, possessive marker." The recent popularity of the use of *noun/adjective + punya* among trendy youths bears witness to the pervasive influence of PIM.

The Vocabulary of Pre-Indonesian Malay

The vocabulary of PIM contains words that are spelled or pronounced differently in SM, such as *belon* or *beloen* (SM *beloem*), "not yet"; *koetika* (SM *ketika*), "when" (as a conjunction); *kombali* (SM *kembali*), "return"; and *misih* (SM *masih*), "still, yet." A few words have a different meaning in PIM; for example, PIM *koetika* means "chance, opportunity" in addition to "when" (as a conjunction), which is its sole meaning in SM.

PIM also uses words that are considered colloquial or nonstandard in SM, such as *kasi[h]*, "give" (SM *beri*) and *bikin*, "make, do" (SM *boeat, kerdjakan*). Incidentally, these PIM words are used in combination with other words to signify the causative as in *kasi[h] lihat*, "cause to see (i.e., show)" and *bikin betoel*, "cause to be in order (i.e., repair)." The same causative meaning is expressed in SM with the suffix *-kan* and/or the prefix *per-* (thus, *per +lihat +kan* for *kasi[h] lihat*; *mem +betoel +kan* for *bikin betoel*). One should note, however, that such PIM words have survived in the spoken language and in the past fifteen years or so have been revived by publications like *Tempo* magazine.

The main difference between a PIM vocabulary and that of SM is the freer borrowing from other languages one finds in PIM. PIM generally borrows more freely from Javanese and Dutch, whereas in the SM of Balai Poestaka publications, one notices a conscious attempt to avoid using loan words whenever possible. More accurately, one must point out that the Balai Poestaka editors, many of whom had a Minang language background, tended to borrow from that language as well. One can then argue that whether from Javanese or from Minang, PIM or SM does borrow vocabulary items.

When one takes into account the existence of borrowed words, one may say that there are subdialects of PIM, in the sense that ethnic Chinese authors tend to sprinkle their Malay with borrowings from Hokkien Chinese. Only in this context can one speak of a "Chinese Malay" or a Chinese subdialect of PIM. But perhaps, then, one must also speak of a "Javanese Malay" or "Arab Malay" as subdialects because these groups also borrow from their original languages.

What many people mistakenly call "Chinese-Malay," structurally and in formal language use, has only been a variety of Malay/Indonesian (pre-Indonesian Malay) widely used by the bourgeoisie in colonial urban centers.

The Chinese of Java, together with other bourgeois population groups in the colony, did develop a mixed colloquial Javanese-Malay language. But it should be emphasized that the Chinese were not the only group to have done that. In fact, now more and more Javanese families are doing so, too.

Pre-Indonesian Malay and Modern Indonesian: The Social Dynamics of Language Development

One sees then how PIM started as the lingua franca of different groups in the colony's urban society. The colonial government, however, planned to purify this variety of Malay,[46] and the culmination was the establishment of the 1901 Van Ophuijsen spelling and the ensuing standardization efforts of the Balai Poestaka.

If one considers the instances described in the preceding section, one may conclude that the results of the colonial effort were largely as follows:

1. In orthography, many indigenous authors did comply, but Chinese authors did not do so until after 1949.

2. In morphology, syntax and vocabulary, however, only those authors whose works were actually published by official publishing houses, mainly Balai Poestaka, showed signs of compliance. Most of these authors were indigenous; many were of Sumatran origin. Chinese authors and indigenous nationalists of Javanese language background retained the use of features typical of PIM, which were stigmatized by the colonial linguistic and literary establishment.

Ironically, after independence the Balai Poestaka variety continued to be regarded as standard Indonesian. However, in Java, preindependence Malay has survived in informal and intimate speech. Java Indonesian has had different subvarieties. If one concentrates on just the variety used by those with Javanese language background, one finds that both eth-

---

[46]Cf. John Hoffman, "A Foreign Investment: Indies Malay to 1901," *Indonesia* 27 (1979): 65–92, passim.

nic Javanese and Chinese use basically the same variety in interethnic encounters. But when one examines the domains of language usage, one finds differences.

The Chinese of Java, who adopted Malay earlier than most indigenous speakers, developed a mixed Javanese-Malay home language when most indigenous families still spoke Javanese at home. This mixed language was not used exclusively by the Chinese. Eurasians and other Foreign Orientals, such as Arabs and ethnic South Asians, who participated in bourgeois, colonial life, also used it in their homes. As noted previously, commercial advertisements in indigenous publications tended to use nonstandardized Malay although standardized Malay, was used throughout the text. Similarly, in business circles people use nonstandardized Indonesian with heavy Javanese influence. Especially in the marketplace and retail shops, indigenous traders and employees use the mixed Javanese-Malay variety.

In more formal domains, everyone tries to speak a variety of Indonesian as close as possible to the prescribed standard. Failure to meet the standard is usually because the speaker has not been educated in the postindependence system, in which standardized Indonesian has been the medium of instruction. It may be true that some Chinese have been less concerned about standardizing their Indonesian, but the same can also be said about quite a few Javanese.

With the increasing modernization and capitalization of Indonesian life, more and more urban, middle-class, indigenous families in Java—and apparently elsewhere—are adopting Indonesian as the home language.[47] In Javanese-speaking areas, this means that for the first time, these families are using Indonesian and Javanese side by side in the home. Interestingly enough, but perhaps not surprisingly, the type of Javanese-Malay/Indonesian mixture that has long been spoken at home by Eurasians, Chinese, and Arabs can now also be heard in Javanese families. It is remarkable that one Javanese grandmother commented on how her children and grandchildren are speaking "like Chinese" (*koyok Cino*).

It is, then, another irony that as many Chinese families are becoming better educated in the Indonesian system and, hence, adopting a variety of Java Indonesian in the home that is closer to the standardized norm, more and more middle-class Javanese families are acquiring the variety stereotypically labeled "Chinese Malay" or "Chinese Indonesian."

In Java, then, and perhaps in other areas, such as Madura, Bali, and elsewhere, where the indigenous population mostly spoke a regional language, the Chinese of Indonesia have played a significant role in the development of modern Indonesian; they have been by far the largest group to communicate in a variety of Malay, admittedly not the one condoned by the colonial government, which later developed into a specific variety of modern colloquial Indonesian. Their role is, of course, more significant if one considers that with Malay they provided their own group as well as others in both pre- and postindependence Indonesia with a literature, a press, and various genres of performing arts more accessible to the general population than those provided by the colonial government.

---

[47]See Dédé Oetomo, "Bahasa Indonesia dan Kelas Menengah Indonesia," *Prisma* 18 (1) (1989): 17–29.

Appendix 1
Corpus Materials

Periodicals

Bintang Barat (Batavia), 1.iv.1879 (reprinted in *Jayakarta*, 11.vi.1990).
Doenia Achirat (Fort de Kock), 19.x.1923.
Doenia Kita (Batavia-Centrum), Maart 1938.
Han Po (Palembang), 8.xi.1926.
Indonesia Raja (Batavia-Centrum), December 1937.
Isteri Indonesia (Batavia), no. 6, June 1939.
Kaoem Moeda (Bandoeng), 2.i.1915.
Keng Po (Batavia/Djakarta), 4.ii.1931, 3.xi.1940, 2.i.1947, 12.vii.1947, 24.ii.1950.
Kung Yung Pao (Djakarta), 23.viii.1943.
Medan-Prijaji (Batavia), 1909, 21.v.1910.
Mimbar Indonesia (Djakarta), 10.xi.1947.
Palembang Sinboen (Palembang), 7.xi.1944.
Patriot (Jogjakarta), 23.v.1946.
Pembrita Betawi (Batavia), 7.ii.1879 (reprinted in *Jayakarta*, 6.vi.1990).
Pewarta Pertoekangan ("Het Ambachtsblad") (Jogjakarta), 5.iv.1937.
Siasat (Djakarta), 14.vi.1947, 28.ix.1947.
Sin Min (Semarang), 1.ii.1947, 16.vii.1956.
Sin Po (Batavia/Djakarta), 1.vii.1914, 18.ii.1919, 1.vii.1924, 2.vii.1924, 2.vii.1930, 3.vii.1930, 15.ii.1935, 15.vii.1939, 2.i.1953, 2.i.1958.
Sin Po Oost-Java/Sin Tit Po (Soerabaia), 1.vii.1922, 16.xii.1941.
Soeara Berkala "Alhambra" (Roman jang modern) (Belawan-Deli), no. 2, ca. 1930.
Soeara Oemoem (Djakarta), 4.ii.1947.
Soeara Timoer - Madjallah PPRK (Perikatan Perkoempoelan Radio Ketimoeran) (Batavia), 28.xii.1940, 11.i.1941.
Soeara Tsing Niën (Batavia), no. 10, 1937.
Warta Bhakti (Djakarta), 2.i.1963.

Monographs

Commissie voor het adatrecht. "Perdjandjian dèsa dalam kaboepatèn Sidoardjo." In *Adatrechtbundel* II (Java en Madoera), pp. 272–85. The Hague: Nijhoff, 1911.
Kartodikromo, Mas Marco. 1914. *Mata gelap: tjerita jang soenggoeh kedjadian ditanah Djawa*, pt. 3. Bandoeng: Drukkerij Insulinde.
———. *Sair rempah-rempah*. Vols. 1, 2. Semarang: Sinar Djawa, 1918.
———. *Persdelict dan soerat perlawanan dari Marco Kartodikromo (di persidangan oemoem Landraad Djokjakarta pada hari Kemis 8 December 1921 dengan poetoesan vonnis tanggal 8 December 1921, no. 989/1921)*. Yogyakarta: Tijp. Sneldrukkerij Pakoealaman, 1922.
Meursinge, A. *Maleisch leesboek voor eerstbeginnenden en meergevorderden*. 2d ed. Leiden: S. en J. Luchtmans, 1845.
"Patriot" Cheribon. *Siapa Dia Itoe? Gadis Bangsawan Indonesia atau Hati Wadja*. Palembang: Raden Bratanata/Pertja Selatan, n. d.
Pramoedya Ananta Toer, ed. *Tempo Doeloe: Antologi Sastra Pra-Indonesia*. Jakarta: Hasta Mitra, 1982.
Semaoen. *Hikajat Kadiroen*. Semarang: Kantoor PKI., 1920.
Sukarno. *Dibawah Bendera Revolusi*, vols. 1, 2. Jakarta: Panitya Penerbit Dibawah Bendera Revolusi, 1959–1964.
Verslag Boedi Oetomo, Tahoen Kesepoeloeh 1917–1918. Solo: Albert Rusche, 1919.

Forms of Censorship in the Dutch Indies: The Marginalization of Chinese-Malay Literature

Hendrik M. J. Maier

The Minister of Colonial Affairs in the Hague wrote to the Governor-General of the Netherlands East Indies in Batavia on June 2, 1913:

> Strong action should be taken against the public preaching of revolt against Dutch authorities, against those extremely tiresome efforts to discredit the best intentions of the Government, against the sowing of hate and discordance between the various races which has become the order of the day. Tolerating these manifestations or leaving their repression to the constantly varying opinion of the judiciary in the Indies—which in practice amounts to the same thing—is like committing political suicide. Moreover, it seems to me that such regulations should be applied without distinction even though the non-European press which causes the greatest possible danger for order and tranquility requires a stricter control than the European press that does not reach so far and needs the help of the native and the Chinese press to penetrate those layers of the population. Introduction of a preventive control has, of course, been made impossible by the changes in the Press regulations of 1906. Therefore, a new means of repression should be looked for, not by the judiciary but by administrative authorities.[1]

It was yet another comment in the continuous correspondence between authorities in The Hague and Batavia on a subject of constant anxiety—the freedom of the press. Beyond circles of administration and mission, awareness of the possibilities printing techniques offered to enterprising persons had only been awakened around 1870. Then, Dutch, Eurasian, and Chinese businessmen had initiated attempts to make money in the business of printing and publishing, their example being followed by natives some thirty years later. An increasingly wide variety of printed materials was being produced not only in Dutch but also in native languages. Of the latter, Malay had been the most important one from the beginning. This should not come as a surprise: various forms of Malay had long been the

---

[1] S. L. van der Wall, ed., *De opkomst van de Nationalistische Beweging in Nederlands-Indië* (Bronnenpublicaties) (Grongingen: Wolters, 1967), p. 239.

main vehicles of communication in the urban centers where the first printing plants were established: Batavia, Soerabaja, and Semarang.

Troubles for authorities had formally started in 1906 when freedom of expression was sanctioned by a royal decree in the spirit of the time in the wake of Wilhelmina's memorable speech on the ethical mission the Dutch people were to carry out in the Indies. All obstructing regulations had been removed, and "an end had been made to any sort of preventive supervision of the printed word," as Kleintjes aptly summarized it in the sixth edition of his handbook on constitutional law in the Dutch Indies in 1932.[2]

In theory, the decree meant that administrative intervention was no longer permitted; authorities in the Indies had to resort to criminal persecution when they opined that an author or a journalist had gone too far in discrediting the best intentions of the government and should, therefore, be accused of attempting to disrupt public order and tranquility. In practice, however, authorities could still resort to the tried and tested method of intimidation; it was just a matter of giving allegedly subversive publishers or authors strong hints that unpleasant things were going to happen to them unless they stopped pen or press. No doubt this form of intimidation more often involved newspapers than literary works, but it did happen, for instance, to Tan Boen Kim and his publisher Tjiong Koen Bie in 1915 after the publication of the first part of a sequel to the novel *Nona Fientje de Fenix*; a couple of days after its publication the publisher was given an urgent message by local authorities to stop its distribution. To prevent this from happening again Tjiong and Tan decided to send the subsequent installments to the local council for inspection before they were printed. The irony of this case is that Tjiong was free to insert this story of censorship in the introduction of another sequel. Sometimes power moves in mysterious ways indeed.

Implementing the decree of 1906 meant asking for trouble; journalists and authors challenged authorities in a variety of ways that Batavia and the Hague could not have foreseen and did not know how to counteract effectively. Events around activities of the Inlandsch Comité tot herdenking van Nederlands honderdjarige vrijheid (Native Committee for the Commemoration of One Hundred Years of Liberty of the Netherlands), or the Comité Boemi Poetra (Native Committee), founded in 1913, were a provisional climax in this game of cat and mouse. The committee announced its determination to devote itself to the establishment of a parliament in the Indies, and for the occasion one of its members, Soewardi Soerjaningrat, published an article in Dutch entitled "Als ik eens Nederlander was" (If I were a Dutchman) that could well be read as a mockery of the Dutch-sponsored activities in the colony in celebration of the Netherlands' independence.[3] The article itself was trenchant enough to create an outburst of anger and indignation in Batavia; when the committee then had the audacity to publish a Malay translation as well, Dutch authorities decided that the time had come to intervene—although not without extensive deliberations about the ideological implications of such a move. The press and its complement—literature—were a constant source of concern. Obviously, the authorities were unable to keep all discursive forces under control; they could try to steer them, and that is what they did. The Dutch distrusted the printed word, which could spread like a moorland fire, invisible but subversive; they feared a domino effect that could bring about the end of the colonial adventure. Yet the methods that the colonizers resorted to in order to neutralize native and Chinese challenges

---

[2]Ph. Kleintjes, *Staatsinstellingen van Nederlandsch-Indië* (Amsterdam: J. H. de Bussy, 1932), p. 163.

[3]See, for example, Kenji Tsuchiya, *Democracy and Leadership—The Rise of the Taman Siswa Movement in Indonesia* (Honolulu: University of Hawaii Press, 1987).

to European wisdom and insight at times revealed a paranoia disproportionate to the capacities of the new literates to mobilize the population.

Official bureaucratic correspondence goes slowly, secret and confidential letters go faster, and telegrams go still faster: in the twentieth century a kind of triple-entry bookkeeping evolved among people who usually knew each other very well not only professionally but also personally. It was hard to follow for outsiders and difficult to interpret for subsequent readers. In reply to the minister's official letter quoted, the Governor-General in Batavia had suggested the possibility of developing methods to "take more effective action against efforts to incite a certain spirit in the public that could endanger the interior safety in the colony." Similar suggestions had already been formulated in a secret letter dated October 11, 1913, but Batavia's official reply was not sent until January 13, 1915—a lapse of more than one year. After seeking the advice of local experts, the Governor-General then wrote to the minister. He was now able to offer two alternative solutions to the problem of controlling the people of the press who appeared to be unable to appreciate freedom of expression in the proper way. One could consider introducing a system of deposit for those who wanted to set up a printing business, a suggestion of the director of the Department of Justice; the other possibility was to the introduce a system of handing out licenses—a suggestion of the Council of the Indies. This official letter was officially answered by the minister on September 17, 1915, half a year later. If the authorities in Batavia had not known that their superior in The Hague was of a different political stamp from his predecessor, they would have been even more puzzled than they already were by the situation in the Indies itself:

> When in 1906 freedom of the Press had been gained in the Indies after a struggle of almost fifty years, there was no native press of any political importance. Since then, it has come into being, and it has developed as a result of currents in native society that have broadened and deepened their bases, showing a tendency to gain ground. Far from obstructing these currents, the Government has tried to remove the impediments in their way . . . because in the Government's endeavours to develop and emancipate native society free expression of a free opinion is the most prominent among the supportive tools. . . . Curbing the press, it has been assumed, serves to stop the worst disasters from happening. I am, however, fully convinced that the gross extravagance of a free press is less dangerous for a community than the dangers which a deeply embittered group of people could create for a society if their mouths are stopped and they are forbidden to speak out. Every opinion expressed in the press that is worth a fight will give rise to objections, objections that in their turn could influence the supporters of that very opinion.[4]

These comments were not only enigmatic for readers in Batavia at the time they were written, for a modern reader of the Bronnenpublicaties, too, they are difficult to interpret. Were they meant to be a noble manifestation of ethical thinking or a marvelous illustration of insincerity? One should note that a new article had already been added to the Penal Code of the Indies as early as March 15, 1914, instigated by the Governor-General, and that the article had been given warm support by His Excellency the Minister of Colonial Affairs in The Hague himself:

---

[4] Van der Wall, *De opkomst*, pp. 396–97.

> He who incites or encourages feelings of hostility, hate or contempt for the Government of the Netherlands or of the Netherlands Indies by way of words or signs or a performance or by any other way will be punished. . . . He who incites or encourages feelings of hostility, hate or contempt between the various groups of Dutch citizens or of inhabitants of the Netherlands Indies will be punished. . . . Any effort to commit this crime is punishable by law.[5]

In other words, at the time the Minister of Colonial Affairs formulated his official answer and called for restraint in governmental efforts to keep the press under control, problems had already been solved. After 1914, the *haatzaai artikelen* (hate-sowing articles) gave authorities the power they needed to take action whenever they thought it necessary to do so. That same Minister of Colonial Affairs did not make a serious effort to keep these articles from the new Penal Code that was imposed in 1918. Looking back in 1932, Kleintjes suggested a direct line between 1906 and the new regulations that were introduced in Dutch Indies society in 1931 and gave the Governor-General the right to ban a periodical for up to a year without being required to ask prior advice from the judiciary; those who were directly involved were not given the right to appeal. Interestingly enough, Kleintjes is silent on the introduction of the haatzaai artikelen in 1914—a curious omission indeed, the more so when one realizes that this book was written by a professor of law and was meant to serve as a compass for those who had to work in the Dutch Indies bureaucracy. Events in 1906, 1914, and 1931 could well serve as the framework for a narrative about the changes that the introduction of print brought about in the Indies. In this narrative about literary life, the texts written by Indies inhabitants of Chinese descent were to play an uneasy role, and several forms of censorship were resorted to in order to disqualify the corpus of Chinese-Malay literature as a whole.

Early twentieth-century Indies society was full of tensions and possible conflicts; colonial society was supported and suspended by a complicated network of discursive forces that were constantly on the verge of running out of control. Batavia and The Hague were confronted by a growing number of problems and irritations. The primary criterion by which the Dutch leaders maintained order and tranquility in the colony was a policy of racial classification and segregation. Here were the white Europeans, over there were their brown native subjects—and somewhere in between were the groups that were hard to classify: Eurasians, Arabs, and Chinese. This distinction was reflected in and further imposed through the judiciary system; its maintenance was to become an obsession for Dutch authorities, and if the elaborate discussions about the legal status of subjects of the Indies had not been so painful for those who were directly involved at the time, they could have been a source of great amusement for those who are now looking back. In the twentieth century, the Dutch Indies was made a "plural society," as Furnivall called it in 1939, "comprising two or more elements or social orders which live side by side, yet without mingling, in one political unit."[6] "A divided society" is the term that Van Doorn used some forty years later: "Colonial societies are by definition internally divided. They emerge and exist, after all, in virtue of the encounter between the world of the colonizer and the colonized. A dualism is, therefore, always apparent; one which ranges from conflict to cooperation."[7] How exactly

---

[5] For example, see W. A. Engelbrecht, *De Nederlandsch-Indische wetboeken* (Soerabaja: Führi, 1917), p. 1,086.

[6] S. Furnivall, *Netherlands India. A Study of Plural Economy* (Cambridge: Cambridge University Press, 1939), p. 446.

[7] J. van Doorn, *A Divided Society: Segmentation and Mediation in Late-Colonial Indonesia* (Rotterdam: CASP, 1983), p. 3.

this division took shape in the Indies has already been described by Furnivall, Van Doorn, and many others. Of concern here is the result of this policy of the Dutch, which is very well summarized in the famous report of the Visman Commission, *Verslag van de commissie ter bestudering van staatsrechterlijke hervormingen* of 1941:

> Social intercourse between persons of different race but similar education is, in general, slight, according to the unanimous conclusion of everyone questioned. There is a difference of opinion over the question of whether the developments of the last twenty years should be considered as having brought an improvement or a worsening of conditions. For the rest it is acknowledged that the corporate life of the Indonesian and Chinese population is segregated by race, preventing further social intercourse.[8]

Following these and other witnesses, Van Doorn concludes that late-colonial Indonesia had become a "collection of self-aware population groups, guided by group nationalism."[9] Inhabitants of Chinese descent, too, were increasingly turning inward, keeping to themselves, building group identity, and developing a certain indifference to events that did not directly concern their group interests. Intolerance or ignorance, misunderstanding or indifference, fear or hate—all these words can be used to describe and analyze how the Dutch authorities expressed their opinions about natives and Chinese in the continuous correspondence between Batavia and The Hague. It would, however, be inappropriate to read these reports, letters, and telegrams as only an exchange of views, information, questions, and orders within a small Dutch elite. It could be equally relevant to read texts like the Bronnenpublicaties—only a minimal selection from the archival stacks—as indirect discussions with voices and letters that were emerging "in words, signs and performances" outside the offices in the Indies. Many things were happening "out there" that caused distrust and uneasiness—and called for objection, reaction, and repression. Obviously, newspapers and their editors were to be important discussion partners for the Dutch elite. Their growth in number and variety alarmed authorities. The papers were hard to control, hard to follow, hard to understand; their editors were often invisible and elusive. Bestsellers for a day or two, they were constantly replaced by others, thus creating a new concept of time measured by clocks and calenders rather than by God and rituals. The press contributed to the creation of new imagined communities, opening up and channeling forces that had never been explored before.[10] The Dutch did not really know how to deal with these changes.

The above quotations from the ongoing correspondence may exemplify Dutch policy in controlling the press: a fluctuating combination of prevention and repression, motivated by a strange amalgam of sentiments—self-righteousness, most of all, but also guilt, insecurity, and the conviction of being among the Lord's selected few. No matter how enlightened administrators in Batavia and politicians in The Hague claimed to be, they believed that administrative repression should remain possible for the sake of order and tranquility, so that economic life and the elevation of the natives could progress undisturbed, and for the sake of quality, so that the natives would develop proper concepts of beauty and morality. These were the two lines of argument in defense of censorship.

Political and moral motivations, both closely related to economic considerations, were equally questionable for the authors and journalists involved. Which was preferable, direct

---

[8] As quoted in Van Doorn, *Divided Society*, p. 13.
[9] Van Doorn, *Divided Society*, pp. 15–16.
[10] Benedict Anderson, *Imagined Communities: Reflections on the Origin and Spread of Nationalism* (London: Verso, 1983).

censorship or criminal persecution after the hate had already been sown? The answers that the authorities formulated to this question were varied and made a univocal policy impossible. What exactly was to be the role of the judiciary? What about simple intimidation? Should these noisy upstarts be silenced right away? It should be pointed out that Batavia may not always have been aware that such doubts could be turned to its advantage as long as they were covered elegantly. After all, a certain degree of capriciousness and arbitrariness is often a more effective tool in keeping people under control than strict maintenance of rules and regulations. Authorities could be challenged, their tolerance tested, but by making it hard to predict their reactions, authors and journalists could be held in constant uncertainty about how to reach and please their publics without running the risk of being persecuted and imprisoned. Civil servant Rinkes, the brightest of them all, wrote the most incisive report on these problems:

> During the discussions that I have had concerning the press I have come to realize that a certain part of the public seems to demand a somewhat sensational tone, and that self-respecting periodicals are usually less successful than those that let their tongues run away with them, and in weekly talks or other occasions they discuss the Government, civil servants, an exhibition, a lottery in a spicy manner indeed, that is to say: they run them down.... (In the Chinese newspaper *Warna Warta*) the author explains how editors lie between the devil and the deep blue sea and that it is only due to their long experience in matters of criminal offense and their mastery over their pens that they succeed in inserting the required force in their style without running into trouble with a criminal court.[11]

Dutch journalists—white, belonging to the superior caste and often backed by sugar and tobacco—were undoubtedly given more space to criticize authorities, and this caused not only indignation and unrest among ethicists[12] but also cynicism among their native and Chinese colleagues who were offended by this application of double standards. Although advisors in native and Chinese affairs warned their superiors time and again about this embitterment among Chinese and native literates, colonial authorities were not particularly concerned, convinced as they were that Power was sufficiently tolerant and that journalists did not have any real reason to complain. The fire of the ethicians was slowly smothered and reduced to a mere pilot flame. Draconic measures had already been taken to contain unrest, yet on August 17, 1930, the Governor-General still found sufficient reason to complain about administrative complacency in an official letter to his superior in The Hague:

> The fact that both the European and the native press time and again indulge themselves in articles that are directed against the Administration—be it directly or indirectly—with the intention of subverting Authority or belittling office holders in person, doing so in a tone that unnecesarily aggravates and polarizes relationships and tensions between the various races, has for long given cause to consider the question whether and how this could be brought under control.[13]

---

[11] Van der Wall, *De opkomst*, p. 389.

[12] See, for example, Jaap de Moor, "De affaire-Asymptoot en de haatzaai-artikelen," in *Onderscheid en minderheid*, ed. Herman Diederiks and Chris Quispel (Hilversum: Verloren, 1987), pp. 285–302.

[13] R. C. Kwantes, ed., *De ontwikkeling van de Nationalistische beweging in Nederlandsch-Indië* (Bronnenpublikatie) (derde stuk) (Groningen: Wolters-Noordhoff, 1981), p. 474.

And in his 1930 classic on the ethical policy, which reads like a retrospect rather than a defense, De Kat Angelino could claim without the slightest effort at irony that the tolerance of the administration was still so great that

> It is a cause of amazement in native circles—in spite of voices that demand an even greater freedom, and one tends to draw the incorrect conclusion that this tolerance is inspired by fear, guilt or weakness. So that is one of the most dubious consequences of freedom of speech and press in a context which does not yet fully realize the moral implications of a voluntary respect of democratic censorship.[14]

Not only administrative capriciousness, criminal persecution, and pure repression served the Dutch in their efforts to retain power in the Indies. Censorship also took other forms. Racial segregation and the reinforcement of ethnic differences and rivalries resulted in a certain degree of ignorance on all sides, and it was in this atmosphere of mutual distrust that the Dutch succeeded in creating a mystique of *zakelijkheid* (efficiency) and, closely related to it, of white superiority. This was another form of technocracy and rationality, very much focused on problem solving and, therefore, impressive for those who were not given the opportunity to take a look behind the scenes and the masks. One could also call efficiency pretentiousness (*gewichtigheid*) as Rinkes did and disapprove as he did of the excessive reaction to any sort of criticism. ("In everything, even in the most simple things, one prefers to act secretly and pretentiously, defending the inaccessability of those beloved documents stored in impressive and opaque portfolios").[15] In both terms, efficiency and pretentiousness, the fears and uncertainties that so often go with ignorance and misunderstandings are silenced.

Even more effective in the long run than any of the methods mentioned so far was the introduction of an educational system: it was rightly perceived as the method par excellence to provide the population with the appropriate insights and skills. Throughout the years, the system extended and refined its reach by ramifications and furcations, and the variety of school types and subtypes was so dazzling that one could wonder if the director of Education in Batavia himself was able to keep up with the changes and modifications, let alone the educationalists in the schools themselves. The concepts that made the school system work were simple: race, status, and wealth, in that order of importance. In the eyes of the ethicists as well as those with economic interests in the Indies, education should keep the whites aware of their special mission to elevate and civilize the natives and stop these self-educated Chinese from developing their own methods of exploring the wonders of this world. The educational system was another tool to keep the races as separate as possible, to gain control over discourse and discursive practices, and to safeguard a useful ritualization of speech and the relevant distribution of knowledge. Since the first discussions in the Indies around 1850 about the desirability of education, the question of which language could effectively be made the vehicle for administration, knowledge, and politics through the educational system had been the central interest. At the end of the nineteenth century the authorities had reached a consensus on the subject: Dutch was to be restricted to the happy few, whereas "Malay" was to be the common language of the Dutch Indies, preferred to the local languages.

Indies Malay was in reality the outcome of centuries of controversy about when and how Dutch, Portuguese, High or Low Malay, Javanese, and many other Indies vernacu-

---

[14] A.D.A. de Kat Angelino, *Staatkundig beleid en bestuurszorg in Nederlandsch-Indië* (The Hague: Nijhoff, 1930), p. 1, 154.

[15] Van der Wall, *De opkomst*, p. 395.

lar tongues were to be used in trading stations, churches, diplomatic dealings and, later on, in both territorial government and the production of agricultural exports.[16]

What kind of Malay was this "Indies Malay?" What kind of Malay did the Dutch really have in mind? For centuries, the vehicle of communication that in its various local forms held the Malays together in a cultural identity of sorts had spread from the Malay heartland over the archipelago. Particularly in the urban areas around the Java Sea where people of so many ethnicities met, it had become the best discursive vehicle for passing on fragments of information. The interaction of forms of Malay with other local languages resulted in the emergence of a variety of pidgins; some of these pidgins, in turn, gradually developed into creoles in which elements from Malay were the dominant feature, providing its users with a distinct identity. During the nineteenth century, the use of these forms of Malay intensified: interinsular traffic increased, urban centers grew in size and importance, and Dutch Indies authorities further stimulated the use of Malay in their efforts to facilitate communication between representatives of the various ethnicities.

Discussions on what was meant by "the Malay language" were heated and lively, the brawls between scholars like Van der Tuuk, Vondewall, and Klinkert being some of the most amusing in our field. There were sufficient reasons for these emotional exchanges. There were the purely scholarly questions of what Malay essentially was, where it was spoken, and which was its correct form. There was the question of scholarly authority—who was "in the true," to use a Foucouldian term, and who was not. And, not the least important was the question of money: the expanding educational system badly needed textbooks and primers, and no doubt writing these schoolbooks was to be a profitable undertaking. In short, much was at stake. These discussions on Malay, however, were not based on a well-balanced appreciation of the problems involved—and surprisingly enough, up to 1942 they never would be. What exactly were the various forms of Malay? And how could one distinguish them? How should a standard be determined and formulated? How was one to describe and order the continuum between the forms of Malay of the Malay Peninsula and Sumatra? How should one describe and analyze the differences between written and oral forms, between older and contemporaneous forms and, most importantly, between pidgin and creole forms? No observer, no scholar had ever been able to appreciate fully such questions, and the tone of puzzlement that permeates the observations of the philologist Hooykaas on the subject shortly before the fall of Dutch power is quite justified: a solid study of these related forms of discourse that together were called Malay had never been undertaken during the entire colonial period.[17]

Insofar as Malay was seriously studied at all, it was always done with a clearly prescriptive aim to organize this language so that it could uniformly be used in a wide variety of situations: teaching the natives, conducting correspondence with native princes and Chinese captains, performing ritual meetings, and formulating tax forms, advertisements, legal verdicts, and railroad timetables. Those who were given the opportunity to study the language, thanks to an assignment by administration, mission, or company, tended to distinguish between Malay as a "language of communication" (*verkeerstaal*) and Malay as a "language of culture" (*cultuurtaal*). The forms of Malay that administrators usually confronted were seen as examples of the "language of communication"; therefore, they were incomplete and bad, apparently for the simple reason that they were not forms of Malay spoken by the Malays

---

[16]J. Hoffman, "A Foreign Investment, Indies Malay to 1901," *Indonesia* 27 (1979): 65–92.

[17]A retrospective summary can be found in C. Hooykaas, "Modern Maleisch," in *Koloniale studiën* 1939, pp. 405–38.

themselves. The term "Laag Maleis" (Low Malay) alone speaks volumes. People of Chinese descent in the urban centers, for instance, used versions of Malay that were widely regarded as gibberish—mere versions of this Low Malay, not to be taken seriously, not to be studied, and not worth any attention. Originating among Chinese immigrants as forms of pidgin, these versions of Malay had developed through generations of speakers—and writers—into a number of creoles, absorbing and rejecting in the process elements of other discourses around them. Thanks to the spread of newspapers and books that used these versions, they were fast converging into a distinct *cultuurtaal*, the very type of language educationalists and scholars were so desperately trying to create in the 1920s, unaware that they did not have to leave their towns—Batavia, Surabaya, Semarang—to find one in full operation.

The standard Malay-to-be was sought primarily in the Malay homeland, Sumatra's east coast, where Malay was used as a cultuurtaal. It was possible to be even more specific: the search for a standard Malay focused on the Riau archipelago which, as some Malays kept telling their Dutch overlords, was the cradle of Malay culture. Riau was accorded this status largely because of the manuscripts that had been produced there, considered by many to be the climax of the Malay heritage. It is easier to sit in a chair than to stand in the mud of the Sumatran east coast, and should not that written tradition be regarded as the apex of Malay culture, in the same way written texts are seen as the nucleus of European culture? On the instigation of Van Ophuysen, its architect if not its inventor, a form of Malay called "Riouw Maleisch" was proclaimed to be the standard. It was a mere combination of various forms of Malay Van Ophuysen had found and collated during his journey in the Malay world, and, therefore, it was in practice nobody's Malay. This Riouw Maleisch was the form that was prescribed for primary and secondary schools through the text books and reading materials distributed by the authorities. Not until the late twenties, it seems, did administrators realize that these school materials offered a form of Malay that was quite different from the forms of Malay that were used in native circles. In 1927, the Director of Education wrote to his superior:

> There is a yawning abyss between the Riouw Maleisch that is officially prescribed at schools and the civilized Malay *[beschaafd Maleisch]* that here in Java is rather common in daily contacts, in meetings and in the press, be it with local varieties. If education is to serve its purpose and wants to be accepted on a wider scale, Riouw Maleisch should be replaced by a form of Malay that is closer to the more common language of conversation and writing. [Experts agree that] it is possible to design a school Malay that is rooted in living language but... in that case several difficulties have to be solved first, e.g. the fact that outside the Riouw Maleisch of textbooks little unity can be discerned in the way of writing and speaking of the so-called civilized Malay which is developing in the free society and in which Chinese journalists play an important role.[18]

Two years later, the newly appointed Director of Education rejected his predecessor's suggestion of replacing textbooks in Riouw Maleisch with textbooks in another version of Malay. Such a replacement was "practically impossible," he wrote, and did not the Bureau voor de Volkslectuur do very good work indeed in cultivating the new sort of Malay? No, for the time being texts in Riouw Maleisch would suffice, if only because they provided the pupils with an adequate basis for the understanding of any other kind of Malay.[19] One must seriously question, however, whether pupils of Chinese descent were able to understand this Riouw Maleisch and, conversely, whether they were provided with an adequate basis

---

[18] S. L. van der Wall, *Het onderwijsbeleid in Nederlands-Indië* (Groningen: Wolters, 1963), pp. 419–29.
[19] Ibid., p. 485ff.

for understanding other types of Malay. Not without reason did natives call this form of Malay "Bahasa Belanda," as Hooykaas observed with slight amusement, and, with due respect to Van Ophuysen's endeavors, one might add that Riouw Maleisch was not the form of language that was spoken and written in Riau either. "Malay language" is a deceptive term, as the word *language* is in general: it suggests a unity, a basis that simply does not exist in the real world. In Southeast Asia, like anywhere else where there are human communities, all sorts of more or less closely related forms of verbal communication were used by various groups, and each of those forms had a distinct place, discontinuous and juxtaposed with other forms of discourse in a hazy network of constantly changing similarities and differences. In this network of discursive practices it was up to political and economic centers to decide which of these forms were to be varieties of the "Malay language" and which of these varieties of Malay was to have special authority. Riouw Maleisch was a political myth; it was an artificially created form of Malay that belonged to no one. Through the aggressive campaigns of the Dutch Indies government alone it was made to work; as *beschaafd Maleis* (civilized Malay) it was to form the basis for a new culture that would lead the native population of the colony into the modern world.

In this preference for a particular form of Malay, procedures of exclusion, selection, and prohibition were effected; not everybody had the right to speak up about everything. This was a more delicate manner of censorship, of which even those in power were not always fully aware. A matter of hegemony, censorship worked in the Indies as it works everywhere else. The introduction of this new Malay through textbooks and readers had far-reaching consequences: a generation of well-educated literates emerged that in due course gained a very effective influence over the language policy that authorities developed in their efforts to bring the process of disintegration and segregation within colonial society to a halt. This process could be described in the reverse as well: other forms of Malay were pushed into the margin because they lacked the authority to maintain themselves in the center. Literary life, too, took on a new configuration. Particularly as a result of the spread of print, two groups were able to seize power over the written word and, accordingly, over the distribution of knowledge. One group consisted of the Chinese Malays who were developing their own identity on the basis of a version of Low Malay, a colonial term they tended to regard as a term of honor. The second group comprised the native intellectuals who had become familiar with the standard of Riouw Maleisch through their education and who operated in close cooperation with government institutions. In 1927, Kwee Tek Hoay still had the courage to write, "We believe that Low Malay will eventually overcome and completely destroy Riau Malay or Ophuysen Malay which is now still protected by the Administration," but this expectation did not come true.[20] In the thirties, the leading proponent of the new Malay, Takdir Alisjahbana, educated by the Dutch and employed by Balai Poestaka, a government-supported institution,[21] could write in that eerie tone of self-confident distrust so characteristic of the Indies' native intelligentsia:

> Moreover, the integration of Indonesian with Chinese Malay will take place faster if only certain groups within the community of people of Chinese descent regarded this land as their fatherland and dissociated themselves from Chinese nationalists. . . . If only their children sat with Indonesian children in the benches of national Indonesian schools that

---

[20] Quoted in Claudine Salmon, *Literature in Malay by the Chinese of Indonesia—A Provisional Annotated Bibliography* (Paris: Éditions de la Maison des Sciences de l'homme, 1981), p. 116.

[21] For a (positive) description of Balai Poestaka and its activities see A. Teeuw, "The Impact of Balai Pustaka on Modern Indonesian Literature," in *Bulletin of the School of Oriental and African Studies* 35 (1972): 111–27.

emphasized the importance of Indonesian, then Indonesian would automatically become their language, too.[22]

Neither Kwee's expectation nor Takdir's wish was to come true in the near future. Convergence of the varieties of Malay remained a mere dream as long as the Dutch kept the speakers of Malay divided and ruled their colony in growing anxiety. How should they keep discursive formations under control?

Conflicts and tensions among discursive formations can be traced through more than textbooks and political meetings; in literary life, too, the struggle for authority can be found and described to historicize the interactions among societal forces. In the wake of the appearance of newspapers and other periodicals, Malay literary life took on a new configuration after 1870. Malay speakers of Chinese descent played the leading role in this, as authors, publishers, and readers, and through them, Creole-like forms of Malay started to interact with the Malay forms in manuscripts and lithographs, which merely emulated literary elements of the Malay heritage, the *syair* and the *hikayat*. New forms emerged: short verses, short stories, and most importantly, novels, which, both in originals and translations, were to take the most prominent position in these literary developments. In this, Malay literary life followed a familiar pattern. In a convenient gloss on Anderson's *Imagined Communities*,[23] Brennan describes the interrelated emergence of nation, novel, and newspapers as follows:

> It was the novel that historically accompanied the rise of nations by objectifying the "one, yet many" of national life, and by mimicking the structure of the nation, a clearly bordered jumble of languages and styles. Socially, the novel joined the newspaper as the major vehicle of the national print media, helping to standardize language, encourage literacy, and remove mutual incomprehensibility. But it did much more than that. Its manner of presentation allowed people to imagine the special community that was the nation.[24]

Less than one decade after the royal decree had guaranteed freedom to the press, Dutch administrators began to express their worries about quality and about tendencies they discerned in Malay publications, not only in articles and serials in periodicals but also in novels and other texts. These publications were considered politically dangerous, morally suspicious, and, therefore, a threat to peace and tranquility. Then the Bureau van de Volkslectuur (Bureau for Popular Reading)—later renamed Balai Poestaka—was founded. In the words of its main instigator, Rinkes:

> The government has taken the initiative to elevate the population in a systematic manner, and it is to become clear from the application and appreciation of the principles that will be developed by the native population itself whether it wants to continue along this road or not. It is in the interests of its existence as a nation that its development is led along the same path that almost all other nations follow towards progress. A first effort has been made, but it is obviously the task of the more developed persons among the

---

[22] S. Takdir Alisjahbana, "Kedudukan bahasa Melaju-Tionghoa," in *Dari perjuangan dan pertumbuhan Bahasa Indonesia* (Jakarta: Pustaka Rakyat, 1957), p. 61.

[23] Anderson, *Imagined Communities*.

[24] T. Brennan, "The National Longing for Form," in *Nation and Narration*, ed. Homi K. Bhaba, (London: Routledge, 1990), p. 49.

native population itself to show their fellow countrymen the way and to offer them the proper tools to find the proper paths towards progress.[25]

The bureau was meant to stand on its own commercial feet, and apparently it did. Ideologically, however, it was clearly an extension of colonial authorities. Balai Poestaka could nicely serve Batavia's efforts to keep the natives away from all those subversive forces that were emerging throughout society, and, therefore, the bureau was provided with the facilities that it needed to build respect and prestige and fulfill its objectives in the proper manner. *Counterpropaganda* Rinkes had called it in an early proposal; that same term came up some ten years later in a confidential report that circulated in the Department of Interior Affairs about the role this institution could possibly play in the Indies:

> In the case of direct propaganda nothing much can be accomplished for the time being [but in other ways things seem possible]. The Government should see to it that the people who want to educate themselves without being driven by feelings of dissatisfaction are given food for their minds so that they will not end up in the ranks of our rivals. And secondly—more important but also more difficult—one could try to spread the view that anyone who wants to improve his country can do so most effectively by supporting this Government. Up to a point this is counter-propaganda to extremism and communism although in a indirect manner only . . . and by taking "natural" nationalistic emotions into account.[26]

The books that were published by Balai Poestaka constituted the nucleus of the library of every government-sponsored school; they were the logical extension of the textbooks and primers and must have had considerable influence on the thinking of young readers. An aggressive sales policy, sometimes with stickers, lotteries, and other promotional gimmicks, secured the publishers a distribution of their books outside the schools that was difficult for competitors to surpass. Supported by the educational system as a whole, Balai Poestaka was able to play a dominant role in leading the native population toward modernity but also to contribute very actively to the shaping of the canon of modern Malay literature—a native manifestation of the hegemony of the Dutch who, once having achieved direction over the decisive economic nucleus, were able to expand this into a moment of social, political, and cultural leadership and authority throughout Dutch Indies society.[27] Within the discourse imposed by Dutch hegemony, certain procedures could be neutralized, certain channels to knowledge blocked. The use of forms of Malay that differed too much from the standard Balai Poestaka tried to develop was discouraged, for instance. Certain subjects were to be avoided: sex, politics, and religion. These evasions constituted considerable delimitations, if not prohibitions—or should they be called repression? Undesirable discussions could be silenced, and authors who were thought to be subversive, deviating, and mad—dangerous, that is—could be intimidated and disgraced. Such were the techniques authorities resorted to in order to strengthen their hegemony. Reformulating a tradition, shaping a canon—censorship can be implemented by active repression, through prevention, through a well-designed system of education, through an aggressive sales policy, and through pretentiousness and efficiency. All of these are forms of censorship, but they are not enough to ensure success. To push possible rivals into the margin and beyond, those strategies need a complement—possible competitors must be discredited. No doubt, the situation was favorable for the Volkslectuur: in the shadow of Batavia it worked "in the true," and, equally impor-

---

[25] D. Rinkes, *Nota over de Volkslectuur* (Batavia: Volkslectuur, 1912), pp. 3–4.

[26] Van der Wall, *Het onderwijsbeleid*, p. 263.

[27] S. Hall et al., *Culture, Media, Language* (London: Hutchinson, 1980), p. 35.

tant, the main competitor to its publications was the fast-growing corpus of texts produced by Chinese-Malay authors and publishers, which emerged in a circle of readers who were increasingly isolated from both the natives and their colonial masters, politically, economically, and ideologically. This was a strong circle that was certain not to break open again during the colonial period. In their drive to create a canon of "good literature," the European leaders of the newly created Malay literary life were blind, or at least pretended to be blind, to the impressive activities that were taking place outside the buildings of Balai Poestaka. Their attitude is exemplified by the article that Drewes, long the director of the Balai Poestaka, published about contemporary developments in literary life in 1932:

> It would be hard indeed to underestimate the important role that the Administration plays in keeping control over the development of good taste in this time of transition. There is the obvious danger that those who are looking for something they are wanting so badly end up in reading materials of dubious quality. . . . Less conscientious publishers manage to cash in on this tendency to realism (for want of a better term), and with its cheap products the Volkslectuur has been able to exercise a beneficial influence here: it succeeded in pushing back the usually very expensive *Schund literatur* [trashy literature] that those Chinese publishers are trying to sell.[28]

In the paragraph preceding this quotation, Drewer shows that authority had already started to discredit Balai Poestaka's rivals by referring to the dubious role the Chinese-Malay press had played in the formation of the new style of prose, "which only rarely becomes well-polished prose." Chinese-Malay literature was a mere commodity, he suggests; it made use of a language of communication and not of a language of culture, to use the terms of the day, and it tried to sell rather than to elevate—a very effective method to freeze the yawning gap mentioned by the Director of Education, He proposes that a distinction exists between two kinds of literature, two kinds of art: "good art" and "bad art," "real art" and "popular art." Even though in the Dutch Indies this distinction may not have run parallel to the distinction between an educated class and "the rest," the distinction Drewes makes is a relevant one.

Authors like Kwee Tek Hoay and Monsieur d'Amour, to mention just two, may have been unwilling to give in to linguistic and thematic demands, and they lacked the political (and educational) patronage that could have guaranteeed them a place "in the true." In the shadow of such explicit disqualifications by authority, they were excluded. Their position was an ambivalent one. On the one hand, they wanted to operate on a commercial basis and, therefore, had to attract as many readers as possible through more sexual innuendos, more violence, more action. On the other hand, they thought they had a task in their own communities: to make some sort of contribution to a distinct Indies Chinese identity, even in a basically hostile society. Perhaps Chinese-Malay literature should be seen as a counter literature, a corpus of texts that was not accepted by a small group of people whose function in the sociocultural establishment gave them the authority to pass judgment. The most intriguing word in Drewes' remarks is, of course, Schund-literatur, a derogatory reference to a corpus of texts that must have been at least fifty times larger than the production of Balai Poestaka: immoral, sensual, and, therefore, malignant and dangerous. Some mildly pornographic texts were indeed published by Chinese enterprises (the publication of *Perhoeboengan Rasia* in Semarang in 1937 comes to mind), but such books were rare, and it is, there-

---

[28] G.W.J. Drewes, "Oud en nieuw in de hedendaagse Indonesische litteratuur," in *De Gids* 96 (1932): 330. ("Schund literatur" is a German term with a distinctly negative connotation; it could be translated as "trashy literature," "rubbish".)

fore, an inappropriate term for the corpus as a whole. To use so derogatory a term was an embarrassing way to discredit elements that could not be brought under immediate control, and was made even more embarrassing because any illustration in support of this insinuation was lacking.

Schund-literatur—the term occurred again in Hooykaas's *Over Maleise literatuur*, the first handbook on Malay literature for native students, published in 1937:

> Not only did they just write for the sake of writing, in a careless language, but they also treated inappropriate subjects. In short, all sorts of Schund appeared on the market, and in huge quantities. The Government thought it appropriate to interfere: by giving suitable reading material to its tens of thousands of matriculants it wanted to repress whatever was considered politically and morally unsuitable.[29]

This is another quotation that could be used in many ways. In a single sentence, Hooykaas discredited the language of Chinese-Malay literature and the intentions of its authors. *All sorts* and *huge* are slightly exaggerated terms. It is well-nigh possible that the Chinese-Malay literates who are criticized here no longer felt that such a remark was a slap in the face; interaction between them and "the others" had become very rare indeed.

One year after Drewes published his ill-founded disqualification of Chinese-Malay literature as a whole, a new phase in Dutch cultural policy was initiated: a self-proclaimed avant-garde came onto the scene in Batavia in the form of a "cultural journal," *Poedjangga Baroe* (The new poet). Most of its leaders and contributors had received a Dutch-controlled education; it was clearly visible not only in the ideas and concepts they propagated but also in the form of Malay they used, very similar to the Malay used by Balai Poestaka. This similarity is not surprising because its editors were closely associated with this showpiece of colonial wisdom. Following the lead of Dutch authority, Takdir Alisjahbana, too, presented the forms of Malay the Chinese were using in their conversations and their books in a derogatory manner—as though his own "Bahasa Indonesia" were already a full-fledged cultuurtaal and Chinese-Malay were not and never could be.

In the same vein, this group of self-confident young intellectuals was keen to denounce Chinese-Malay literature, if only to establish their own importance in literary life and to create the atmosphere that an avant-garde needs to gain authority and prestige. In and after the Japanese occupation of the archipelago this self-confidence was amply rewarded. Japanese authorities banned the use of Dutch, and in their efforts to stimulate the use of Malay they continued the policy of the Dutch; Takdir and some of his friends were to become important advisors in the continuous construction of a Bahasa Indonesia, and the form of Malay that had been developed by Balai Poestaka (and *Poedjangga Baroe*) was to serve as a standard. Of course, this resulted in a further marginalization of Chinese-Malay language and literature. The derogatory attitude that the *Poedjangga Baroe* people, like the Dutch authorities, had shown for their rivals was continued by the generation of artists that arose in the wake of the Revolution. In their often violent reactions against their forerunners in Balai Poestaka and *Poedjangga Baroe*, authors like Chairil Anwar and Sitor Situmorang did not look for inspiration in the rich Malay-Chinese tradition but preferred to seek it in Western and regional examples. Interaction between the two mainstreams of Malay literature appeared farther away than ever. And to follow the tradition of derogation and disqualification to the end: in this survey of modern Indonesian literature published by the prominent

---

[29] C. Hooykaas, *Over Maleise literatuur* (Leiden: Brill, 1937), p. 193.

Poedjangga Baroe member Armijn Pane in 1949, Chinese-Malay literature was denounced as once again Schund-literatur:

> The newspaper, a Western product, brings the dead prose to life again. The transient everyday life: the news needs to be told, first in the long-winded narrative style of the old prose, later short and powerful, sharp and clear, "to the point": the new style, the new prose was born. Carried along by real life it went astray from the straight and narrow to the Schund-literatur. In 1908 the Commisie voor de Volsklectuur was installed, initially meant to meet the needs of pupils and former pupils of the ... schools, later to be a beacon in the modern world with its new needs.[30]

The disqualification remained the same, as did the fear and distrust. The political and practical problems the Chinese-Malay tradition was to confront in the fifties forced its supporters to keep a low profile. The lack of appreciation and interest from the new literary elites, who so eagerly tried to replace their Dutch masters, was a final blow, it seems, for the continuation of this rich tradition, a tradition that still awaits a careful study.

---

[30] Armijin Pane, *Kort overzicht van de moderne Indonesische literatuur* (Jakarta, Balai Pustaka, 1949), p. 13.

Towkays and Tycoons: The Chinese in Indonesian Economic Life in the 1920s and 1980s

Jamie Mackie

Since the nationalization in 1957–1958 of the Dutch business enterprises that had dominated the colonial economy, including most of the country's largest plantations, mines, banks, and business houses, many Chinese firms previously confined to an intermediate position in the "colonial caste structure," as Wertheim has called it,[1] have been able to advance to the topmost ranks in the present economic structure of Indonesia. Collectively, they now overshadow the previously dominant state sector made up largely of those nationalized enterprises. The two largest Chinese firms, Liem Sioe Liong's vast conglomerate and William Soeryadjaya's Astra Corporation, hold assets that were estimated to be worth Rp. 6.4 trillion and Rp. 2 trillion respectively (US$3.5 billion and $1.2 billion) in 1988, whereas ten others are in the $400–$700 million range and another one hundred or so exceed the $100 million mark.[2] By any measure, international as well as local, the foremost of these men can aptly be called tycoons, "businessmen of extraordinary wealth and power," in the dictionary definition, whose wealth far exceeds that of their predecessors earlier in the century, Dutch as well as Chinese. In contrast, none of the wealthiest Chinese towkay of the 1920s (a word that refers rather indeterminately to "a Chinese big businessman," although not always an especially rich one) could have been compared with the big Dutch capitalists of the colonial era, apart from the almost legendary Oei Tiong Ham, to whom I will return shortly.[3]

Most explanations of how and why this transformation has occurred tend to fall somewhere between two rival camps. On one side are the structural and class interpretations,

---

[1] W. F. Wertheim, *Indonesian Society in Transition* (The Hague: Van Hoeve, 1956), chap. 6.

[2] Figures based on *Warta Ekonomi*, 5 (5), (July 1989): 72, and *Conglomeration Indonesia. A Profile of Indonesia's Largest Business Groupings*, ed. Christianto Wibisono (Jakarta: Pusat Dokumentasi Business Indonesia, 1990). Although all such estimates of company assets must be treated with reserve, these are probably adequate to indicate approximate orders of magnitude.

[3] Definitions of towkay and tycoon are taken from Mary Somers-Heidhues, *Southeast Asia's Chinese Minorities* (Hawthorn, Vic.: Longman Studies in Contemporary Southeast Asia, 1976), p. 114, and *Webster's New Collegiate Dictionary*, respectively.

which weight the close relationships the new tycoons have developed with the New Order political and military authorities. At the other extreme are those explanations that stress ethnic and cultural factors or simply take for granted that the commercial successes of the Southeast Asian Chinese more generally are owing to their seemingly ingrained advantages over their indigenous rivals in business skills and motivations. Both approaches have much to be said for them, and both have their weaknesses; neither is entirely adequate in itself. A complex interplay of ethnic and class factors has shaped the development of Chinese business enterprises in Southeast Asia over the last century or more, which is not easily reduced to one-dimensional generalizations at any stage. To understand the processes involved one needs ideally to be able to trace the evolution of the economic roles of particular Chinese businessmen, or broad groups of them, in the particular historical and sociopolitical contexts of their times. That is not easy, however, for it is difficult to get adequate biographical or historical information about even the better-known of them, let alone the more obscure and poor Chinese who remain in the shadows. All one can do is draw inferences from the lives of the few wealthy figures, both past and present, whose stories have been recorded.

In an attempt to sketch changes in the economic situation and roles of the Sino-Indonesian minority as a whole during this century, I will focus here on the two men about whose careers information is most fully available, Oei Tiong Ham and Liem Sioe Liong.[4] Because both were outstandingly successful and wealthy, they cannot be regarded as representative of Chinese businessmen in general, let alone of the entire Chinese minority. But if one can identify the factors that made these men so successful, one may find clues to the successes or failures of others.

One must be wary of the stereotypical notion that the Southeast Asian Chinese have long been predominantly traders because some superior aptitude for commerce and small-scale industry was lacking among the indigenous peoples. It was really only from about the 1920s onward that large numbers of Chinese in Indonesia began to move away from other occupations, mostly less desirable ones, as in the case of thousands of plantation and mining coolies, into what today are commonly regarded as their characteristic roles as small-scale traders, *warung* operators, commodity dealers, and money lenders. There had, of course, been significant numbers of Chinese in those roles in various parts of the colony long before the 1920s, but they were then far less widely or thickly spread geographically, and fewer engaged in petty trade than those in later periods. Since the 1920s, however, they have become almost ubiquitous in those roles. The changes in occupations and economic roles that unfolded between 1900 and 1930 (arrested by the onset of the Great Depression, which caused the cessation of large-scale Chinese immigration) must be seen as the beginning of a long process of adjustment and adaptation to constantly evolving economic and political conditions that can be traced to the present day.

The splendid picture James Rush has given in this volume of the extensive networks or pyramids of Chinese patrons and clients that were established around the great opium concessions (farms) held by the opium "kings" in central and eastern Java in the latter half of the nineteenth century provides us with a good starting point for this story slightly farther back in time. Many of the lower-level participants in that business must have been petty traders in small towns who dealt in opium inter alia through those networks. But because of

---

[4]The term "Sino-Indonesian," rather than "Indonesian Chinese," is used here in the contemporary context by analogy with the generally accepted term "Sino-Thai" to stress nationality not ethnicity. For the years before the 1960s, when the dual nationality issue was still unresolved, the indefinite term "Chinese" is appropriate and more convenient.

their involvement in the networks (frequently illegal and semicriminal in character, Rush observes) they were probably traders of a rather different type from the more modern shophouse owners who operate independently—and in most cases honestly—and who fanned out across entirely new areas of Java and the Outer Islands in the early decades of this century. Rush notes that in addition to the kings who controlled the opium farms, and their numerous retainers in the late nineteenth century, there were also many penniless newcomers and small-scale vendors and tradespeople among the Chinese, who never earned more than modest incomes or rose above menial occupations. But they were nowhere near as numerous or widespread at that time as they became by the 1920s. The big money was in opium until the economic crisis of the 1880s, the product that seems to have attracted the most enterprising or acquisitive of the Chinese with substantial capital. Others, although not many, were engaged in commodity trading and in cultivation, particularly of sugar and tobacco, from much earlier in the century. Most were not yet large-scale operators, however, and if big fortunes were made in these sectors, they did not lead to the emergence of families as wealthy as those produced by the opium trade.

What Rush calls the "dance of collaboration" between the Chinese opium kings and the local Dutch and Javanese officials, especially his observation that the former were located physically close to the powerholders and "nested within the power structure," has much in common with the kinds of relationships that prevail today between leading Chinese capitalists and Indonesian powerholders, both in Jakarta and in the provincial capitals and smaller towns throughout the country. But this system disintegrated in the 1890s, he tells us, as the opium farms collapsed financially, and the authority of the *peranakan* (locally born) elite families waned under the impact of a new wave of *totok* (China-born) immigrants. The economic roles of the Chinese and the character of the various Chinese communities changed significantly over the next forty years as did the entire colonial economy, owing to the vigorous expansion of the Dutch plantation system and the much higher investment levels in all fields between the 1890s and 1929.

Chinese Business in Indonesia in the 1920s

Patterns of Chinese business activity in many parts of the colony were transformed in the years between the collapse of the opium farms in the 1880s and the 1920s, the last prosperous decade before the Great Depression, which brought a radically new set of changes. This was a time of rapid increase in the Chinese population, owing to a high rate of immigration, primarily of indentured laborers for the Sumatran plantation industries.[5] One result was a widening rift within Chinese society between the peranakan and totok communities, both political and economic. At the same time, the dramatic expansion of the Dutch-dominated plantation economy severely constrained the scope of operation for the existing Chinese planters in the sugar and tobacco industries, although it opened up other trading opportunities for them as the plantation frontier expanded into new areas of Java and Sumatra. It was directly associated with an increase in the number of small Chinese warung owners scattered throughout the archipelago. A detailed diachronic account of the economic processes and sociocultural dynamics underlying the changes then taking place would be an illuminating supplement to the several rather static accounts available of Chinese business activities in the last years before World War II. A few of the more prominent individuals who emerged as business leaders are identifiable, but, with the exception of the

---

[5]The Chinese population of the colony rose from 344,000 to 800,000 between 1880 and 1920, then to 1,233,000 in 1930. For fuller details, see J. A. C. Mackie, "The Geographical Dispersal and Occupations of the Indonesian Chinese, 1900–1930," *Asian Culture* (Singapore), 14 (April 1990): 5–22.

biggest towkays like Oei Tiong Ham, Tjong A Fie, and a handful of others, little is known of their business careers.

The disintegration at this time of the symbiotic relationship between wealthy Chinese businessmen and colonial officials noted by Rush was attributable not just to the collapse of the opium kings but also to the fact that the Chinese now found themselves more generally under pressure, even under attack, by the Dutch authorities as exploiters of the native people, a popular theme of Ethical Policy reformers. The point can be carried even farther into the present century. The Chinese minority was regarded with hostility, or at least suspicion, by the various state authorities in Indonesia not only through the last half-century of colonial rule but also throughout the next thirty years of Japanese occupation, the revolution, and the early years of independence. Only since the 1970s has something like that earlier symbiotic relationship with the ruling elite been reestablished. The general thrust of government policy during the period of rapid expansion of the Dutch plantation economy between 1900 and 1930 was to exclude Chinese and indigenous producers from participation in that sector lest they disturb the Dutch planters' access to land, labor, and markets at minimum costs.

Only one Chinese firm succeeded in competing with the Dutch on their own ground at this time, the Oei Tiong Ham Concern. Its story throws light on the scope of and limits upon Chinese big business during that late colonial period of rapid economic expansion, although Oei was quite unlike other Chinese businesssmen of that time in many respects. In his early years he was one of the last of the old-style opium kings, yet he soon transformed himself into a new-style modern capitalist using business techniques similar to those of the Dutch. Oei thus became one of the few Chinese who survived in the fiercely competitive business of sugar cultivation; he also succeeded in establishing a set of mills that were among the most modern and efficient in the colony, which at the time was the most technically advanced sugar producer in the world. He was a remarkably innovative and forward-looking businessman by any standard.

Born in Semarang in 1866, Oei Tiong Ham was the son of a moderately well-to-do, educated Chinese who had fled to Java not long before, after the collapse of the Taiping rebellion in which he had participated. Oei's father, although penniless on his arrival in Semarang, was soon able to build his sugar trading company, Kian Guan. This firm persisted as the core component of the family business until the 1950s, a record in longevity for a major Indonesian Chinese firm. His son, Oei Tiong Ham, was brought into the firm after a period of Chinese-language schooling. By the age of twenty-four, after being appointed lieutenant of the Chinese in Semarang, he was not only managing the firm but was also involved in the opium farm business, presumably by virtue of the standing of his family at that time.[6]

The early stages of Oei Tiong Ham's career and the reasons for his initial success are still obscure. There are several legendary stories about him during this period: that he was a heavy gambler who nearly lost a large sum of his father's money at one point but was saved by the generosity of an old Chinese lady who had confidence in him; and that he was bequeathed a substantial legacy by an old German living in one of his father's houses in Semarang who had taken a liking to him, which enabled him to purchase his first sugar plantation. Regardless of the truth or fantasy behind these anecdotes, it is clear that the most important of these early steps in career advancement must have been his decision to buy several sugar plantations in the early 1890s at a time when the industry was just beginning

---

[6] A useful set of biographical studies on which I have drawn here is compiled in Yoshihara Kunio, ed., *Oei Tiong Ham Concern: the First Business Empire of Southeast Asia* (Kyoto: Centre for Southeast Asian Studies, 1989).

to emerge from its severe 1880s slump, while values were still depressed. In the following years, sugar prices, demand, and production rose steadily so that the five plantations he acquired soon became the basis of a strong, well-integrated group of companies extending from sugar production and trading to a shipping company, warehouses, a bank, and overseas trading offices. It seems unlikely that the opium farm was an especially critical element in his growing fortune because the opium trade was declining by the 1890s. In any case, his family was already quite well off, so the capital needed to build up his business enterprise was not difficult to acquire. But what made him such an outstanding businessman for his time was the way he ran his business once he got started, for in this he was quite untypical of other Chinese businessmen of the late colonial era.

The key factor in his commercial success seems to have been an awareness of the need to adopt Dutch business methods and technical skills combined with a shrewd sense of timing in his purchases and sales. In the latter respect he was perhaps not very different from other Chinese traders of his time, but he was far ahead of them in the former (although it is puzzling that no others followed him on that score). One of his mills was the first in Java to be electrified. He employed Dutch mill technicians, accountants, and lawyers extensively, and also used Dutch-trained Chinese with similar qualifications in due course. He avoided excessive diversification into activities unrelated to his sugar-based enterprise, although Kian Guan's overseas trading interests expanded and diversified considerably after World War I.

Oei Tiong Ham's relations with the Dutch authorities appear to have been reasonably cordial but never particularly close, not at all comparable with the symbiotic relationships with national political leaders that later developed in the 1970s and 1980s. He did not speak Dutch and appears not to have associated socially with Dutch officials in Semarang, although he entertained lavishly, including visiting state guests such as King Chulalongkorn. Yet he received little help from the government and was sufficiently outraged by its imposition of a stiff excess profits tax on him after he had made a killing from the steep increase in sugar prices during World War I that he moved permanently to Singapore in protest. He died there, still in his fifties, in 1924.

Although the Oei Tiong Ham Concern survived his death and continued to operate into the 1950s under the leadership of the two most competent of his many sons (he had twenty-five children in all), it gradually became a less successful business enterprise and was finally nationalized in 1961 after running into political problems with the Sukarno government. It survived the difficult years of depression, World War II, and the struggle for independence that followed with only moderate setbacks but faced increasing problems in adapting to the radically different conditions that emerged after independence. Above all, it was weakened at that critical juncture by the universal problem of generational change within a Chinese family firm, which gave rise to debilitating intrafamily disputes in the 1950s over matters of control and business strategy. It is hard to avoid the conclusion that leadership and personality factors were crucially important in both the rise and decline of this first great Indonesian Chinese corporate enterprise.

None of the other leading Chinese merchant families of the early twentieth century achieved anything like the eminence of Oei Tiong Ham. His nearest rival was Kwik Hoo Tong, a very successful trader in sugar and other agricultural commodities during the boom years of the 1920s (until he went bankrupt) also based in Semarang. (The prominence of Semarang Chinese at that time is interesting, for the only Chinese firms that actually cultivated plantation crops in East Java, where the biggest Dutch agricultural enterprises were concentrated, seem to have been much smaller than those in Central Java.) Kwik's company did not compete directly with modern Dutch enterprises in plantation agriculture, however.

He was more an old-style towkay than a modern tycoon. Much the same could be said of the famous Tjong A Fie, an influential *Kapitien der Chineezen* in Medan, who had diverse business interests and close relations with the Dutch local authorities but no particular and enduring base to his enterprise comparable to that of Oei.[7]

A few Chinese planters cultivated sugar and other plantation crops in Java on a small scale until the 1920s, but none approached the stature of the Oei Tiong Ham Concern. The expansion of large Dutch corporate plantations from the 1880s on crippled the embryonic class of Chinese sugar and tobacco planters who had previously been able to compete against Dutch planters in significant numbers at a time when most of those enterprises were quite small and rudimentary, generally between 17–30 ha. for sugar or 3.5–7.0 ha. for tobacco. But the introduction of large steam-driven sugar mills required huge capital outlays and a vast expansion in the size of sugar plantations during the last quarter of the nineteenth century; most of them were between 350–700 ha. and some of the largest were twice that size. Small privately owned plantations merged into larger ones during the consolidation and corporatization that accompanied the severe slump in the sugar industry in the mid-1880s. Only a handful of Chinese mills were able to survive under those circumstances—Oei Tiong Ham's the foremost among them, along with several much smaller ones—but the latter all collapsed soon after the onset of the depression of the 1930s.

For tobacco and other cash crops, consolidation was less dramatic but equally devastating to the few Chinese planters who survived on the fringes of the plantation economy into the 1920s. (In rice milling and trading, however, they became dominant at about this time for the Dutch were never significant competitors there.) Few if any Chinese planters were able to establish large-scale rubber plantations during the rubber booms of the early twentieth century, although many Chinese played important roles as traders and rubber remillers in the fast-expanding indigenous smallholder rubber industry of South Sumatra and elsewhere.[8] Government policy was less important than technological and financial factors in bringing about their exclusion from the Dutch-dominated plantation sector, but there is no doubt that the colonial economy no longer needed Chinese participation in that sector as it had in the mid-nineteenth century. Whereas the larger Chinese plantations of the nineteenth century had been able to compete with their Dutch rivals, they were increasingly forced out of business in the early twentieth century. Thus Chinese capitalists in Java found it easier to survive in fields like retail trading and petty industries, where they were competing only with Indonesians.

One other factor that affected the pattern of economic roles at that time was the change in the character of the Chinese population: the number of China-born (totok) members increased sharply. This increase resulted from the very high immigration rates of the 1920s, mostly to Sumatra but also to Java. Many of these newcomers, nearly all single men, became petty traders or artisans, often in the more remote rural areas where peranakan had been reluctant to operate. Many others moved into the newly expanding plantation areas of Java or rubber-growing areas of Sumatra where business opportunities were most plentiful. The totok were almost solely responsible for the great expansion of Chinese commercial enterprise across Indonesia in the early twentieth century, taking on the classic economic roles with which they have been most commonly associated since then. Few peranakan were

---

[7]See Onghokham, "Chinese Capitalism in Dutch Java" in Yoshihara, *Oei Tiong Ham Concern*, pp. 50–71; he mentions also the Be, Liem, and Tan families in Semarang and the Han, Kwee, Tjoa, and The families in Surabaya as the foremost to produce Chinese officers and revenue farmers over long periods.

[8]See K. D. Thomas and J. Panglaykim, "The Chinese in the South Sumatran Rubber Industry: A Case Study in Economic Nationalism," in *The Chinese in Indonesia: Five Essays*, ed. J. A. C. Mackie (Melbourne: Nelson, 1976).

attracted toward the risks and discomforts of such activities; their greater access to education and a more settled lifestyle inclined them toward salaried and professional jobs, wherever possible.[9]

It is surely not coincidental, therefore, that a high proportion of the most dynamic and successful Chinese businessmen who have emerged in Indonesia since that time have been either China-born or from totok family backgrounds. They have pushed aside the old peranakan families and often bought up their old-style mansions. Although they had little scope for dramatic expansion or enrichment during the forty years of disruption and stagnant economic conditions that followed the onset of the depression in 1930, many were able to survive those years more successfully than the peranakan. When favorable economic conditions returned after about 1970, these men were well placed by experience and adaptability to seize the rich opportunities for business expansion that arose in the Suharto era.

Disruptions and Transitions, 1930–1965

During the twenty years covering the depression, Japanese occupation, and struggle for independence, many of the Chinese in Indonesia were forced to move into new and different economic roles—or in a few cases now found themselves able to do so—as the economy underwent a series of major upheavals that shattered the old colonial economic structure. New types of industries developed in the 1930s, most of them quite small and predominantly Chinese owned (e.g., textiles, food processing, soap, cigarettes), as the colony's capacity to import shrank drastically and protective barriers created new markets. As the Dutch-owned businesses that had dominated the modern sector of the economy collapsed or contracted, there was more space for Chinese businessmen to move into their places, especially during the 1940s. But their opportunities for upward social mobility were still effectively closed by the economic dominance of the Dutch over the huge plantation sector and the capital-intensive banking, financial, and commercial spheres, a state of affairs that continued into the late 1950s, well after Indonesia had proclaimed her independence. No fundamental reshaping of the patterns of ownership and control of the country's productive resources occurred until 1957–1958, when all Dutch enterprises were suddenly nationalized at a tense moment in the struggle to recover West Irian.

The elimination of the Dutch opened new opportunities for the wealthier Chinese to take their places in various niches along the higher slopes of the commanding heights of the economy, but as the nationalized enterprises were almost wholly state controlled and private enterprise generally was under an ideological cloud in the era of President Sukarno's "Socialism à la Indonesia," the Chinese did not gain very dramatically from the new situation until after the New Order regime took over in 1965–1966. The steadily intensifying economic and administrative decline of 1958–1965 meant that everyone in the country was living more or less hand-to-mouth, from one crisis to the next. Almost no significant new investment was occurring to stimulate economic activity, and real incomes per capita were declining in most regions. Many Chinese were able to cope with these conditions more skillfully than indigenous Indonesians, thanks to their greater commercial experience, but few became especially rich at this time. At best, they were treading water.

No new tycoons of any real substance emerged during those troubled decades—Mas Agung was the nearest approach to one, perhaps, but was not yet the wealthy tycoon he became later—although some Chinese got rich by smuggling goods to Singapore and else-

---

[9] See David Willmott, *The Chinese of Semarang* (Ithaca, N.Y.: Cornell University Press, 1960), chap. 3. For further details on occupations and location, see Mackie, "Geographical Dispersal."

where during the 1940s and by engaging in "barter trade" (a euphemism for smuggling at a time of high black market foreign exchange rates) in the 1950s. Many of them took their money, and often their families and entire businesses, to Singapore or Malaysia. Because of the generally stagnant condition of the economy throughout those decades, there were few opportunities to tap expanding markets and thereby build substantial business empires as in the earlier years of the century or in the post-1970 period. Even the old, established family firms found it difficult to survive in those circumstances, and many of them collapsed during the war and revolution, particularly those that had depended heavily on Dutch suppliers or customers. According to Twang Peck-yang, the businessmen who succeeded best in the disrupted circumstances of the 1940s had small small businesses and the ability to adapt. Of these, members of the Hok-cia subgroup were the most outstanding. One of them was Liem Sioe Liong.[10]

Above all, the political vulnerablity of the Indonesian Chinese was worse than at any other time during those middle decades of the century, particularly in the unsettled conditions of the Japanese occupation and the revolution, when anti-Chinese violence was widespread. The strong nationalist sentiments aroused by the struggle for independence were directed against the Chinese as well as the Dutch, at times fanned by right-wing groups against which neither President Sukarno nor the Communist party, the only political forces inclined to defend them, were able to mount any effective defense. There was almost no scope for the kinds of close conections with the political authorities that have characterized the New Order, or the earlier relationships described by Rush between the opium kings and the colonial authorities.

Sino-Indonesian Businessmen under the New Order

The earliest years of the New Order were a period of terrifying insecurity and spasmodic violence for the Indonesian Chinese. The victors in the 1965–1966 power struggle were the very people who had earlier been their most feared enemies, the military and the Muslim right wing.[11] It would scarcely have been imaginable in 1966–1967 that anti-Chinese antagonisms in the society would soon be damped down almost completely by the military authorities or that within twenty years the Chinese would be prospering as they have in the vanguard of the country's "economic miracle." Least of all was it then foreseeable that the foremost of the big Chinese towkays would be able to grow so extraordinarily rich in an intimate alliance with the new military-political elite.

It is worth posing the hypothetical question whether that pattern of alliance would ever have been achieved without an accident of history, if only to underline what a crucially important and fortuitous quirk of fate it was: President Suharto and Liem Sioe Liong quickly began to build an enduring relationship on the basis of the slender personal and financial links first established between them in Central Java many years earlier. The businessman who was destined to become the greatest tycoon in the nation's history, thanks to that relationship, happened already to have achieved a degree of mutual trust with the man who was destined to become president (and remain so for a quarter-century). The personal element in the president's relationship with Liem seems to have been enormously important

---

[10]The Hok-cia are a small but unusually interesting subgroup of immigrants from Fujian, reputedly very close-knit, who proved highly successful as traders and smugglers during the years 1945–1949. A disproportionate number of them are now prominent among Indonesia's businessmen; see Twang Peck-yang, "The Transformation of the Trading Minorities in Indonesia, 1940–50" (Ph.D. diss., Australian National University, 1988).

[11]See Charles Coppel, *Indonesian Chinese in Crisis* (Kuala Lumpur: Oxford University Press, 1983) and J. A. C. Mackie, "Anti-Chinese Outbreaks in Indonesia, 1959–1968," in Mackie, *Chinese in Indonesia*, chap. 3.

from the beginning right down to the present. Someone else might have been equally able to fill Liem's shoes, for instance, one of the various other *cukong* who became notorious around 1970–1971 because of their financial connections with various military and political leaders, not solely President Suharto.[12] But one suspects that it would have been a significantly different kind of relationship, with Suharto the intensely reserved kind of man he is and trust one of the key values for old-style Chinese like Liem.[13] The consequences, too, might have been quite different, at least in the early unsettled years of the New Order. Of the dozen or so cukong most commonly mentioned at that time, only Bob Hasan has achieved the same intimacy of access to the president and his family as Liem, and that fairly recently after he established the powerful grip over the timber and forest products industries that he has had since 1980. William Soeryadjaya, the second largest of the tycoons, has never had links as close with the palace as those of Liem, according to Jakarta gossip, nor have any of the other top ten tycoons.

What matters in the long run, however, is not so much the accidents of personality involved, important though they appear to have been here, but the structural ties that have bound together the two elements. On one side are the Sino-Indonesian business enterprises with their money and commercial skills, which were desperately needed in the early years of the New Order; on the other side are the military and political leaders of the new regime, with their capacity to supply protection and social stability, creating a tight symbiotic relationship that had been impossible prior to 1965. Yet that kind of alliance might not have developed as it did if the political structure established by the initially loose New Order coalition of military and civilian elements that overthrew Sukarno had resulted in a more pluralistic or less state-dominated system, one in which political parties and other social groups might have been able to play a larger part, instead of the highly centralized and increasingly authoritarian, patrimonialist structure that came into being in the early 1970s.[14] It was not a predetermined outcome but one shaped by the political struggles of the years 1966–1974. The political vulnerability of the Chinese during those years combined with that precarious political balance and the straitened economic circumstances of the late 1960s all stacked the odds heavily toward the emergence of some such pattern of relationships.

The government's decision to reverse the economic policies of the Sukarno era and to embark on a market-oriented economic strategy could not have succeeded, however, unless the way was opened for the Chinese to participate as fully as possible in economic life because they alone had the commercial experience and ready access to foreign capital. Their contribution to the economic transformation of the country since 1966–1967 has far exceeded that of the *pribumi* businessmen and state enterprises. Yet the most distinctive feature of the

---

[12]Coppel gives the best account of these relationships in *Indonesian Chinese in Crisis*, pp. 153–54, defining a cukong simply as a "Chinese businessman in alliance with Indonesian power holders"; for lists of the names current in 1970–1971, see Leo Suryadinata, "Chinese Economic Elites in Indonesia: a Preliminary Study" in *Changing Ethnic Identities of the Southeast Asian Chinese since World War II*, ed. Jennifer Cushman and Wang Gangwu (Hong Kong: University of Hong Kong Press, 1988), pp. 261–88.

[13]See the discussion of *sun yungi* (Cantonese, "interpersonal trust" or "confidence," the key concept in business relations among Chinese), Clifton Barton, "Trust and Credit: Some Observations Regarding Business Strategies of Overseas Chinese," in *The Chinese in Southeast Asia*, ed. Linda Lim and J. A. Peter Gosling (Singapore: Marnuzen, 1983).

[14]See Harold Crouch, *The Army and Politics in Indonesia* (Ithaca, N.Y.: Cornell University Press, 1978) for the best account of political developments in the early New Order period. He has also used the term *patrimonialism* to refer to the political system as it developed in the late 1970s, with a high degree of concentration of both decision-making power and control over the allocation of key financial and economic resources (capital, bank credits, licenses, etc.) at the apex of the political structure.

emergence of the big Sino-Indonesian conglomerates since that time has been the extent to which they have been able to benefit from deviations from free-market principles by taking advantage of privileged access to resources (particularly subsidized loans), quasi-monopoly situations, and rent-seeking opportunities. They have been able to leverage the huge profits generated from them into enormous capital gains.[15]

The consequences of this situation for the Sino-Indonesian community in general have been immense. Political connections and protection have been an almost essential condition of economic success for Indonesian businessmen of all races since early in the New Order, very blatantly so in some instances but never to be ignored entirely for Riggs's ugly term "pariah capitalist" is appropriate in Indonesia not only to the Chinese. At the same time, the entire Sino-Indonesian minority has been subject to various forms of discrimination and exclusion from educational, social, and employment rights, ostensibly on the grounds of promoting the economic advance of the pribumi, measures that the wealthy Chinese have been powerless to prevent or protest. (They avoid them by having their children educated overseas, at great expense to the country.) The net effect has been to keep the Chinese dependent, politically powerless, and easily controllable.

The huge corporate conglomerates that have come to dominate many areas of the country's economic life began to emerge in the early 1980s, after the momentum of development induced by the oil boom began to diversify the national economy dramatically for the first time since the 1920s. About one dozen of these groups are now outstandingly large and wealthy, whereas several hundred would exceed in size any of the earlier Chinese firms in Indonesia, except perhaps the Oei Tiong Ham Concern at its peak in the 1920s. Almost all are family firms rather than joint stock companies with multiple holdings, and all of them have been created by "new men" who have made their fortunes since the Suharto regime took over in 1965–1966. "Old wealth" is conspicuously absent at this level. Surprisingly few of the top thirty or forty firms have failed over the last twenty years, although most of them have relied on highly leveraged bank loans or speculative property dealings to provide the capital bases from which they have expanded. All have had to rely to some degree on political connections for privileges or protection.

It is much easier to put together a picture of the Sino-Indonesian big business class, impressionistic and blurred in many details though it may be, than it is to depict the Sino-Indonesian minority as a whole or the condition of their scores of thousands of smaller business enterprises. It is probably true that nearly all Sino-Indonesians at every level of society have experienced substantial improvements in their standards of living (except in some rural areas, perhaps) as has the urban population in general. They now constitute a core element in the newly emerging Indonesian urban, educated middle class. But reliable statistical data are too scanty to enable one to sketch the socioeconomic conditions of the entire ethnic minority with any precision. Only by the crudest guesswork could one attempt to estimate how many adult Sino-Indonesians were engaged in business activities in the 1980s or how many hold professional or salaried jobs or are still engaged in agricultural, fishing, or mining activities (as some are). It is well documented that very few indeed are employed in government service and that the educational levels of Sino-Indonesians are generally much higher than those of the indigenous people. In those respects the situation in the 1980s does not differ greatly from that of the 1920s, except in degree. Citizenship, however, has undergone a fundamental change. Well over 90 percent of Sino-Indonesians are

---

[15] On rent-seeking capitalists, see Yoshihara Kunio, *The Rise of Ersatz Capitalism in Southeast Asia* (Singapore: Oxford University Press, 1988), pp. 3–4, 68–98.

now Indonesian citizens, increasingly identified with the economic and social future of the country as the old links with China fray.

At this point it is appropriate to turn to the life story of Liem Sioe Liong for clues to the emergence of the great tycoons. But there is one big difference between Liem Sioe Liong and Oei Tiong Ham. For all his later eminence, Liem has had more in common with his peers than Oei did, except in the key factor of his close and long-standing relationship with the president. And like many of them, but unlike Oei, his life has been a classic case of the Horatio Alger rags-to-riches myth of a man who started from the very lowest rungs of the socioeconomic ladder and has ascended to the top. His story falls into two parts: an unremarkable life as an ordinary Indonesian Chinese trader during his first fifty years, followed by an utterly extraordinary rise to immense wealth over the last twenty years under the Suharto regime.[16]

Liem came to Central Java from Fujian in 1938, aged twenty, as an almost penniless immigrant, living and working initially with his brother in Kudus as a petty trader during the difficult years of the Great Depression and World War II. They started out in a form of rural small-scale hawking on a buy-now-pay-later basis, known as *Cina mindering*, to which many Hok-cias across Java had turned because, as one of the smallest of the Chinese emigrant groups and among the last to come to Java in any number, they were forced to find a livelihood in the less-favored occupations. Although their returns were small and the risks of loss high, the experience paid off in the disrupted conditions of Japanese occupation, war, and revolution that followed soon after for these traders were well acquainted with the countryside. They knew where to go for goods that were in short supply and had wide-ranging networks of former customers and clients who were obligated to them.

Soon after the Japanese took over, the mindering business was banned and Liem had to find other forms of small-scale trade to make a living, including trade in cloves for *kretek* factories. He did well enough even in those difficult times to be able to marry and move into better accommodations. He achieved a reputation for being hardworking, modest, and discreet and became sufficiently well regarded in both the local Chinese community and among the Indonesians to have his first great stroke of luck, which opened the way to his later fame and fortune. The local independence committee was asked to provide a refuge during the struggle for independence for a mysterious visitor from Jakarta. The visitor turned out to be Hassan Din, President Sukarno's father-in-law, for whom Liem's household was chosen as a safe haven. This twist of fate brought him into contact with various TNI military officers and established his credentials as a sympathizer with the republic and its leaders. As one result, he became a supplier to the Republican forces. He thereby established contact with officers of the Diponegoro Division, including Sudjono Humardani, later a close associate of Suharto, and he continued to supply various commodities to it throughout the 1950s. He claims, however, that he did not actually meet Lieutenant Colonel Suharto, as he was then known, until around 1952, several years before the latter was appointed military commander in Central Java and based in Semarang.

Supplying the armed forces was not Liem's only activity in those years for he continued to deal in cloves, importing them from the Outer Islands of Indonesia or from Singapore, in some cases smuggling them past the Dutch authorities. Risky though it was, this business must have been lucrative (kretek consumption was increasing steadily even then), and by the early 1950s, Liem's business activities had expanded sufficiently to make it worthwhile

---

[16]See Eddy Soetiyono, *Kisah Sukses Liem Sioe Liong* (Jakarta: Indomedia, 1989) and Sori Esa Siregar and K. T. Widya, *Liem Sioe Liong: Dari Futjing ke Mancanegara* (Jakarta: Pustaka Merdeka, 1989).

to move his entire household to Jakarta. Thence he embarked upon a series of more substantial manufacturing ventures in both Jakarta and Semarang. Significantly, none of these was particularly successful at that time, although he still maintained his clove business in the Kudus-Semarang region. In the late 1950s, when Suharto was military commander in Semarang, Liem began to build his close relationship with him. The Semarang phase of his business career must have been quite important for him, although relatively little is known about it apart from the fact that he then acquired two small private banks including Bank Central Asia (BCA), which was later to become one of his crown jewels. Yet it made little money for him until 1975, when Liem was able to entice Mochtar Riady to leave a rival bank and manage BCA; he rapidly turned it into the money-spinner it has since become.

Prior to 1965, Liem was a moderately successful Jakarta businessman, but not at all an outstanding or well-known one. His story would until then have been broadly similar to those of many other Chinese towkays in Indonesia at that time. But he rocketed into prominence soon after Suharto became president, obtaining highly controversial monopoly rights to import cloves (along with Probosutedjo, the president's half-brother, who has shown little love for him in later years) and to manufacture flour, the springboard from which his other business interests, many in conjunction with members of the Suharto family, rapidly expanded. All this gave rise to widespread criticism of him as the foremost of the notorious cukong said to be bankrolling the new regime from behind the scenes, to a point where his close associations with members of the Suharto family circle soon became public scandal. But the president simply disregarded the criticism, and Liem survived unscathed, even during the anti-Chinese outbreaks known as the Malari affair in 1974.

Liem's business empire began to grow rapidly in the early 1970s as he diversified his investments into general trading, real estate, textile manufacturing, crumb rubber milling, and logging, all of them fast-growing sectors of the Indonesian economy when it recovered from its mid-1960s chaos. His achievements in these fields were not especially remarkable, however, and in several other sectors his record was curiously checkered. He was relatively slow to enter the profitable motor vehicle assembling industry, long after the Astra and Krama Yudha groups had established strong positions there. His banking enterprises were not at all successful until after 1975, when Mochtar Riady was brought in to manage BCA. From then on, BCA rose rapidly to become the most dynamic of the private banks, with a string of associated insurance and financial enterprises attached to it; but the credit for that is attributable more to Riady, who is generally regarded as an outstanding banker, than to Liem himself.

In the early 1980s, Liem's business interests were already estimated to be worth more than US$2 billion, and he was branching out into several offshore investments, of which the Hong Kong–based First Pacific group was in time to prove highly successful. But he also had serious problems in the 1980s, most notably his loss-incurring involvement (imposed upon him by the president in return for other favors) in the government-owned Krakatau Steel complex and the overextension of his huge Indocement group of cement factories, which had to be bailed out by the government at the cost of billions of rupiah during the slump of 1984–1985.

One cannot help wondering, in light of these episodes, whether Liem's great fortune has been due to his outstanding business acumen (as Oei Tiong Ham's appears to have been, as well as those of several big tycoons of the 1980s) or whether he has just been an "ersatz" rent-seeking capitalist, as Yoshihara claims all Southeast Asian businessmen are, relying primarily on political connections for privileges and subsidies to rake in unearned income. It would be absurd to suggest that such a man has not displayed considerable business skills of some kind, but are they the skills of the small-scale towkay or of the modern corporate tycoon? It is not easy to identify any other factor that would account for his astonishingly rapid growth since 1968. The principal sources of cash flow or profits that have enabled his empire to expand so much faster than any of his rivals' are hard to pin down. The Indocement group of cement plants, one of his largest investments, serving the country's leading growth sector, urban construction, has probably lost about as much money in the 1980s as it has generated. Property deals have certainly been bringing in big profits for him, although he is only one of many large-scale operators in that field. The flour and clove monopolies are presumably still lucrative money-spinners for the group but would account for no more than a small part of its growth. His other trading and manufacturing ventures may be yielding high rates of return—many of them were undertaken in conjunction with other leading business groups in recent years—and it may be that the extraordinary diversity of his holdings proved advantageous during difficult times in the mid-1980s, enabling him to snap up bargains. He is said to have picked up many ailing companies that turned to him for help during the economic downturn, so he must have made big capital gains when they returned to profits later. By 1989, Liem's group included more than 243 companies, whereas it had less than one-quarter that number earlier in the decade. His total assets had grown to US$ 3.5 billion, almost double what they had been a decade earlier. Yet there is a magpie-like quality to these ill-assorted acquisitions, what seems like a grabbing at bargains reminiscent of the old towkay mentality, rather than a sign of deliberately planned corporate logic.

Is Liem at all typical of the other big tycoons of the New Order era? In several respects he is, despite the sheer scale of his activities and his close links with the palace that make him exceptional. He does not stand in a class apart from his contemporaries in the way that Oei Tiong Ham did by his forward-looking business strategy and managerial techniques. In fact, several others seem to be ahead of him in this respect, the Astra and Dharmala groups, in particular.[17] The diversity of Liem's vast array of companies is a feature of at least half the second-ranking groups that make up the top fifty, although on a lesser scale. And it may be significant that such diversity is more characteristic of the wheeler-dealer rent-seeking types than of the groups built by the more highly regarded businessmen who have minimized their reliance on political connections.

On the controversial matter of just how much political influence he wields, Liem again differs from other tycoons in degree more than in kind. Almost all promote their special interests at the highest levels they can reach, some vigorously or scandalously, others much less so. Although Liem has certainly had unrivalled access to President Suharto for a long time, it is impossible to assess how far he has been able to impact the determination of the government's economic policies in general, as distinct from particularistic decisions about the allocation of contracts, credits, subsidies, and so on (relatively little in the early years, one would guess, when the technocrats carried more clout, although that may no longer have been the case in the 1980s). Other leading tycoons who seem to have similar access and influence include Bob Hasan, the timber king, Ir. Ciputra, Prayogo Pangestu, the fast-rising pulp and paper baron, now in league with Suharto's daughter, Mbak Tutut, but relatively few others these days. A recent development of potentially great importance has been the

---

[17]Liem's is the only group in the top six that is not based primarily on one line of business but on a bewildering diversity of firms and product lines. Most of the biggest groups have several divisions—real estate, finance, banking, or trading as well as manufacturing—but all others of the top six are relatively concentrated; for instance, the core business of Astra lies unequivocally in auto assembling, of Sinar Mas in palm-oil plantations and cooking oil, of Lippo in banking and finance, whereas the two kretek giants, Djarum and Gudang Garam, are into cigarette-related activities.

tendency for other big business groups to go into partnership with Liem's companies in many of their new ventures, partly as a means of insurance and access to influence or protection, one suspects, so that he is becoming the center of a complex network of new-style patron-client relationships linked indirectly into palace circles.

In short, new elements have constantly been woven into the ever-changing cobweb of personal and financial ties holding the business-political elites together as it has evolved over the last twenty years. And it increasingly seems that Indonesia may be moving toward a pattern of political relationships strikingly similar to Rush's picture of the nineteenth-century opium kings "nested within the power structures" of Java. Nothing like that had occurred during the intervening hundred years, when the Chinese in Indonesia found themselves out of favor with the authorities, initially colonial, later independent Indonesian, who were trying to change the character of the society in various ways. Perhaps in this respect, the course of Southeast Asian history, after colonial era deviations, is returning to its more natural, earlier, direction. If so, it may be going back to something more like the pattern of political and economic relationships Rush has described, to which one should be looking for clues about the shape of things to come, rather than toward the emergence of a conventionally European-style but predominantly Sino-Indonesian bourgeoisie.

BECOMING AN *ORANG INDONESIA SEJATI:* THE POLITICAL JOURNEY OF YAP THIAM HIEN

Daniel S. Lev

Djikaloe pranakan Tionghoa dengan mendengar soeara hatinja maoe lengketken nasibnja bersama-sama orang Indonesier pada tana Indonesia ini, ia poen moesti dianggap Indonesier sedjati.
—Liem Koen Hian, 1934.

Once the curtain of common myths about *peranakan* Chinese in Indonesia is parted sensibly on reality, what appears is a startlingly complex presence in local history, filled with the kinds of contradiction, tension, strength, vulnerability, and tragedy that seem always to surround such diasporas. To say that Indonesian Chinese have enriched Indonesia is a misleading cliché, for it sets them apart still as something other than Indonesian. For the most part, they are understandable nowhere else, as is true of most national minorities anywhere. If they are not unique, they are at least different, as Indonesians generally are different from anybody else.

As it happens, the man I discuss in this paper is about as different from anybody else, in important ways, as one can imagine and yet is more or less understandable in Indonesia—and to many is an authentic Indonesian hero. One measure of his achievement is that by the end of his life, in April 1989, at age seventy-six, few thought his Chinese origins relevant to anything important or even all that interesting. For many of the thousands who mourned him, and certainly for those who created a small furor at his graveside—shouting that this man belonged to the nation, not just his family—Yap had become an extraordinary symbol of the struggle for political change in Indonesia. It did not matter that his name was Yap.

For critical comments, information, and advice on this paper, although I have not been able to absorb all of it, I am grateful to T. Mulya Lubis, Oei Tjoe Tat, Siauw Tiong Djin, Leo Suryadinata, Harry Tjan Silahi, Charles Hirschman, and Arlene O. Lev.

The quotation from Liem is translated as follows: If peranakan Chinese, heeding their hearts, want to join fates together with Indonesians, then they too must be considered true Indonesians.

98 Daniel S. Lev

Yet Yap came to the national scene of Indonesian politics rather late, only in the 1960s, after an apprenticeship in the sideshow of peranakan politics. By no means was he the only one to do so, but his course was peculiar enough to merit attention, in part because one can trace the ideas that guided him through it. Although his early biography is sketched here, the main focus will be on a few issues that marked his way out of a minority periphery towards the national center. For the sake of contrast, much of the paper is built around the tension between Yap and the late Siauw Giok Tjhan, chairman of the peranakan political organization Baperki (Badan Permusjawaratan Kewarganegaraan Indonesia) from its inception in 1954 until it was banned in 1966. For several years these two extraordinary men dominated one range of conflict over a wider continuum of peranakan political experience and thought.

Yap Thiam Hien

As a prelude to a discussion that concentrates on one or two leading figures, rather than peranakan society in general, it may be useful to recall that Indonesian Chinese have never formed a well-integrated community. Other similarly positioned minorities around the world have enjoyed (not always to great advantage) more religious and cultural integrity, or at least less diversity. Peranakan Chinese in Indonesia *are* disparate: geographically spread, religiously and culturally variegated, historically experienced, and locally absorbed and formed in different ways. Group recognition exists, of course, along with ethnic identity—as often as not enforced by external hostility and pressure—but there is relatively little vertical and horizontal solidarity, however differently outside impressions may have it. The social and political history of Indonesian Chinese demonstrates this point well enough. Hard as it is to avoid using the term "the Chinese" or some other inadequate analogue—peranakan, Warga Negara Indonesia (WNI), Indonesian Chinese, *keturunan*—one ought to hold in mind that it almost always produces a caricature, often a racist one at that.[1]

In Yap Thiam Hien's case, except for the presence of an odd foster grandmother, his early life was unexceptional in one stratum of peranakan Chinese society, yet it would seem peculiar anywhere but in the stream of twentieth-century Indonesian history. Three or four items from his biography may help to account for the kind of man he became.

He was well born to the wealth, privilege, and comforts of an *officier* family in Banda Aceh in 1913, but just at the time when the privileges of the officieren were beginning to disappear under the dual pressures of middle class Chinese political awakening and colonial social reforms. His great-grandfather, the *Luitenant*, who had immigrated from Guangdong to Bangka and somehow ended up in Aceh, did well mainly (one suspects) from the opium monopoly, but once this disappeared, he, like many other officieren around the colony, lost the family stake through commercial misadventure—in his case, coconut plantations, then an egregiously bad investment in Aceh. (Then and later, many peranakan, by contrast with immigrant *totok*, gave the lie to the myth of Chinese business prowess, but commercial ineptitude seems to have run especially deep in the Yap line.) Bankrupt, the family lost its position in 1920 to another family, the Han, imported from East Java.

Not long afterwards, when he was nine, Yap's young mother died. He and his younger brother and sister fell to the care of his grandfather's mistress, a Japanese woman, Sato Nakashima, whom the Yap children came to think of as mother, father, and grandmother all in one. If nothing else set Yap apart from others, a Japanese grandmother did, but she was evidently a remarkable person in her own right. There is no space here to trace her influence on the character of the three children, but it was substantial. She provided them, along with much else, the kind of intimacy that extended Chinese families usually lacked, as well as a fairly firm ethical sense that may explain a great deal about the mature Yap.

His father, Sin Eng, the first real peranakan in the Yap line, was a weak figure who won little respect from his son. A trite psychoanalyst might conclude that the mature Yap Thiam Hien was quick to challenge authority because of his relationship with Yap Sin Eng—and might be right, though the authorities whom Yap fought also deserve some credit. If nothing else, however, Sin Eng helped to mold Thiam Hien's life by adopting Dutch legal status (*gelijkstelling*) for his family. European status guaranteed the children's rights to a European education after the family lost its officier status. Yap's education in the schools for Europeans and privileged others was superb, from the ELS primary school in Kutaraja (Banda Aceh), through MULO in Batavia, where his father moved in the 1920s, and on to the AMS-A/2 (Western languages) program in Bandung and Yogyakarta. His education, like his advantaged birth, left him confident and ambitious but also socially at loose ends, for the European education and ethnically mixed experience was followed by few appropriate nonethnic lines of opportunity. None of this was unusual in the small stratum of highly educated non-Europeans in the colony.

---

[1] In Indonesia far more so than in Malaysia, for example, but closer to the Thai, Vietnamese, and Philippine cases, peranakan Chinese are not always easily distinguished from ethnic Indonesians. Sometimes this is as true physically as it is culturally, for many, like Yap himself, have mixed genes, to put it bloodlessly.

In one way or another most were culturally marginalized.[2] For Yap, however, there was little to fall back on. Raised in Aceh but having moved to Jakarta, he had no extended family in Java and little enough of a nuclear family, for only he and his father and brother were there until Sato Nakashima and his sister came in the late 1930s. This may help to explain his conversion to Protestantism in 1938, after his introduction to it a few years earlier in the loving Eurasian family with whom he lived in Yogya.[3] The church, a Chinese *Hervormde Kerk* (Reformed Church) in Jakarta, and associated nonethnic organizations provided him with a secure base that he took to enthusiastically, though he understood little of modern Dutch Calvinism until he began to read and talk about it assiduously in Holland after the war.

As in the church, his vocational chances were also tracked into a Chinese stream. The colonial policy of separating and thus creating ethnic camps made it difficult to cross lines. The most obvious opportunity for Yap, failing work elsewhere during the depression, was in the Dutch-Chinese Teachers School (HCK) in Jakarta, which prepared him to teach in the Dutch-Chinese schools (HCS). Finishing the HCK curriculum in one year, he taught in private (*wilde scholen*) HCS in Cirebon and Rembang for four years until 1938. Returning to Jakarta, he found other work and enrolled in the Rechtshogeschool to study law. Here too, though he was then unaware of it, he was also implicitly channeled into a Chinese tunnel. Although Yap eventually became one of Indonesia's most prominent professional advocates, neither in the Rechtshogeschool nor at the law faculty in Leiden did he think of joining the advocacy. It was not initially a calling for him but in time became one. As few ethnic Chinese were recruited into the colonial legal bureaucracy, the one profession clearly open to ethnic Chinese law students was private lawyering.

After working his way to the Netherlands on a repatriation ship in early 1946, Yap finished his law degree in Leiden in 1947. He did a great deal more than study law, however, which may have been less on his mind than religion and politics. Living at the *Zendingshuis* in Oogstgeest, just outside of Leiden, he read widely in modern Protestant theology and talked endlessly with students preparing for mission work. His commitment to the church, but also to his own independent reading of the religion, deepened. The church offered him further training at Selly Oakes in England if he would commit himself also to church work in Indonesia. He agreed and paid that debt many times over, beyond a period as a church youth leader in Jakarta during the late 1940s, in his dedicated labors in the reorganization of the Protestant churches and in the ecumenical movement (including the Council of Churches [DGI], now the Alliance of Churches [PGI]) in Indonesia.

Yap also became a committed nationalist during his Leiden period, opposing the Dutch effort to restore their colony and siding outspokenly (a tautology in Yap's case) with the revolution. In this he was neither alone nor in the majority among peranakan students in

---

[2] Yap first got an inkling of the discomforts of marginalization as his name kept changing: from Yap Thiam Hien to Thiam Hien Yap when his father converted to European legal status; Jaap when he moved to Java; and John as a nickname during the 1930s, when adopting European given names or nicknames was something of a fashion among the educated.

[3] But his younger brother, Bong, lived with the same family and never converted. His sister became Catholic after studying in a Catholic school in Banda Aceh. Yap was one of relatively few peranakan converts to Protestantism before the war, but explaining why he or others adopted the religion is not easy. The missiologist Hendrik Kraemer may have fathomed one basic reason for conversion among ethnic Chinese, particularly in Jakarta and Cirebon, by relating it to the noticeable decline of the extended family in those areas. The Chinese family, he reasoned, was fundamentally analogous to religion among other groups, and when it broke down, its members would be ready for conversion. See Hendrik Kraemer, *From Missionfield to Independent Church* (The Hague: Boekencentrum, 1958), pp. 149–58, on "The Chinese Question" in West Java.

Holland. Peranakan Chinese were generally suspicious of politics under the best of conditions, and the news from home of anti-Chinese violence during the revolution was upsetting. But for Yap (as for his brother, who followed him to Holland) anticolonialism came easily, though thoughtfully, and nationalism no less so. There was never any doubt that he would return home nor that the revolution was right. At the same time, he began to develop a political orientation, basically democratic socialist, through his association with other Indonesian students connected with the Dutch Partij van de Arbeid (Labor Party).[4]

After returning to Jakarta in 1948, Yap packed a huge supply of life crises into a short year or so. He married. His father Sin Eng and Sato Nakashima both died in 1949. He worked in the church. And he decided to practice as a professional advocate, eventually joining a small but prominent law firm all of whose partners were publicly engaged in and beyond Chinese affairs.[5] Yap was not likely to sit back. He saw himself as a public man, with too many ideas to ignore the mountain of difficult issues around him and too much energy to sit quietly in one office. Moreover, the relative lack of willing Chinese leaders placed a premium on the few who were available. Yet he was utterly unprepared for politics, without experience or essential knowledge, contacts, understanding, or even the suppleness of character and sense of easy compromise and humor that would have made him a quick political study.

Although the revolution eliminated the explicit ethnic segregation of political life, this change did not mean a great deal. Only a few peranakan Chinese joined national parties. Most of those who were at all inclined to act politically, themselves a small minority, knew or sensed that they either would not be welcome or would swing little weight. Yap joined neither the PSI nor the Protestant Parkindo, though he was invited into the latter by Dr. Leimena. Suspicious of insider politics and doubtful about the ethics of political life, he, moreover, refused to be bound by party discipline. In addition, he was afraid that ethnic Indonesians would not accept him at face value, a burden of doubt from which he was relieved only in the 1960s in the circle of professional advocates.

Despite his own nonethnic predilections, he had no choice but to retreat into the few Chinese opportunities for public service. What was available, apart from one or two ineffectual Chinese parties in which he had no interest, was the Sin Ming Hui, the social service association founded in 1946 that fed into each of the Chinese political organizations established thereafter. During the early 1950s, until Baperki came along, Yap worked for a legal assistance office sponsored by the Sin Ming Hui to advise ethnic Chinese, particularly on citizenship problems. It was the citizenship question, more than anything else, that drew Yap to grand issues of Indonesian state and society.

Citizenship marked peranakan vulnerability as nothing else could. It went to the heart of peranakan identity and security, preceding every other issue of significance to those who thought they belonged in Indonesia and nowhere else. No one could escape the abysmal

---

[4] It was not a surprising choice, of course. Many Indonesian professionals and intellectuals moved towards democratic socialism during this period. Among peranakan Chinese, a few joined the Indonesian Socialist Party (PSI), but most did not, probably mainly for ethnic reasons.

[5] All members of the firm were Chinese, as were its clients, a fairly common pattern until the 1960s. Yap's more senior partners included Lie Hwee Yoe, founder of the firm in the 1930s, the West Javanese Tan Po Goan, who had actively supported the revolution and become a member of the PSI, and the much younger Solonese Oei Tjoe Tat. Oei was prominent in the Sin Ming Hui, and later in Baperki and Partindo, and a member of Soekarno's cabinet from 1963 through early 1966, when he was imprisoned for over a decade. His politically active partners no doubt helped to educate Yap and to encourage his own public bent.

threat posed in the ups and downs of the legal rules as they changed under political pressure nor, for that matter, the miserable, costly, and humiliating charges and treatment that accompanied the documentary requirements of each change. But any serious consideration of the citizenship question was bound to raise others about how and where peranakan Chinese fit in Indonesia.

During the early 1950s, such questions arose more insistently and openly than at any time thereafter in the then still-active peranakan press, above all *Star Weekly* in Jakarta. It was a time of uncertainty and surprise, when Chinese, lumped together without differentiation, became fair political game as an accessible, live symbol of colonial privilege.[6] Chinese responses to the unsettling situation sorted along a continuum that included emigration, hard-nosed refusal to recognize any need for adaptation, and reflective, often painful soul searching, largely in the pages of *Star Weekly*, about peranakan Chinese history, culture, sins, virtues, exigencies, and about what must be done to adapt as a legitimate part of Indonesian life. In themselves, the discussions of that period are a fascinating study in intellectual history as commentators explored peranakan history and culture, the invidious effects of colonialism in molding the minority, and the problem of who had to adjust to whom and over what obstructions created either by ethnic Indonesian or ethnic Chinese mentalities. Yap himself wrote mainly about the law of citizenship but as an avid and thoughtful reader must have been absorbed in the debates.

Baperki was established in March 1954 as pressure grew on peranakan Chinese—above all the question of citizenship but also Chinese schools and commercial influence—and their lack of preparation to deal with it became apparent.[7] It was the first organization to bring together nearly all strands of peranakan politics, though not all that effectively nor for long. Yap was a founding member, primarily as a representative of the Protestant stream. Auwyong Peng Koen, another HCK graduate, the capable and influential editor of *Star Weekly*, was there for Catholics. Still others spoke for the old right, left, and center of a thin political tradition begun in the 1910s. No less than before the war, successful peranakan Chinese leadership fell to those best connected with the regime, which in the colonial period meant the established wealth of the Chung Hua Hui but in the 1950s meant, in a dramatic shift of personnel and ideology, those who had joined the revolution.

A natural choice for chairman of Baperki was Siauw Giok Tjhan from Surabaya, a journalist, politically experienced on the left in the prewar, pronationalist Partai Tionghoa Indonesia (led by Liem Koen Hian), and briefly a minister in the revolutionary Amir Sjarifuddin cabinet in Yogya. Politically acute, well connected with and respected by national political leaders, Siauw turned Baperki into the most highly mobilized political organization ever of

---

[6] In August 1951, Liem Koen Hian (quoted at the beginning of this article), long a supporter of Indonesian nationalism and of the revolution, was arrested in the Sukiman anti-Communist razzia. Angry and bitter, he publicly rejected Indonesian citizenship. He remained in the country as a businessman but died soon after in Medan. The tragic incident rocked politically conscious peranakan Chinese, making any who were confident about their acceptance more aware of just how vulnerable even the most patriotic peranakan actually were.

[7] On Baperki see, among others, Mary F. Somers, "Peranakan Chinese Politics in Indonesia" (Ph.D. diss., Cornell University, 1965); idem, *Peranakan Chinese Politics in Indonesia*, (Cornell Modern Indonesia Project Interim Reports Series, Ithaca, N.Y. 1964); Charles A. Coppel, "Patterns of Chinese Political Activity in Indonesia," in *The Chinese in Indonesia: Five Essays*, ed., J. A. C. Mackie (Honolulu: University Press of Hawaii, 1976); and Go Gien Tjwan, "De historische wortels van de Baperki-beweging," in *Buiten de Grenzen: Sociologische opstellen aangeboden aan Prof. Dr. W. F. Wertheim* (Amsterdam: Boom Meppel, 1971).

Indonesian Chinese, though without much more influence in the political system than before.

Baperki, which provided the setting for the Siauw-Yap debates, closely approximated general Indonesian political patterns. It was, for example, utterly dominated by Javanese peranakan and, significantly, by the politically dynamic, experienced, and mobilized East Javanese peranakan. No less in Baperki than the PNI, for instance, local, family, and personal intimacies bore weight, and often could be traced back over decades.[8] Finally, like other parties, Baperki tended to circle increasingly tightly around the personal leadership of Siauw.

The peculiar situation of the peranakan minority entrapped Baperki in inextricable contradictions. In one example, often cited, Siauw persuaded the founders that the organization must be presented as multiethnic; hence its name, which emphasizes the citizenship issue but does not mention Chinese. Yap disagreed at first, typically on grounds that if it was a Chinese organization, it should say so, but he quickly came to recognize the symbolic significance of Siauw's stroke. A few non-Chinese were recruited into Baperki's councils, as the Sin Ming Hui before it had also done for the sake of protection. But the gesture remained a gesture. Baperki could be no more multiethnic than ethnic antagonisms would allow it to be, which was very little. Overwhelmingly, it was, and was understood to be, a Chinese organization.

Beyond this fundamental problem was another. Founded not as a party but as a "mass organization" in order to avoid ideological conflict among its members, in a short time, nevertheless, it was behaving much like a political party and paying the price in defections, internal conflict—much of it caused by Yap—and political disunity within the community it meant to represent. But the advantages of acting like a party were too attractive to ignore, as was true also of the apparent rewards for choosing ideological sides in the political system at large. The tensions caused by these developments defined the issues over which Siauw and Yap fought, and their bitter, protracted battles in turn helped to locate the varying dimensions and limits of peranakan participation in the Indonesian universe.

Oddly, despite appearances, the two men were much alike and in agreement on a few fundamentals that set them both apart from others, including close associates. Siauw, by far the more politically knowledgeable and experienced, was supple, personable, emotional, and intimate. The better educated and intellectually avid Yap, religiously devout, a loner, and not much given to small talk, tended toward rigid and uncompromising (and occasionally self-righteous) principle, rigorous logic, and detached argument. But both men were personally modest, unself-serving, serious, and responsible—qualities they recognized and respected in one another. Siauw was probably more comfortable with a Chinese identity, whereas Yap, who did not regret being Chinese, nevertheless took it more lightly. But neither was naive or particularly chauvinistic about the peranakan minority in Indonesia nor given to justifying the privileges many Chinese had gained in the colony and maintained thereafter. Both, indeed, tended to be censorious of bloated wealth, Chinese or other. They defended not Chinese commercial advantage but Chinese minority rights.[9]

---

[8]One example is the relationship between Siauw and Go Gien Tjwan. Given the closeness of many Javanese peranakan and *priyayi* families, it is not surprising that personal connections extended into the PNI and a few other organizations. Siauw himself, whatever his ideological affinity to the PKI, was personally quite close to Sartono, the PNI speaker of Parliament.

[9]Yap was both impressed and puzzled by Siauw's defense of Chinese rice millers when they came under attack by government policy, for it indicated Siauw's even-handedness in protecting all Chinese, even if this seemed to

Moreover, their defense of the minority's human rights did not stop there at all. From different starting points—Siauw's a Marxist critique, Yap's a more eclectically democratic socialist and idiosyncratically Christian—both assumed that Indonesian economy and society had to change in principle. On what kind of change was needed they disagreed monumentally, but each had principles that were significant beyond merely defending peranakan. Siauw, however, who won hands down in every conflict with Yap, ultimately could not escape the peranakan circle to speak to a larger Indonesia. Yap did.

Yap lost out in the Baperki struggles largely because of Siauw's greater political skill and appeal but also because he was rather alone, without effective support, without any of the connections that counted, and without much understanding of everyday politics. Always an outsider and a persistent stranger to the styles of Javanese peranakan politics—which is to say, Javanese politics—Yap never figured out how to play that game well.[10] He had nothing more, really, than substantial resources of personal courage, principle, and learning. Several of the liberal allies he found in Baperki in 1954 fled soon after the completeness of Siauw's control of the organization became clear. Partly out of unrealistic optimism but also from a stubborn disinclination to give up on anything, Yap stayed, biting heels until he was swept away in 1960. But Yap lost too because his vision of peranakan problems and solutions made less sense to many ethnic Chinese than did those of Siauw.

The issues in the Siauw-Yap debate ran a gamut from those having to do with Baperki, reflecting differences over how best to represent the peranakan minority, to political principles of the Indonesian state. Of the first order was Baperki's steady evolution into a political party, as Yap saw it, that assumed increasing responsibility for Chinese affairs. Yap did not object to the decision to contest the elections of 1955, which installed a specific voice for peranakan interests in Parliament and the Constituent Assembly. He himself took a seat in the Constituent Assembly, though technically not in Baperki's delegation but in the Fraksi Lima Orang, all of them Baperki members. But he did oppose any further extension of Baperki's political reach.

Why? The answer illustrates a fundamental disagreement over conceptions of the relationship between community and leadership and, by extension, between society and state. Siauw sought to mobilize unified support—even at the cost of defections—in defense of peranakan interests, for this seemed essential particularly during the period of Guided Democracy. Yap was more skeptical than Siauw about political possibilities and less willing to take risks on behalf of the peranakan community. In addition, however, he was convinced that the community itself, as much as possible, had to assume responsibility for its own affairs.[11] This issue came to a head over the establishment of Res Publica University, sponsored by Baperki over Yap's fierce opposition.[12]

---

contradict his Marxist commitment to deprived classes. It is worth noting that Siauw got along quite well with the totok community, which trusted him and from which he evidently obtained substantial contributions for various Baperki projects. Yap had few contacts, if any, among totok Chinese and tended to distance himself from them. Neither Yap nor Siauw spoke Chinese.

[10] Although Yap's wife Khing was a Javanese speaker from Semarang, and servants in their home were Javanese, he never learned to speak or understand Javanese.

[11] In Yap's mind there may have been an analogy between the peranakan condition and that of the Protestant churches immediately after independence. In the church he had been instrumental in establishing a school system independent of the corporate church to separate their fates, and assure the schools' survival if the churches came under attack.

[12] The issue of principle was mixed with personal pique on Yap's part. Beginning in 1957, as alien Chinese schools came under attack, Baperki was able to take over and run many of them under its own umbrella. At the

The same problem—to Yap's mind, how best to represent peranakan Chinese without making them more vulnerable—attached to the question of Baperki's support for the Communist party (PKI). A few complexities around this issue need sorting. Much was made of Siauw's Communist sympathies, not least by Yap, but Siauw's communism came with a lower case "c," and it is likely that the Chinese factor counted for more in his commitments than ideology.[13] Yap was anti-Communist but not rabidly or unthinkingly so. His religious education in Oegstgeest and training for church work thereafter in Holland and England contained a strong anti-Communist bias. But he doubted party ideologies of any sort. He placed his trust mainly in personal character, which allowed him to respect Siauw as a man while challenging his political views and attachments. (Siauw reciprocated, admiring Yap for his honesty and courage even as he thought him a terrific pain.)[14] Before the 1955 elections, Yap and Go Gien Tjwan, who he knew was Communist, campaigned as a team to demonstrate that men of different political views could work together. Yap thought this proved that Baperki was nonideological.

He fought bitterly with the Siauw group as Baperki seemed to move closer to the PKI after 1956. For Siauw, ideological attraction apart, what counted was that only the PKI among the major parties explicitly rejected ethnic bigotry and publicly supported Baperki initiatives. Moreover, PKI support for Soekarno, to whom Siauw attached great importance, also made sense of a political alignment with the party. But for Yap, though his own ideological biases naturally made a difference, the primary consideration was that the Chinese minority must not risk taking ideological sides. To do so would split the community more than it was already and envelop it in political danger. Baperki's drift to the left drove some of its most prominent centrist figures out and alienated more, yet it alone symbolically

---

same time, because of informal quota restrictions on the matriculation of ethnic Chinese students in the universities, it was agreed that a new university should be created in which there would be no discrimination against Chinese students. Yap was a member of the committee that set about organizing a private effort. Before it got far, however, the Baperki inner council—Siauw himself, Go Gien Tjwan, and the secretary, Buyung Saleh—quietly but quickly undertook their own effort, undercut that of Yap's committee, and successfully put together the land and funds to set up Res Publica University. Apart from his personal outrage at the flanking maneuver, Yap thought that by establishing its own university, Baperki endangered the school (and peranakan interests generally) by association. In this he eventually proved to be right. At the time, however, along with the urgent need for a university—and as well the ability of Siauw et al. to mobilize quickly the funds and energy it required—education was too important a political issue for Baperki leaders to allow anyone else to take credit for resolving it.

[13]Siauw evidently had been attracted to communism since the 1930s, when Tan Ling Djie, to whom he remained quite close, influenced his ideological education. Until 1953, he edited *Harian Rakyat*, after it had been sold to the PKI. Questions were raised about whether he was a secret member of the party, but in fact he may have resented the Aidit leadership for having ousted Tan Ling Djie, if Siauw thought this was inspired by anti-Chinese animus or too much sensitivity to anti-Chinese sentiments. See Siauw Giok Tjhan, *Lima Jaman: Perwujudan Integrasi Wajar* (Jakarta and Amsterdam: Yayasan Teratai, 1981), pp. 296–97. My point, however, is that Siauw was rather more devoted to the survival of peranakan Chinese than he was to communism. One of the issues between Yap and Siauw had to do with the latter's support of the People's Republic of China, which he visited, and to which he sent some of his children to study. Yap thought Siauw's connections with China were wrong, partly on ideological grounds but also because it reinforced the myth that Indonesian Chinese were loyal to China. Yap himself refused to go to China, though he was intellectually interested in it, precisely for this reason. It is an interesting question whether Siauw was attracted to China for ideological or ethnic-cultural reasons. Yap evidently thought the former influence more important, but it may well have been the latter.

[14]Siauw, *Lima Jaman*, p. 241.

represented the entire minority.[15] The danger was that in case of ideological warfare, the Chinese minority would be politically exposed and without a means to defend itself.[16]

The tensest battle between Siauw and Yap took place in 1959 over the issue of the restoration of the 1945 Constitution, which clearly demarcated their understandings of stakes and possibilities. Yap's thinking about minority issues took a critical turn as a result of this debate, which started in late 1956 and early 1957, as the parliamentary system collapsed and Soekarno pressed his *Konsepsi*. To clarify the implications of their divergence, however, it may help to call attention to the principles on which they agreed. Because they shared a commitment to human rights, including the Universal Declaration, both quite naturally asserted the rights of minorities. With different emphases, both also were essentially egalitarian. Neither had any taste for the corruption, inefficiency, economic waste, and self-aggrandizing tendencies of party conflict during the parliamentary period.[17]

But Siauw supported Soekarno, whereas Yap condemned Guided Democracy. In neither case was the position simple. Siauw was convinced that the parliamentary system had failed, that its insoluble conflict of ideologies and partisan advantage would lead to national disaster, and that adequate evidence for its dangers existed in the escalating attacks on the Chinese minority. Soekarno he knew to be free of prejudice, as were many PNI leaders associated with the president, and so was the PKI, which Soekarno insisted should be in the government. But beyond all this, Siauw was no less drawn to Soekarno and his vision than were many other Javanese. It is essential to recognize this Javanese influence in the trust that Siauw placed in Soekarno's person. Siauw believed that Indonesia needed revolutionary change, whose principles would secure the Chinese minority in a political-economic order from which ethnic issues would disappear, and that Soekarno was the key figure to bring all this about. Consequently, as Guided Democracy evolved, Siauw consistently brought Baperki along behind the president. Whatever his doubts about the 1945 Constitution, of which there must have been many, like others he brushed them aside for the sake of Soekarno's ascendancy.

Yap, however, worked from the lawyerly assumption that persons are less promising than sound institutions and legal processes. He too admired Soekarno as unprejudiced but stopped short of wanting to vest more authority in the man. Rather, he insisted that the most secure hope for Indonesia and its Chinese minority rested in effective law, which required the constitution to be taken more seriously than political figures. On this issue Yap and Siauw split completely. In the Constituent Assembly, every member of Baperki except Yap voted to restore the 1945 Constitution. Yap was the only member of the *Konstituante* to vote "no" contrary to his *fraksi*. Yap's opposition to the 1945 Constitution was not focused solely on Article 6, which provides that only an indigenous Indonesian may become president.[18] This was an important issue, and one that had to trouble Baperki, which, as Yap

---

[15] In his dramatic speech to the Baperki congress of December 1960 in Semarang, Yap angrily accused the Siauw leadership of having driven out many of the respected founders of the organization. In fact, those who left initially were mainly from the *Keng Po* group: Auwjong Peng Koen, Khoe Woen Sioe, and Injo Beng Goat. Others on the center and center-right remained almost to the end but with little influence.

[16] As it happened, after 1965, Chinese suffered less than Yap feared precisely because the community was politically divided. Baperki, suddenly naked on the left, was obliterated, but its defectors and opponents were safe, active, and, in some cases, remarkably influential.

[17] The voluminous evidence for Siauw's views can be found in his *Lima Jaman*. Yap developed his arguments in writings scattered over the years from 1959 through 1988, but I am relying also on interviews with him.

[18] Actually, the objection on grounds of discrimination was to both Articles 6 and 26, the latter of which provides that "(1) Citizens are indigenous Indonesians and others certified [*disahkan*] as citizens by statute."

argued, was established to fight against all forms of discrimination. What could be more discriminatory than Article 6? Unlike others in the organization, including Siauw, who tried to defuse the issue by waving it aside, Yap refused on principle to dismiss it.[19] But Article 6 was not the end of Yap's case against the 1945 Constitution, as he made clear in May 1959 during the *Konstituante* debate:

> The history of constitutional states is the history of the struggle of people against tyranny, despotism, and absolutism. The struggle for fundamental human rights and freedoms against absolute power. The constitution is a manifestation of the victory of justice over arbitrariness, the victory of "Recht" over "Macht." Therefore a constitution is intended to establish and guarantee in its body fundamental human rights and freedoms, to formulate and limit Government authority, and to control the exercise of that authority....
>
> The history of the struggle for independence of the Indonesian people is also a struggle for the supremacy of "Law" over "Power," of justice over arbitrariness. Therefore, the Indonesian Constitution must share the same character and purpose as other constitutions.
>
> What good were the sacrifices of the Indonesian people for the sake of independence, if Indonesians can still be detained at will, without knowing what they are guilty of, without trial, and then released just like that without the right to sue for revision and damages, just as in the colony?
>
> What good are the sacrifices of the Indonesian people in the struggle for independence, if, as in the colonial period, Indonesians do not have the right and freedom to think, to write, to organize, to hold meetings, to join political parties, to act in opposition, to strike, and so on.[20]

And so on in the same vein. Yap detailed the shortcomings of the 1945 Constitution, particularly with respect to executive authority, and sharply criticized the limitation of rights already evident in the early Guided Democracy period. Finally, he excerpted from his earlier speech in the Constituent Assembly:

> In English I once quoted the saying that ... if human beings were angels, then Government would be unnecessary. And I added: There would also be no need for Constitutions. But humans are not angels. Indeed, humans often do evil things, and do not always do virtuous things. We realize that all authority may be abused, and that as authority increases, so does its abuse. Consequently, humans in authority must have limits imposed on their authority in order to protect them against themselves and to protect others against them.

---

[19] In his memoirs, Siauw points out that in the preparatory committee discussions in August 1945, the initial draft of Article 6 required the president to be both Muslim and *asli*. On August 18, it was agreed that the religious qualification should be removed, for it was understood that as Indonesia's population is overwhelmingly Muslim, the president was bound to be a Muslim anyway. The same reasoning should have applied to the ethnic qualification, Siauw agrees, but no one raised the issue. At that session of the preparatory committee one peranakan member was present, Yap Tjwan Bing, later on the PNI council, but according to the record he did not object. See Muhammad Yamin, *Naskah-Persiapan Undang-Undang Dasar 1945* (Jakarta: Yayasan Prapantja, 1959) 1: 402, 418. Siauw claimed in 1959, repeating the point in his memoirs, that one reason for the asli qualification was to avoid the possibility that a Japanese president might be imposed. Siauw, *Lima Jaman*, p. 286. I know of no corroborating evidence for this assertion.

[20] *Risalah Konstituante*, 1959, Sidang ke–I, Rapat ke–12, May 12, 1959, 612–19, at 613–14.

The debate over this issue, among others, transplanted to the Baperki Congress in Semarang in December 1960 led to Yap's departure from the organization.[21] It also indicated Yap's departure from the strategic thinking of many peranakan leaders about the relationship of the Chinese minority to the Indonesian state. Siauw represented—or better, formulated—the choice of a substantial Javanese peranakan intellectual stratum to bet optimistically on the ability of Soekarno and his support on the left to bring about the fundamental change that would secure peranakan chances. But Yap, skeptical outsider and much puzzled by the intricacies of Javanese political habits, had little faith in this kind of prognosis. Moreover, he was already moving beyond peranakan grounds toward the larger and less confining arena of Indonesian state and society, a point to return to later.

One last debate over peranakan issues is worth recounting, in which Yap confronted not only Siauw but Siauw's critics, made up largely of "assimilators." It came to a head in the pages of *Star Weekly* in 1960, at a time when the Chinese minority was under attack, uncertain, and tense, largely as a result of the turmoil over the alien traders restrictions of 1959 (PP 10 [government regulation 10, 1959]) but also, still, in connection with issues of citizenship and education. In this period of angst, the long debate over peranakan choices sharpened considerably.

In *Star Weekly*, a group of ten well-known peranakan figures published a statement favoring voluntary "assimilation" as the way out of the minority dilemma. By this view, peranakan should in effect disappear through absorption by adopting "Indonesian" names, shedding Chinese distinctions, and becoming essentially "Indonesian."[22] After all, said its proponents, Chinese had long mixed biologically and culturally with indigenous Indonesians, and artificial obstacles to the continuing process, whether in the form of Chinese "exclusiveness" or anti-Chinese prejudice, should be eliminated. It was not an insensible position.

But it clashed frontally with the equally compelling "integrationist" view, which had it that the Chinese minority, no less than any other minority in a country made up of minorities, should be accepted as part of the Indonesian universe, without additional prejudicial encumbrances. This was Baperki's argument. Here Yap and Siauw were agreed, and both were particularly incensed by the proposal that Chinese should adopt "Indonesian" names.[23] But agreement stopped there, for how integration was to be achieved divided Siauw and Yap (and many others) sharply. Siauw, again, was convinced that only a radical restructuring of Indonesian economy and society would make effective integration possible, for the problem, he believed, was a side effect of the economic injustice and exploitation

---

[21] At the Semarang Congress, Yap delivered a speech in which he attacked Siauw unremittingly for supporting the PKI and Soekarno. Siauw did not reply, but Yap was hooted down mercilessly by the membership and vilified personally in a speech by Buyung Saleh. Yap attended no meetings of Baperki thereafter, but he never resigned his vice-presidency or membership, insisting that he would have to be ousted formally, which Siauw and other officers refused to do. In 1968, when Yap was accused of Communist associations through his connection with Baperki, his speech at the 1960 Congress helped to vitiate the charge.

[22] *Star Weekly*, March 26, 1960.

[23] Again and again in his memoirs Siauw returns to the name-changing issue, which he mistakenly attributes entirely to Catholic peranakan, castigating its proponents in undisguised anger and contempt. During the late 1960s, when the pressure on peranakan to adopt "Indonesian" names became particularly heavy, both from within and without the community, no one opposed it more fiercely than Yap, though the issue will not be taken up in detail here. I use quotation marks around "Indonesian" here simply to make the point that, from one perspective, in Indonesia "Chinese" names are no less "Indonesian" than "Batak," "Javanese," "Balinese," or "Menadonese" names.

caused by colonialism and imperialism.[24] Yap was equally convinced that the Communist cure he believed Siauw offered would kill all the patients.

In a series of articles for *Star Weekly* entitled "The Three Therapies," which stimulated more (and more acrimonious) correspondence than the journal had ever received, Yap attacked what he probably conceived as left and right extremes.[25] In the first piece, published as a brief letter, Yap dismissed Siauw's "Communist" therapy partly on grounds that it was totalitarian and, therefore, ideologically unacceptable but also more subtly because opposition to it by the majority of Islamic and Christian Indonesians made it unrealistic. In the second letter, he challenged the "assimilationist" position of the ten *tokoh* (prominents). First, he wrote, although voluntary assimilation was one way of resolving the minority problem, there were other means of doing so: the legal elimination of all forms of discrimination and education in democracy and human rights, policies that would foster good racial and ethnic relations. Second, and more emphatically, social-political conditions and the temper of the country were not conducive to assimilation. In his criticism of both therapies, Yap eventually proved quite right, even prescient.

The third article, in which Yap offered his own solution, is remarkable for its acute analysis of the peranakan problem and of minority relations generally. In some ways it represents Yap at his best: detached, analytical, rigorous, even-handed, and unremittingly critical. Yap was most concerned here not with Siauw's argument but with that of the assimilators, which he probably (and correctly) thought the more dangerous illusion because it seemed more obvious and compellingly simple. Drawing on the work of Louis Wirth, Arnold Rose, Lévi-Strauss, the Declaration of Human Rights, and much else, he presented minorities as the creation of dominant majorities—defined by their power, as in the case of the Dutch colonial "majority"—that would themselves be affected by their treatment of minorities. In a concise comparative review of the experience of minorities around the world—Jews in Europe and blacks in the United States, among others—he pointed out that physical or cultural differences were the bases on which groups of citizens were turned into minorities. For this reason, he wrote, the ten tokoh wanted to get rid of the differences they perceived to be grounds for discrimination against peranakan. But were they right in supposing that this was the only way to do it? No, for Switzerland, Hawaii, the Soviet Union, and China demonstrated that national unity and coexistence were possible without a culturally destructive leveling (*nivellering*) in the kind of "brave new world" Hitler sought to create.[26] Replying to the arguments of Lauw Tjoan Tho, one of the ten tokoh, Yap agreed that under optimum circumstances assimilation, as a multidirectional process of give-and-take, was desirable, but

> assimilation of a minority into a "dominant group" cannot possibly be achieved if only the minority wishes it while this objective is rejected by the "dominant group." And if we do not hesitate to point out that at present there is a part of the "dominant group" that rejects assimilation of the Chinese minority, it is because the facts speak loud and

---

[24]Siauw's commitment to this analysis was genuine. In his memoirs he returns to it endlessly, to the point of making his autobiography more pedantic and boring than it ought to have been. Siauw, *Lima Jaman*, passim.

[25]Yap's three articles appeared in *Star Weekly* on April 16 and 30 and May 21, 1960. The critical responses, including one by Siauw, went on through June. Buyung Saleh wrote a generally vituperative but occasionally reasoned reply in the pages of *Berita Baperki*, May 15, 1960.

[26]Nazi Germany, which Yap thought the epitome of evil, was much on his mind during this period. In an original draft of the first installment of the "Three Therapies," a long introductory paragraph deals with "Nazi-fascists" and their treatment of Indonesian citizens of Chinese descent. In the published version, this paragraph and all references to "Nazi-fascists" are excised, probably at the request of *Star Weekly's* publishers.

clear. Up to the present Indonesian citizens of Chinese descent still experience "restriction of employment opportunities, lack of access to facilities that are meant to serve the population in general, the presence of bias and antagonism among law enforcement officials and many other manifestations of prejudice" (Arnold Rose, UNESCO study). Can this "discrimination and exclusion" be regarded as signs of the acceptance of the proposal of Lauw Tjoan Tho et al.? If there is no discrimination based on physical and cultural differences, then there are no more minorities and no "dominant group." And if there are no minorities and dominant group, isn't the problem done with? ... We do not oppose assimilation *an sich*. We are only trying to explain that assimilation, as a means of resolving the minority problem, is not now appropriate. For discrimination has damaged the relations between groups, and bad interrelations are not the right soil and climate for the cultivation and sprouting of assimilation.[27]

After following a clearheaded and sustained argument for several impressive passages, however, suddenly the conclusion takes an astonishing leap into an abyss of confusion as Yap proposes his own way out. It may indicate how many blind alleys thinkers about the minority problem ran into and how desperate they were for promising solutions. Having rejected simple structural and simpler assimilationist analyses, Yap decided that "the problem is man himself," and his diagnosis was that the human soul is sick. The remedy was "Not 'brainwashing' but 'heart-cleansing'; not a change in the structure of society but a change from the materialistic and homocentric to a Christocentric view of man; not the elimination of physical and cultural differences, but the elimination of prejudice, egoism, and hypocrisy; that there no longer be a 'dominant group' but instead a 'ministering elite' (*dienende elite*); not the retooling of man, but the rebirth of man in Jesus Christ."[28]

Yet in the dizzying unreality of this statement, there is an inkling of another solution that helped to pave Yap's road out of the confinement of ethnic politics and attachments.

Even among peranakan intellectuals and professionals, Yap was less well suited than most, and uncomfortable, in a world defined mainly by ethnic boundaries. By upbringing, education, culture, and experience he had little reason to feel at home in a Chinese, or even "Indonesian-Chinese," setting. He found himself there, as a public man, largely for lack of an alternative that offered no resistance either in a larger Indonesian universe or in his own mind. Siauw, more experienced and familiar in the peranakan (and totok) world, used his knowledge of and connections in the political system to incorporate the minority into national politics. Ultimately, however, his position in Baperki and his devotion to its causes, though it did not narrow his ideological commitments, did limit the reach of his voice. He donned an identity and was held to it. Yap, who had more reluctantly accepted the same identity, was less bound by it and freer to pursue an ideological course that was not exactly

---

[27]Yap, "Three Therapies," from the typescript version, p. 7. Yap goes on: "That assimilation of individuals has occurred in the past, now too, and will in the future, despite everything, cannot be denied. But these... exceptions prove the rule."

[28]*Star Weekly*, May 21, 1960, p. 6; p. 7 of the original typscript manuscript. What exactly was in Yap's mind when he wrote this and to whom precisely he directed it is not at all clear. Did he mean that Chinese had to turn to Christ or that all Indonesians should do so? Did he really believe any of this made sense? or did he, failing all else, simply fall back on the religious purpose that had become so important in his own life? We never talked about the article, at least not directly, and so I have no idea what he meant. It was, however, a time of great stress for him because of his battle within Baperki, his anger at the politics of Guided Democracy, and his anxieties over the persecution of Chinese. The church, in which, as always, he was hard at work on other matters, may have been the one place where he found any satisfaction.

divorced from, but independent of, the accident of having been born Chinese. Ideologically, he was capable of thinking beyond the interests of the Chinese community to consider the character of Indonesian state and society, as his discussions in the "Three Therapies" show. So, clearly, was Siauw, though politically Siauw risked principle for what appeared to be political necessity. Yap stuck to principle, partly because he was in a better position to do so but also because he had little else to fall back on.

The ideology that finally counted, however, was not Christianity, which was another blind minority alley, but law. Once squeezed out of Baperki, Yap did not put the peranakan problem out of mind but, with a slight push, leapt to a different, Indonesian, stage on which minority questions were significant but submerged in a more complex network fashioned from rule of law and human rights issues.

If, as he argued in *Star Weekly*, the minority problem was largely a "dominant group" problem, then it had to be approached through an opening of principle to the Indonesian state and its responsibilities to Indonesian society. This turn of thought entailed another, which was perhaps more important—the problems of the Chinese minority were not sui generis. They could not, or should not, be construed separately from human rights problems generally. The appropriate struggle was not for Chinese alone, but for all Indonesians.

Yap's own opening was through the professional advocacy. He became widely known beyond the peranakan community quite suddenly, in 1966, for his defense of Subandrio before the Military Tribunal-Extraordinary. Instead of a pro forma show, Yap turned out a stunning defense replete with fine legal edges, which the judges ignored, and powerful political criticism, which the audience did not. Yap had appeared, with another advocate, in the name of PERADIN, the Indonesian Association of Advocates. Although a founding member of PERADIN in 1963–64, he remained uncertain that indigenous Indonesian advocates could ever accept a peranakan colleague on equal terms. It was more his problem than theirs. Few senior advocates of that generation—of the character of Lukman Wiriadinata, Hasjim Mahdan, Soemarno P. Wirjanto, Ani Abas Manoppo, Suardi Tasrif, and others—were much infected by ethnic bigotry.[29] Or, to the extent that they were infected, professional and collegial loyalties nevertheless took precedence. In PERADIN, at long last, even more perhaps than in the church, which itself remained troubled by ethnic cleavage, Yap found the kind of nonethnic setting that helped free him from the suffocating asthma of ethnic identity. The proof came in 1968, when Yap himself was illegally detained by a corrupt prosecutor and police official whom he had accused of extortion. After his release, they had him prosecuted for criminal libel. His PERADIN colleagues—Zainal Abidin, Djamaluddin Singomangkuto, and Hasjim Mahdan—stepped forward voluntarily to defend him. For the skeptical Yap, who always respected action more than words alone, it was revelation and liberation, more important to him, I suspect, than he ever admitted to his attorneys. Thereafter, his closest friends came from the intimate circle of senior professional advocates.

Thereafter, too, he spent less and less time on Chinese issues and more and more on those of legal process and human rights. The last major Chinese issue he took up had to do

---

[29]The point is worth making that in general, the higher reaches of the priyayi class to which most senior advocates were born had always gotten along quite well, even intimately, with Javanese peranakan. It was for this reason that during the parliamentary period, when priyayi scions dominated the political elite, the Chinese minority, though under pressure, could expect more sympathy and help than was the case later, when middle-class elements that had long competed with and were hostile to Chinese economic advantage rose to prominence, particularly via the army.

with the controversy over pressure to adopt "Indonesian" names, which he continued to excoriate unequivocally.[30] It was not that Yap had lost interest, by any means, and when the occasion arose, he remained adamant in defense of Chinese citizens but now as citizens more than as an isolated minority and more as a general principle of human rights than as a specific issue in ethnic relations. This position followed naturally from his own political evolution. Liberated from the rigid limits of ethnic identity, he himself now spoke as an Indonesian citizen.

He spoke, moreover, and acted with all the courage, bluntness, forthrightness, passion, and tenacity that had driven his antagonists in Baperki (and occasionally in church circles) to distraction. In PERADIN, the Legal Aid Institute, the Institute for the Defense of Human Rights, in the press, parliament, in court, in the World Council of Churches and the International Commission of Jurists, and elsewhere, he simply never stopped—to the day of his death in April 1989—defending imperative values of human rights and justice. He became a living symbol of the human rights struggle, widely known and appreciated for his integrity, courage, and refusal to be quiet. Beyond a certain point, few thought of him any longer as the Chinese Yap. The thousands who paid respects at his funeral and the activist students who shouted then that Yap belonged to the nation clearly thought of him as a special kind of Indonesian, not a peculiar kind of Chinese. By the end of his life, Yap himself felt comfortable with this view.

---

[30] By this time, in the early New Order, Baperki was gone, its leadership scattered among various jails and prisons. Siauw was detained until the mid-1970s, when he was released and went to Holland, where he died in the 1980s. He and Yap had one last, rather miserable confrontation in 1980, in Holland, where Yap had gone to receive an honorary degree from the Vrije Universiteit. At a meeting of Indonesian Chinese immigrants to which Yap was asked to speak, with Siauw present, he harshly condemned the political consequences that Baperki bequeathed to the citizens of Chinese descent. Siauw, perhaps angry but undoubtedly hurt, briefly defended the organization's achievements.

THE SOCIAL AND CULTURAL DIMENSIONS OF THE ROLE OF ETHNIC CHINESE IN INDONESIAN SOCIETY

Mély G. Tan

Interest in the ethnic Chinese in Indonesia and in other Southeast Asian countries has continued unabated largely because of the important role they continue to play in the economy, and in at least one country, in the polity. Not surprisingly, most studies of the ethnic Chinese have concentrated on these two areas.

However, the social and cultural dimensions of their role have not been entirely neglected.[1] In Indonesia, the interest in these dimensions is, perhaps, also generated by the

---

This is a revised and updated version of a paper presented at the Symposium on the Role of Indonesian Chinese in Indonesian Life, Cornell University, July 13–15, 1990. This paper with the same title, was originally presented at the joint CCSEAS/NWRSEA Conference at the Asian Centre of the University of British Columbia, Vancouver, B.C., Canada, November 3–5, 1989.

[1] See an early sociological study by Ong Eng Die, *De Chineezen in Nederlandsch Indië: Sociografie van een Indonesische bevolkingsgroep* (The Chinese in the Dutch East Indies) (Assen: Van Gorcum, 1943), his doctoral dissertation, written from secondary sources while he was in the Netherlands during World War II; Edward J. Ryan, "The Value System of a Chinese Community in Java" (Ph.D. diss., Harvard University, 1961). See more recent studies on the role of ethnic Chinese in the development of the press in Indonesia, on education, and on religion in Leo Suryadinata, *The Pre-World War II Peranakan Chinese Press of Java: A Preliminary Survey* (Athens: Ohio University Center for International Studies, Southeast Asia Paper No. 18, 1971); idem, *The Chinese Minority in Indonesia, 7 papers.* (Singapore: Chopmen Enterprises, 1978); idem, *Kebudayaan Minoritas Tionghoa di Indonesia*, (The culture of the Chinese minority in Indonesia), trans. Dédé Oetomo (Jakarta: Gramedia, 1988). Jennifer W. Cushman and Wang Gungwu, eds., *Changing Identities of Southeast Asian Chinese Since World War II*, (Hong Kong: Hong Kong University Press, 1988); L. A. Peter Gosling and Linda Y. C. Lim, *The Chinese in Southeast Asia*, vol. 2, *Identity, Culture and Politics* (Singapore: Maruzen, 1983); the monumental work on what has been referred to as "Chinese-Malay," "Sino-Malay," or "Melayu-Tionghoa" literature, in Claudine Salmon, *Literature in Malay by the Chinese of Indonesia: A Provisional Annotated Bibliography* (Paris: de la Maison des Sciences de l'Homme, 1981). See also Myra Sidharta, ed., *100 Tahun Kwee Tek Hoay, Dari Penjaja Tekstil Sampai ke Pendekar Pena* (100th anniversary of Kwee Tek Hoay, from textile peddler to fighter with the pen) (Jakarta: Pustaka Sinar Harapan, 1989). Since the 1980s, a number of theses and dissertations have been written by Indonesian students at universities in Indonesia or abroad focusing on the social and cultural lives of the ethnic Chinese and their relations with the majority population. These include: Danny Indrakusuma, "Posisi berbeda agama dalam hubungan Cina-Pribumi: Suatu studi tentang persepsi masyarakat Cina di Kota Solo" (Skripsi Sarjana Sosiologi, Fisipol, Universitas Airlangga, Surabaya, 1987); A. H. Kurniawan, "Identifikasi Pelajar SMA Keturunan Tionghoa di Jakarta" (Skripsi Sarjana

realization that twenty-three years have passed since the New Order government implemented a series of regulations with the expressed intent of accelerating the process of *pembauran*, or assimilation.[2] These regulations were announced in the form of instructions or decisions on the presidential and ministerial level. The first, on "The Basic Policy for the Solution of the Chinese Problem" was promulgated in June 1967 and was followed in December of the same year by another on religion, beliefs, and Chinese customs.[3] In addition, a number of specific regulations pertained to the education of ethnic Chinese children whose parents were Indonesian citizens as well as those whose parents were aliens.

From these regulations it is clear that for the government, assimilation, defined as the eventual disappearance of a group as a sociocultural entity, is the best way to resolve what is usually referred to as the "Chinese problem" *(masalah Cina)*. This legacy of the colonial past has persisted and in some ways has been aggravated since independence. The problem is the existence in society of a relatively small (estimated at around 3 percent) but highly significant group, which the ethnic Indonesian majority perceive as alien in appearance and culture. In their view, the group's grip on the economy is disproportionate to its numbers, and it tends to segregate itself socially and residentially, a behavior they see as an arrogant expression of feelings of superiority. These perceived characteristics have generated resentment towards the group, which at times has exploded into actions of violence against them.

One should be aware that this policy is not a product of the New Order government alone. President Sukarno also espoused the idea of assimilation, although he was not as insistent about it as the present government. At the time, he also allowed an opposing view to flourish, no doubt to balance the assimilationist view. This opposite view, propounded by the ethnic Chinese mass organization Baperki, supported integration rather than assimilation.[4] Baperki defined integration to mean the acceptance of the ethnic Chinese as an integral part of Indonesian society by recognizing the validity of their existence as a social entity similar to indigenous ethnic groups. In the aftermath of the 1965 abortive coup, this organization was banned because of its close relations with the Indonesian Communist party.

Since 1965, assimilationist perspective has prevailed, and the present government seems determined to accelerate the process through regulation. It is evident that the cultural factor

---

Sosiologi, Fisip-UI, 1984); Dédé Oetomo, "The Chinese of Pasuruan: A Study of Language and Identity in a Minority Community in Transition" (Ph.D. diss., Cornell University, 1984); Stephen Suleeman, "Persepsi golongan keturunan Tionghoa Indonesia terhadap golongan bumi putera" (Skripsi Sarjana Ilmu Komunikasi, 1986); and Hendra Sutedjo, "Komunikasi dan tingkat suami-istri perkawinan campuran" (Skripsi Sarjana Ilmu Komunikasi, Fisip-UI, 1984).

[2] The root of this word is *baur*, meaning to mix. In the context of intergroup relations in Indonesia, it means "to assimilate."

[3] Instruction of the Cabinet Presidium no. 37/U/IN/6/1967, "The Basic Policy for the Solution of the Chinese Problem," sanctioned in Jakarta on June 7, 1967, and signed by Suharto as chairman of the Ampera Cabinet Presidium; Instruction of the president of the Republic of Indonesia no. 14, 1967, on religion, beliefs, and Chinese customs sanctioned in Jakarta on December 6, 1967, and signed by Suharto as acting president of the Republic of Indonesia; Coordinating Body for the Chinese Problem—Coordinating Body for National Intelligence, comp., *Pedoman penyelesaian masalah Cina di Indonesia* (Handbook for the resolution of the Chinese problem in Indonesia), vol. 1 (Bakin: Jakarta, 1979). Volume 1 comprises the policies for the resolution of the Chinese problem, the technical instructions, and a compilation of the laws for the basic policies. Volume 2 is a compilation of the laws concerning the general handbook *(pedoman umum)*, and volume 3 is a compilation of the laws concerning policy implementation and implementation organization.

[4] The Badan Permusjawaratan Kewarganegaraan Indonesia (Consultative Body for Indonesian Citizenship) was established in March 1954. It participated in the national elections of 1955 and received wide support in the ethnic Chinese community.

is considered the main obstacle to this process. Hence as stated in the regulations, "Guidance in assimilation in the framework of the realization of unity of the nation should be geared towards the establishment of unity in the value system." To this end, "All forms of cultural affinity based on the country of origin should be removed, in order to give all elements of culture in Indonesia the opportunity to develop according to the Pancasila."[5]

In view of the importance given to the cultural factor it seems appropriate to assess how these regulations have been implemented and how the ethnic Chinese have responded to them. No doubt these responses have varied in time and place by age and cultural orientation. Nonetheless, indications are that the general response has been compliance, albeit sometimes mixed with covert reluctance. Whenever possible, however, people also attempt to ignore or get around the regulations.

This attitude of compliance can be seen as a manifestation of the powerlessness of the ethnic Chinese and their total lack of bargaining power. Although they are perceived by the ethnic Indonesian majority to dominate the economy, a recent event vividly illustrates their weak position—the response of ethnic Chinese big businessmen to the appeal of President Suharto on March 4, 1990, to sell up to 25 percent of the shares of their companies to cooperatives. Although their immediate response was positive, recognizing the validity of Suharto's expressed motivation—the concern for the effects of social inequity—they later noted privately as well as publicly the grave uncertainties in the implementation of the idea. Still, their overall response again was compliance.[6]

An assessment of the persistent Chinese problem is pertinent now that the Indonesian government has finally resumed diplomatic relations with the People's Republic of China after freezing relations for twenty-three years. This prolonged freeze is alleged to be owing to the view, espoused especially among the military, that normalization should be contingent on the resolution of this problem within the country.

The Memorandum of Understanding was duly signed by the respective foreign ministers in Jakarta on August 8, 1990, and witnessed by President Suharto and Prime Minister Li Peng of the PRC. Interestingly, of the four paragraphs of the document, two deal with dual nationality (referring to Indonesian citizens of Chinese origin) and noninterference with each other's domestic affairs.[7] This mention is widely seen as a recognition of the existence of the Chinese problem in Indonesia as indicated by the writings on ethnic Chinese that proliferated in the mass media around the event.

In view of this development, one might ask whether the government considers this problem resolved, in other words, that assimilation has been achieved, or that other considerations have prevailed and under the circumstances it is simply considered irrelevant. The

---

[5] Coordinating Body for the Chinese Problem, *Pedoman*, vol. 1.

[6] This appeal was made on March 4, 1990, when President Suharto invited thirty-one big businessmen (now popularly referred to as "conglomerates"), twenty-nine of them ethnic Chinese, to his cattle ranch, Tapos, in the Bogor area. In a speech that lasted about 1.5 hours and was broadcast in its entirety on national TV the same evening, he exhorted them, now that they had become wealthy, not the least because of the opportunities given by the New Order government, to express their gratitude for this good fortune. The gist of his appeal was that big businesses should sell up to 25 percent of their shares to cooperatives. In this way, he contended, "social envy" (*kecemburuan sosial*), which can lead to social unrest, could be avoided. Small businesses, represented by cooperatives, would feel that they had a share in big business and that, therefore, they also had a stake in keeping them going. See *Tempo*, especially March 10 and April 14, 1990, for the names of the businessmen invited; see also *Editor*, April 14, 1990.

[7] From the English translation of the document.

latter seems to be the case if one looks at trade relations, which have flourished since the signing of the Memorandum of Understanding on trade between the Chamber of Commerce and Industry of Indonesia and the PRC in 1985.[8]

A review of the regulations enacted by the New Order government to resolve the Chinese problem, how they have been implemented, and how the ethnic Chinese have responded to them follows.

Regulations Concerning the Ethnic Chinese

As indicated, the most comprehensive regulation was contained in the instruction of June 1967 on the basic policies for the resolution of the Chinese problem. This regulation spells out the rationale for allowing foreign nationals to continue to operate in Indonesia. The considerations put forward are as follows:

> that in the framework of development, all resources should be marshalled, including those belonging to foreign nationals; that to accelerate the process of development the efforts of citizens should be increased, while the capital/financial resources and enterprises of foreign nationals should be put to use correctly in the right proportion; that in the spirit of the Pancasila philosophy, the principles of a state based on law, and motivated by the desire to have good relations with all countries . . . it is necessary to reevaluate, review, the policies concerning foreign nationals, in particular the Chinese problem.[9]

These instructions were to be implemented by "all bodies and the apparatus of the government, both civil and military, by the central as well as the local governments."[10] It was also stipulated that they were specifically directed toward Chinese foreign nationals. They deal with the requirements for obtaining a work permit and a license to operate an enterprise and with foreign capital that is considered "foreign domestic capital" and is, therefore, "national wealth that is in the hands of foreign inhabitants, and as such should be marshalled, developed and made use of, for the benefit of rehabilitation and development." The government does not permit this foreign domestic capital to be transferred abroad.

The regulation includes a section that urges children of foreign nationals who have become residents of Indonesia to attend government as well as private schools that follow the national curriculum. An item on organization stipulates that with the permission and control of local authorities, only organizations related to health, religion, death, sports, and recreation will be allowed in certain areas with a sufficient number of foreign nationals. In addition, there is a special section on relations with the PRC; relations at that time were extremely strained but not yet severed (they dissolved four months later in October 1967).

The final part of this instruction concerned the implementation of the regulation and the August 1967 establishment of a special staff, Staf Khusus Urusan Cina, or SKUT (Special Staff for Chinese Affairs), which was directly responsible to the chairman of the Cabinet Presidium, that is, the president. Charged with the task of assisting the minister of political affairs in the resolution of the Chinese Problem, the special staff was responsible for coordinating and monitoring the implementation of the policies, especially those related to the

---

[8]Signed by the Indonesian Chamber of Commerce and Industry and the China Council for the Promotion of International Trade on July 5, 1988, in Singapore. After the historic meeting in Tokyo in April 1988 between President Suharto and the foreign minister of the PRC, when the foundation was laid for the resumption of diplomatic relations, technical follow-up meetings occurred.

[9]See n. 3, this article.

[10]Ibid.

Chinese Problem. In the discharge of its task, the special staff could cooperate with other government agencies or with relevant private organizations.[11]

Two regulations, which could be considered elaborations on the instruction, were probably generated by this special staff: the instruction on religion, beliefs, and Chinese customs implemented in December 1967 and the basic policies concerning Indonesian citizens of foreign descent.[12] The first document was directed to the ministers of Religious Affairs and Internal Affairs and to other relevant government agencies on the central and local levels and concerned those aspects of Chinese religious behavior that showed cultural affinity with their country of origin. According to this instruction, such religious beliefs should only be expressed privately, and festivals related to Chinese religion and Chinese tradition should be celebrated within the confines of the home.

The second document deals specifically with Indonesian citizens of Chinese descent. It reiterates that before the law all citizens, including those of foreign descent, have the same rights and responsibilities. It also stipulates that they should be guided through the process of assimilation in order to avoid so-called racial exclusiveness. Furthermore, it states that discrimination does not exist because citizens of foreign descent are given the same opportunity as indigenous citizens "to marshall resources in all fields in order to accelerate development." Those with Chinese names, however, are urged to change them to Indonesian-sounding names.

Another regulation included in the Resolution of the Provisional People's Consultative Assembly no. 32, 1966 concerns the use of Chinese language and script in the mass media. It states that there will be only one Chinese-language newspaper (subsequently called *Harian Indonesia*), sponsored and controlled by the government.

As mentioned earlier, a number of regulations concerned education. Because Chinese-language schools had been central to the perpetuation of Chinese culture, these regulations deserve careful attention. Chinese schools have had a history of trials and tribulations that dates to the late 1950s, when the Central Military Command ordered all schools set up by organizations of "orang-orang Tionghoa Perantauan (Hoa Kiaw)" who were not citizens of a country that had diplomatic relations with Indonesia (in this case, Taiwan) to be closed. They were closed in October 1958. In 1957, schools with the same type of sponsorship in the Nusa Tenggara area were prohibited by order of the regional military command.[13] These actions put an end to all schools set up by the Kuomintang or its sympathizers. In line with Indonesia's one-China policy, however, schools sponsored by PRC organizations were still allowed to operate. In the aftermath of the 1965 upheaval, violence was directed toward them, and they were also ordered to close. This prohibition was formalized by the decision of the minister of Education and Culture in July 1966.

---

[11]*Laporan Tahunan 1968*, Staf Urusan Cina (Jakarta: Kabinet Pembangunan Republik Indonesia, 1968).

[12]See Presidential Instruction no. 14/1967 signed by Suharto, then acting president on December 6, 1967, and Presidential Decision no. 240/1967 on basic policies concerning Indonesian citizens of foreign descent.

[13]Sardjono Sigit, Asimilasi Pendidikan: Pokok-pokok Riwayat dan Permasalahannya (Jakarta: Departemen Pendidikan dan Kebudayaan, 1981) relates the history of foreign schools or international schools in Indonesia—the actions taken against the Dutch language schools in 1957, the Kuomintang Chinese language schools in 1957–1958, and the schools sponsored by the PRC and PRC sympathizers in 1965–1966; the banning of all Chinese language schools from 1966–1968 and the Special Project National Schools from 1968–1974; and the history of the laws for implementing assimilation in education and the regulations concerning foreign language and international schools.

Nonetheless, in 1968, the government allowed a group of wealthy Chinese (known Taiwan sympathizers) to establish schools for the students of the banned schools because many of them could not be accommodated by existing schools. The Sekolah Nasional Proyek Khusus (Special Project National Schools) had to follow the national curriculum but were allowed to teach the Chinese language as an extracurricular activity. They became very popular; in 1970 there were eight schools in Jakarta, and by 1973 there were thirty-five schools in Sumatra alone.[14]

This development alarmed the government because some of the schools allegedly used Chinese as the medium of instruction. In 1974, the government closed them; the reason given was that the transitional period for the adjustment of former Chinese school pupils had terminated. This regulation marked the end of formal education in the Chinese language, thereby closing any avenue for systematic Chinese enculturation. Nonetheless, the government still thought that special instruction toward assimilation was necessary. The minister of Education then set up an assistance team for the implementation of assimilation in education and the regulation of foreign schools. These schools became known as Sekolah Pembauran.[15]

The implementation of the regulations concerned with the social and cultural lives of the ethnic Chinese was not as definitive and consistent as it was for regulations on education. In many situations, implementation was determined by the attitude of the local authorities toward ethnic Chinese. For example, activities in Chinese temples continued, and in some of the renowned ones—among others, the temple at Tanjungkait on the northern coast of Banten in West Java and the Sam Po Kong Temple in Semarang in Central Java—festivals are still drawing visitors from surrounding cities. These festivities have also started to spill outside the temple grounds, which could not have happened without permits from the local authorities.

On the other hand, in the beginning of 1989, a performance in Medan of the Chinese play *Sam Pek Eng Thai* (the Chinese version of Romeo and Juliette) adapted (the location was old-time Batavia) by the playwright Riantiarno of Teater Koma was abruptly canceled. Only on opening day did the authorities inform him that permission for the performance was not granted. The reason given was that because the opening day happened to be a national holiday, it would be inappropriate to have a public performance of a Chinese play. The authorities appeared to object also to the dragon dance in the play. It is interesting to note that the same play had been performed to wide acclaim in Jakarta in the prestigious Gedung Kesenian. Some months before that event, a similar fate befell an opera troupe from Taiwan. They were informed about the refusal of their permit after they had arrived in Jakarta.

The denial of permits in these two cases, in which the objection was against the Chineseness of the play or show, gives an impression of arbitrariness on the part of the authorities. Yet Mandarin movies and video cassettes from Hongkong may be shown or rented, and Mandarin-speaking entertainers regularly perform in hotels and nightclubs.

---

[14] Ibid.

[15] For a number of years when these schools began, I lectured to their supervisors *(pengawas)* on the cultural background of the ethnic Chinese to improve the supervisors' understanding of Chinese culture. During the discussion period, invariably at least one participant would comment on the problem faced of teaching the students Pancasila at school, only to have them influenced by Chinese culture at home. The question then raised was What can be done to eliminate this influence of Chinese culture?

A review of the implementation of the regulations indicates that the government has enforced most consistently restrictions on Chinese-language schools, the use of Chinese script in public places, and the sale of Chinese-language publications.

Responses of the Ethnic Chinese

Scholars studying the ethnic Chinese[16] still tend to treat them as a monolithic entity by referring to all of them as "Chinese" or "overseas Chinese." In Indonesia, this tendency is apparent among the majority population in the use of the terms *orang Cina, orang Tionghoa,* or even *hoakiau.*[17] I contend that these terms only apply to those who are alien, not of mixed ancestry, and who initially do not plan to stay in Indonesia permanently. The terms and the definition used for this group have important implications culturally, socially, and psychologically, especially for policy considerations and policy implementation.

As indicated in recent writings, the term commonly used today to refer to the group as a whole is "ethnic Chinese," regardless of citizenship, cultural orientation, or social identification. "Ethnic Chinese" refers to a group with cultural elements recognizable as or attributable to Chinese culture, whereas socially, members of this group identify with and are identified by others as a distinct group.

To identify the ethnic Chinese in Indonesia, however, is not easy. First they must be differentiated by citizenship into aliens and citizens and then by cultural orientation and social identification. Cultural orientation and social identification are a continuum. At one end are those, mostly of the younger generation, who identify completely and solely as Indonesian and whose cultural orientation is also Indonesian. Examples of individuals in this category are the late Soe Hok Gie, a student activist during the 1965–1966 upheaval, and his social scientist brother, Arief Budiman, who is known for his critical views of the development process in Indonesia, and who is married to a Minangkabau woman. Then there are Jusuf Wanandi, one of the directors of the Center for Strategic and International Studies, his brother, Sofjan Wanandi, one of the big businessmen, and Christianto Wibisono, director and owner of the nationally known Indonesian Business Data Center. All of them were prominent student activists during the 1965–1966 upheaval and are known as members of the "1966 generation."

There are also artists, like the nationally renowned playwright and film director Teguh Karya; Teguh Srimulat, the owner-director of the long highly popular folk theater, Srimulat; and the famous comedian, Ateng. One should also mention sports figures like Verawati Fadjrin, who several times became women's champion in international badminton competitions; she is a convert to Islam and is married to an ethnic Indonesian businessman.[18]

A number of exceptional figures belong at this end of the continuum. K. Sindhunata, a Catholic peranakan, is a lawyer and officer in the Indonesian Navy (now retired), who in the

---

[16]This section on the responses of the ethnic Chinese to the aforementioned government regulations is based mainly on Mély G. Tan, "The Role of the [sic] Ethnic Chinese Minority in Development: The Indonesian Case," *Southeast Asian Studies*, 25, (3) (December 1987): 63–83.

[17]The terms *orang Cina* and *orang Tionghoa* are Indonesian for "Chinese," whereas *hoakiau* is a Chinese (Hokkien) term meaning "overseas Chinese." It should be noted that the term *Cina,* or *Cino* in Javanese, is still considered by ethnic Chinese to have a derogatory meaning, especially in Java.

[18]These names can be found in *Apa dan Siapa Sejumlah Orang Indonesia 1983–84* (Who's Who in Indonesia 1983–84), comp. *Tempo* (Jakarta: Grafitipers, 1984). A biography recently appeared of Teguh Srimulat, who is not generally known to be of Chinese origin, which mentions the Chinese names of his parents. See Herry Gendut Janarto, *Teguh Srimulat. Berpacu dalam Komedi dan Melodi* (Jakarta: Gramedia, 1990), p. 24.

early sixties was one of the initiators of a group that became known as *assimilationists*. Haji Junus Jahja, a Dutch-educated economist, became known because of his well-publicized view that the solution to the Chinese problem is the mass conversion of the ethnic Chinese to Islam. Yet another exceptional figure is the businessman Bob Hasan, known as the "Rattan King," who also is the main promoter and financier of popular sports events.

At the other end of the continuum are those people usually referred to as *totok*, who are Chinese oriented culturally. They typically have had a Chinese-language education and speak Mandarin or one of the Chinese dialects with one another. Most have Indonesian citizenship through naturalization or, if born in Indonesia, through the various laws enacted and implemented in the 1950s and 1960s. Some of the businessmen often referred to in the foreign press fall in this category: Liem Sioe Liong, or Sudono Salim; Mochtar Riady; The Nin King; Go Swie Kie; and Eka Tjipta Wijaya, among others.[19]

Between these two categories is a whole range of people in various stages of acculturation to and identification with Indonesian society, who are commonly referred to as *peranakan*, people of mixed ancestry. Their daily language is Indonesian, spoken often along with the local language of the region in which they were born. Many have become Protestant or Catholic; more recently, some have converted to Islam.

How have the ethnic Chinese responded to these measures that directly or indirectly affect their cultural and social lives? A brief review of their thinking and actions shows that they have been by no means united in their efforts to find a solution to the Chinese problem. Four lines of thought have emerged since independence.[20]

The most notable line of thought was propounded by Baperki, the ethnic Chinese mass organization mentioned earlier, which was formed in March 1954. From the beginning, this organization received the support of the ethnic Chinese, but when it became closely associated with the Indonesian Communist party under the leadership of the late Siauw Giok Tjhan, many of the other leading figures resigned. The line of thought proposed by this organization was *integration*, by which they meant the acceptance of the ethnic Chinese as a *suku*, or ethnic group, similar to indigenous ethnic groups. Thus, the group would be considered an integral part of Indonesian society without being dissolved as a sociocultural entity. In Siauw's view, this situation would be achieved only when Indonesia became a Socialist state. After the 1965 coup, Baperki was banned, and its leaders were detained.

The opposite view was expounded by a group mostly of young intellectuals, who in March 1960 announced a "statement of assimilation" in the magazine *Star Weekly*. This proclamation was the start of a movement that espoused the complete dissolution of the group and its absorption into various indigenous ethnic groups. Members of this group

---

[19]For an exposé of the business activities of these figures see, among others, Richard Robison, *Indonesia: The Rise of Capital* (North Sydney: Allen and Unwin, 1986); Yoshihara Kunio, *The Rise of Ersatz Capitalism in Southeast Asia* (Singapore: Oxford University Press, 1988); and Yoon Hwan Shin, "Demystifying the Capitalist State: Political Patronage, Bureaucratic Interests, and Capitalist-in-Formation in Soeharto's Indonesia" (Ph.D. diss., Yale University, 1989).

[20]The ideas propounded by Baperki, Yap Thiam Hien, and the assimilationists are based on various writings in Leo Suryadinata, *Political Thinking of the Indonesian Chinese 1900–1977, A Source Book* (Singapore: Singapore University Press, 1979). For the assimilationists, see also Charles Coppel, *Indonesian Chinese in Crisis* (Kuala Lumpur: Oxford University Press, 1983). The ideas of Junus Jahja are taken from Junus Jahja, *Zamam harapan bagi keturunan Tionghoa: Rekaman dakwah Islamiyah 1979–1984* (Era of hope for the people of Chinese descent: A recording of the propagation of Islam 1979–1984), ed. Junus Jahja (Jakarta: Yayasan Ukhuwah Islamiyah, 1984). See also, idem, *Catatan Seorang WNI. Otobiografi* (Notes of an Indonesian citizen. Autobiography) (Jakarta: Yayasan Tunas Bangsa, 1988).

became part of the Lembaga Pembinaan Kesatuan Bangsa (Institute for the Promotion of National Unity), or LPKB. This group was not a mass organization but consisted of a full board of officers with specified tasks. Known as the *assimilationists*, they received the support of the government and especially of the military. From its inception to the present, the leading figure in this group has been K. Sindhunata, mentioned earlier. After 1965, the group continued to receive support from the government, and in 1977, changed its name to Bakom-PKB (Badan Komunikasi Penghayatan Kesatuan Bangsa or Communication Body for the Appreciation of National Unity). This organization came under the aegis of the Department of Internal Affairs.

Yet another view was proposed by the late Yap Thiam Hien, a prominent lawyer and Christian church leader. His ideas have been called *pluralist* by Suryadinata. I prefer the term *religionist*, however, for they are based on his deep sense of religion and his total commitment to fundamental human rights. The "therapies" he proposed were "heart-cleansing," a change in attitude to becoming "Christian-centered" and "the rebirth of man in Jesus Christ," hence the term *religionist*. His was a rather lone voice because most ethnic Chinese consider it improbable that a Christian approach would receive a favorable response in a predominantly Muslim society.

More recently, another religionist approach emerged with the ideas of Junus Jahja, an activist of the LPKB who continued as an officer of the Bakom-PKB. He became a Muslim in June 1979, married a Muslim woman a few years later, and served as a member of the prestigious Majelis Ulama Indonesia Pusat (Central Council of Indonesian Ulamas) for the period 1980–1985.[21] Junus espouses the idea that the solution to the Chinese problem lies in the mass conversion of the group to Islam. In his opinion, sharing the same religion would remove all the barriers between the majority ethnic Indonesians and the minority ethnic Chinese. To this end, he set up a foundation called Yayasan Ukhuwah Islamiyah (Foundation for Islamic Brotherhood) as the vehicle to spread Islam among the ethnic Chinese. He is quite realistic about its limited prospects for success, however, and acknowledges that despite favorable press coverage from 1979 through 1984 only an estimated twenty thousand converted; at one point he had mentioned a target of about two hundred thousand.

Of these four lines of thought, only the Bakom-PKB and Junus Jahja's Muslim group are still active and vocal today. The Bakom-PKB has an executive board in most cities that have sizable ethnic Chinese communities. The appointment of prominent ethnic Chinese to the board is with the blessing of the local office of the Bureau for Social and Political Affairs of the Department of Internal Affairs. In many ways, this board functions as a liaison between the government and the ethnic Chinese community. Junus Jahja with his Ukhuwah Islamiyah foundation seeks to recruit new converts and deepen the knowledge of Islam of those already converted by encouraging them to open their homes for prayer meetings and religious study. Junus's efforts have the full support of the Muslim leadership and prominent people in the government.

To what extent do ethnic Chinese share the idea of assimilation either through absorption in the various ethnic groups of their regions as propounded by the assimilationists or through conversion to Islam as advocated by Junus Jahja? Neither of these approaches appears to be attractive to most ethnic Chinese; they see the first as having coercive

---

[21] Another ethnic Chinese who served in the council was the late Abdul Karim Oey, a Moslem of long standing. No doubt the late Hamka, prominent Moslem leader and thinker, played an important role in these conversions and in bringing these new converts into the mainstream Moslem group.

elements and the second, conversion to Islam, as too drastic, a measure that would require a complete change in one's way of life.

The approach most favored is usually stated as "secara wajar" (in a natural way), through a process of sharing important aspects of life in education, work, and organizational spheres with indigenous Indonesians. This approach is carried out primarily on the individual level. This natural process is facilitated, for example, by participation in the activities of mainstream social organizations and political parties. This phenomenon is by no means new; after independence, individual ethnic Chinese became active members of existing political parties. Following the 1965 abortive coup, however, ethnic Chinese as a group tended to refrain from active participation in politics, although a few individuals continued to do so in a low-key way.

Recently, however, this low-profile attitude has given way to a more visible stance. For example, during the campaign period in the parliamentary election of April 1987, Dutch-educated economist and businessman Kwik Kian Gie came to the fore in the smallest camp of the three contestants in the election, the Partai Demokrasi Indonesia (PDI), or Indonesian Democratic Party. His activities rated mention in the *Far Eastern Economic Review*: "The diverse nature of the party's appeal has been symbolized by the appearance of Chinese-Indonesian PDI leader Kwik Kian Gie at major rallies." The article also noted that "Kwik, a leading businessman, has even highlighted his Chinese origin in at least one PDI rally."[22] It remains to be seen whether this is an isolated phenomenon or the beginning of a trend toward greater participation and fuller acceptance for ethnic Chinese in the sociopolitical arena.

Other changes are taking place in the social and cultural lives of the ethnic Chinese, especially among the younger generation. For instance, changing patterns of education have led to generational differences in language use at home and among members of the ethnic Chinese community, especially in Java. Whereas among the older generation some still speak good Mandarin or a mixture of Mandarin, Malay-Indonesian, and Javanese; and a very few speak fluent Dutch or a mixture of Malay-Indonesian with Dutch loanwords, the younger generation speaks only Indonesian or a mixture of Malay-Indonesian.[23]

There have also been changes in religion. The younger generation is moving away from traditional "Chinese religion," which in Indonesia consists primarily of ancestor veneration at home and of certain Chinese festivals, toward conversion to Catholicism or Protestantism and, more recently, to Islam. It is not uncommon in ethnic Chinese families today to find the children Catholic or Protestant, the mother still adhering to Chinese religion, and the father not professing any religion at all. Yet, on his identity card he may claim to be Buddhist or even Protestant, for since the 1965 upheaval, to leave the category for religion blank exposes him to suspicion that he is a Communist.

Interethnic marriage is also occurring but mostly when both parties are Christian. The incidence of marriage when one of the parties is Muslim is much lower. For instance, a study in Jakarta shows that of the 175 ethnic Chinese–ethnic Indonesian marriages recorded

---

[22]*Far Eastern Economic Review*, April 23, 1987. Recently, Kwik sold his business, an agency for European electronic equipment, apparently "in order to devote himself entirely to politics." He was rumored to be on the verge of bankruptcy, probably because his outspoken criticism of certain business policies and practices made it difficult for him to keep his business going.

[23]This language use by ethnic Chinese in Pasuruan, a small town in East Java, is described in Oetomo, "Chinese of Pasuruan," pp. 455–63, 467–527. This is a clear example of the cultural variety within the ethnic Chinese group, which is also based on age and "social class."

at the Civil Registration Office in 1982 only 13 percent were between Christians and Moslems.[24] Apparently, the parents of both parties play an important role in these cases. On the Muslim side is the requirement that the non-Muslim party convert to Islam, whereas on the non-Muslim side, especially if the child is a daughter, the gravest parental concern is that, because in Muslim law a man is allowed to have more than one wife, she may find herself in the position of having to share her husband, or if she refuses to be made a co-wife, requesting a divorce.

An aspect that has not changed much is the persistence of stereotypes. Among ethnic Chinese the view persists that ethnic Indonesians are unwilling to work hard, that they are wasteful, and that "if they have no money, they will ask from us, sometimes with a veiled threat"; hence "as long as they like money, we are safe."[25] Conversely, the stereotypes among ethnic Indonesians about ethnic Chinese also persist that they are very rich; that they are only out to make as much money as possible; that they are arrogant and feel superior, which is reflected in their tendency to be "exclusive," that is, to segregate in plush real estate areas and to stay away from neighborhood mutual help activities.

Mutually negative stereotypes also persist among totok and peranakan that reflect the continuing lack of social interaction between them. In a study in Solo, researchers found that more totok than peranakan have become Muslim. Peranakans who were asked about this finding opined that the totok convert to Islam because they think it is advantageous for business, intimating that the totok will do anything to promote their businesses. The totok, on the other hand, look down on peranakan as "wong londo" (Dutch) because they speak Dutch among themselves, or as *pribumi* because they speak Malay-Indonesian or Javanese only. The totok especially resent Dutch-speaking peranakan because they see such language use as an expression of peranakan feelings of superiority.[26]

The attitude of the younger generation of ethnic Chinese toward their position in Indonesian society deserves closer examination. This group experienced neither the colonial regime, when the population was systematically divided by race, the Japanese occupation, when all ethnic Chinese were treated as one group, the turbulence of the revolution, when ethnic Chinese were accused of collaborating with the Dutch, nor the controversy about assimilation and integration in the latter part of the Sukarno era. They do know that during the upheaval of 1965–1966, ethnic Chinese youths participated in the demonstrations against the Sukarno government and that some of them were recognized as leading figures in the then strong and influential student movement.

As a result, they seem more positive about their identity as Indonesians. At the same time, this identification makes them feel more frustrated when they experience discrimination. For instance, a special code is attached to the serial number of their identity cards and passports, indicating that they are citizens of foreign descent.[27] They resent the fact that

---

[24]Sutedjo, "Komunikasi," pp. 66–68.

[25]Oetomo, "Chinese of Pasuruan," pp. 134–41.

[26]Indrakusuma, "Posisi berbeda agama," pp. 63–76. See also, Oetomo, "Chinese of Pasuruan," p. 436.

[27]This matter came up at a seminar organized by Tarumanegara University (a private university with a predominantly ethnic Chinese student body) on March 10, 1990, on the occasion of the establishment of a center for the study of nation building (Pusat Kajian Kesatuan dan Persatuan Bangsa). The keynote speech was given by Minister of Internal Affairs Rudini. During the discussion period, one of the faculty members, a pribumi who teaches *kewiraan*, which includes civics, asked about the special codes. As he put it, when his students asked him about this, he was at a loss about how to answer them. The minister replied that he would look into it, and if this really were true, it should immediately be stopped. Apparently, in Jakarta, those of foreign descent (Chinese, Arab, Indian, Dutch) have a zero in the group of numbers after the serial number of the village (*kelurahan*). According to

assimilation is a one-way process; only they are expected to adjust and comply. Hence according to the results of a recent study in Sukabumi,[28] the younger generation tends to withdraw within its own group and to strengthen its ethnic Chinese identity. If they don't emphasize their Chineseness, they at least see themselves as different from the ethnic Indonesians.

The feeling of being discriminated against, even after having complied with all the New Order regulations pertaining to their social and cultural lives, has given rise to an assertiveness that is new to the ethnic Chinese. This attitude is expressed in an insistence on the consistent implementation of the principle of two types of citizenship only: the Warga Negara Republik Indonesia or WNRI or WNI (Indonesian citizen) and the Warga Negara Asing or WNA (alien), meaning that all citizens should be treated the same, regardless of ethnic origin, and similarly, all aliens should be treated the same, including those of Chinese origin. This view has been stated on many occasions by Sindhunata as chairman of the Bakom-PKB and by Lie Tek Tjeng, a historian affiliated with the Indonesian Institute of Sciences (LIPI) and a widely recognized (including by the military) expert on Indonesia-China relations.

Furthermore, expression of the view that assimilation should not necessarily mean the disappearance of the ethnic Chinese as a group is increasingly open. For instance, Harry Tjan Silalahi, one of the directors of the Center for Strategic and International Studies and a former member of the People's Consultative Assembly (MPR), was quoted in an interview in *Suara Pembaruan*, the major afternoon paper, as saying, "Assimilation should not eliminate diversity" (pembauran jangan menghilangkan kebhinekaan). He stated that assimilation cannot be forced on people but should be promoted through persuasion and regulation. He went on to say that this should be done by creating situations in which the two groups can interact more freely. He suggested that this approach means providing more opportunities for ethnic Chinese to enter government schools, the army, and the civil service.

Sofjan Wanandi, who subsequently became the spokesman for the group of businessmen invited to Tapos, was quoted in a meeting of the Indonesian Chamber of Commerce and Industry as raising the question of why more pribumi big businessmen were not included in the meeting at Tapos, suggesting perhaps that this could be seen as exclusivism in reverse.

This kind of open questioning of the policy of assimilation and its implementation indicates a feeling among the ethnic Chinese of greater security in their identification as Indonesians, accompanied by a sense of being treated unfairly. Despite full compliance with the regulations governing their social and cultural lives, they feel they are still not appreciated, recognized, or accepted as full-fledged fellow citizens by the ethnic Indonesian majority. They now insist more strongly that assimilation should be a two-way street.

Conclusion

Clearly, basic changes are occurring among the ethnic Chinese in Indonesia. Changes are especially noted among the younger generation, many of whom have become Protestant, Catholic, and more recently, Muslim. These changes may reduce their visibility as ethnic Chinese, remove some of the sources of resentment, and thereby lead to reduced hostility

---

K. Sindhunata, chairperson of Bakom-PKB, the passports of those of foreign descent also have a special code (*Tempo*, March 17, 1990, also April 14 and April 28, 1990, in "Letters to the Editor").

[28]Suleeman, "Persepsi golongan keturunan," pp. 201–6.

toward this group. No doubt the assimilationist policy of the government has been responsible for many of the changes.

It is clear that acculturation is an irreversible process and is continuing at a rapid pace. One must distinguish, however, between the process of acculturation and the process of social integration as indicated by social interaction. The former is proceeding linearly as Chinese cultural elements disappear and elements of local culture are adopted. One can even talk about the emergence of an "urban culture," in particular, "Jakarta culture," to which the ethnic Chinese have contributed. However, the process of social integration as manifested in social interaction is still not going smoothly. Contrary to their expectations, although members of the younger generation of ethnic Chinese state that they identify as Indonesians, they do not feel entirely appreciated and accepted by the ethnic Indonesian majority. Frustration has generated an assertiveness expressed in an insistence that the principle of two types of citizenship, Indonesian citizens (WNRI) and aliens (WNA), be implemented consistently and that efforts be mutual.

One should be mindful that the role of ethnic Chinese in the Indonesian economy is still perceived by the ethnic Indonesian majority as very powerful. With the recent policies of deregulation, especially in banking, generating a proliferation of new banks or new branches of existing banks and causing the rush of companies (many of which are owned by ethnic Chinese) to "go public," their role in the economy is viewed as even more pervasive than before. The stereotype that all ethnic Chinese are wealthy and that they have benefited most from "facilities" made available by the New Order government and become big businessmen in the process has undoubtedly been reinforced by the event at Tapos. Hence although basic changes are occurring in the social and cultural dimensions of their lives, their role in the economy is the most visible to ethnic Indonesians and is the major source of resentment against them. It is imperative, therefore, that changes also occur in the economic arena.

Does normalization of relations with the PRC have any relevance to the Chinese problem? It is implicitly recognized in the Memorandum of Understanding that marked the resumption of diplomatic relations between the two countries. Yet as indicated in the many writings on the ethnic Chinese in Indonesia that appeared in the media at the time, it is uncertain the Chinese problem has been resolved.

However, ultimately the government, its policies, and the implementation of these policies will determine whether relations between the ethnic Chinese minority and the ethnic Indonesian majority will continue to be characterized by periodic outbursts of social unrest with the ethnic Chinese remaining victims of scapegoating and deflected aggression or whether a gradual but continuous reduction in conflict situations will occur.

The ethnic Chinese should realize that it is imperative to diversify occupationally and residentially and to move away from overconcentration in economic activities and certain exclusive neighborhoods. They should realize that, having elected to become Indonesian citizens, they must pay equal attention to their responsibilities as well as their rights as citizens. Furthermore, as a minority group they are compelled to find ways to achieve an acceptable accommodation with the majority population. On the other hand, for individuals, total assimilation is a course of action still as open today as it was in the past.

THE ROLE OF ELITES IN CREATING CAPITALIST HEGEMONY IN POST–OIL BOOM INDONESIA

Yoon Hwan Shin

The rapid growth of the Indonesian economy during the 1970s accompanied the emergence of what I called elsewhere a new capitalist class.[1] This class differs from its pre–New Order counterpart in many respects.[2] Although ethnic Chinese remain a dominant segment, those who comprise the capitalist class have increasingly included a substantial number of indigenous *(pribumi)* business people, who have accumulated sufficient capital to affect the fate of Indonesian capitalism and have entrenched themselves deep in strategic sectors of the economy.

It is important to note, however, that the development of this new capitalist class has come about in a sociopolitical and cultural environment that is amiable neither to capitalism nor to the Chinese minority. When the Indonesian economy encountered economic crises in the 1980s, the disparity between the economic prowess of the new capitalists and their political and ideological weaknesses loomed large. The increasing role of the private sector as the savior of the post–oil boom economy was called for more emphatically than ever, but anti-Chinese sentiment and lack of a "capitalist hegemony" in Indonesian society constrained the active contribution of the new capitalists.[3] It was against this contradictory backdrop that

---

[1] Yoon Hwan Shin, "Demystifying the Capitalist State: Political Patronage, Bureaucratic Interests, and Capitalists-in-Formation in Soeharto's Indonesia" (Ph.D. diss., Yale University, 1989).

[2] Ibid., chap. 6. See also Richard Robison, *Indonesia: The Rise of Capital* (Sydney: Allen and Unwin, 1986), p. 3, and Yuri Sato, "The Development of Business Groups in Indonesia, 1967–1989" (Master's thesis, University of Indonesia, 1989).

[3] Antonio Gramsci, *Selections from the Prison Notebooks*, ed. and trans. Quintin Hoarse and Geoffrey Norwell Smith (New York: International Publishers, 1971). Here I follow Allex Callinicos in defining Gramsci's *hegemony:* "an 'organizing principle,' or world-view (or combination of such world-views), that is diffused by agencies of ideological control and socialization into every area of daily life," or "this prevailing consciousness . . . internalized by the broad masses." "As all ruling elites seek to perpetuate their power, wealth, and status," Callinicos explains, "they necessarily attempt to popularize their own philosophy, culture, morality, etc. and render them unchallengeable, part of the natural order of things." See Allex Callinicos, *Gramsci's Marxism* (London: Pluto Press, 1976), p. 39. For an opposing interpretation of Gramsci's hegemony, see Anne Showstack Sassoon, "Hegemony,

political and business elites and procapitalist intellectuals came to the fore to advocate a market-oriented economic system and ideology. Capitalist hegemony must be *created* by noneconomic forces, especially by the state, as John Saul found in postcolonial societies, because these societies lack the time and experience required to develop a capitalist culture "slowly and surely."[4]

The creation of capitalist hegemony could not be more opportune than in post–oil boom Indonesia. Substantively, the sluggish and strained economy called upon the private sector to undertake the leading role in economic growth, which had been played by the state with its rich oil revenue. Furthermore, the growing frustration and aggression among small-scale business people and the popular sector had to be politically and ideologically accommodated to provide secure situations for the new capitalists and multinationals to invest.

The "ideological modes of economic domination" described here refer to the political and cultural efforts elites undertake to insure and perpetuate the economic dominance of an emerging new capitalist class. That these efforts were increasingly evident in the 1980s reflects that Indonesian capitalism is moving into a more stabilizing stage with a supportive ideology. I discuss in this paper: (1) the sociopolitical implications of the recent trend toward interracial economic cooperation; (2) the dissemination of capitalist ideas and ethics among business people, intellectuals, and government officials; and, most importantly, (3) the phaseout of anti-Chinese, indigenist economic policies and their implications.

Toward a National Business Class

Since independence, the concept of private capitalism has had negative connotations in Indonesia. Because the Indonesian usage of the term *capitalism* often accompanies such modifiers as free fight after Sukarno used it that way, many Indonesian elites exploited the term politically and implanted connotations of inherent chaos, unfairness, and selfishness in it. Their suspicion of capitalism was frequently expressed in creative but unsubstantiated conceptual forms. During Parliamentary Democracy, there was Assatism; Sukarno popularized communalistic Marhaenism; now under the New Order, much ink has been spilled to debate the Pancasila Economic System *(Sistem Perekonomian Pancasila)*. These expressions, despite the different emphases and nuances among them, share at least one connotation: a hatred of a social stratum that the indigenous society lacks and that was and is occupied by the former colonizers and their collaborators. An economic system that leaves or helps them go their way was believed to undermine the well-being of the indigenous population. Thus alternative ideas were mobilized and put to test. On every trial, however, the result was dismal. It is against this hostile historical and social backdrop that the new capitalists, appearing more balanced in racial representation than before, have emerged in the New Order and have been remarkably successful in taking root in the Indonesian economy and, to a lesser degree, in society.

The ideological efforts to create and maintain a stable capitalist system are succinctly expressed in one concept, *pengusaha nasional* (national entrepreneur), which is replacing previously popular, racial terms to designate business people belonging to different social and economic groups. The stress is on the imported word *nasional*, which is antithetical to *asli* or

---

War of Position and Political Intervention," in *Approaches to Gramsci,* ed. Ann Showstack Sassoon (London: Writers and Readers, 1982).

[4]"The State in Postcolonial Societies: Tanzania," in the *Socialist Register 1974,* ed. Ralph Miliband and John Saville (New York: Monthly Review Press; London: Merlin Press, 1974); reprinted in *The State and Revolution in Eastern Africa: Essays by John S. Saul,* ed. John S. Saul (New York and London: Monthly Review Press, 1979), p. 170. See also Hamza Alavi, "The State in Post-Colonial Societies: Pakistan and Bangladesh," *New Left Review* 74 (1972).

pribumi. This observation does not imply that this officially promoted term will soon remove such still prevalent terms as *nonpribumi, orang Cina, orang Tionghoa,* or *WNI (keturunan) Cina* (or, simply, *WNI*) from everyday conversation.[5] I am simply arguing that the disappearance of these terms from the media and government decrees will at least discourage state officials, business people, and intellectuals from making issues of the Chinese problem. Reduced usage also marks a beginning of the end for the government to blame only the Chinese for their "exclusivism." It does not, of course, guarantee that ordinary Indonesians will soon accept the new usage. Even so, it should be seen as an effort by the state and the new capitalists to *create* the hegemony of capitalist ideology and culture in society. The term implicitly suggests that the entrepreneurs, whether Chinese or indigenous, serve the common interests of the nation, not their respective racial interests. On a general level, it also conveys the concept that capitalism realizes the interests of all, not just the capitalists' class interests.

The nomenclatural development has been substantiated by a change in the world of business, that is, the increased commercial cooperation among the private business people, especially between pribumi and Chinese.[6] In a sense, it is an acceptable compromise between the sobering reality of the invincible Chinese economic position and the unwarranted ideal of indigenism.

This cooperation takes the forms of an intrafirm partnership and an interfirm market cartel. Joint ventures among big corporations now go beyond racial or ethnic differences. The partnership between pribumi and nonpribumi is not new in Indonesia, but what I refer to here is a somewhat sincere one, unlike the cukong, Ali-Baba, and Baba-Ali arrangements, which are convenient bypasses of legal obstacles. With more pribumi in business and with more Chinese confident in the New Order's commitment to the capitalist path, business people of the two races have become engaged in a more lasting and earnest form of business partnership. In this new form, the indigenous partner is not merely a political contributor but a true partner in ownership and management.

Most of the Chinese big business people seem to have increasingly realized that their exclusive domination of the economy would spread sentiments of economic indigenism and eventually influence the policy making of the state, the signs of which surfaced in the wake of the Malari affair. In this sense, it can be argued, it is in their economic as well as political interest to see a strong indigenous business sector develop. The establishment of a powerful, racially intertwined economic class may revive an anticapitalist mood in society but will help prevent racist feelings from besieging the indigenous population. As long as the military is firmly in power, the Communists will never be able to regain political vigor. By contrast, racial prejudices would easily inflame social unrest and even gain influence among the governing elite within the state.

---

[5]Both orang Cina and orang Tionghoa refer to a Chinese; the former is considered pejorative by the Chinese Indonesians. Immediately after Soeharto assumed power, his regime deliberately discouraged the use of orang Tionghoa, which is recently regaining ground. See Charles A. Coppel, *Indonesian Chinese in Crisis* (Kuala Lumpur: Oxford University Press, 1983), p. 157. WNI, pronounced weh-en-ih, stands for *Warga Negara Indonesia*, literally meaning an Indonesian citizen but, in practice, referring only to ethnic Chinese who have obtained Indonesian nationality.

[6]A phrase coined to express the Chinese-pribumi cooperation in business is "pembauran di bidang usaha." *Pembauran*, literally mixing, association, or social intercourse, has been primarily used to mean cultural assimilation of "non-native" Indonesians. In business, however,—"di bidang usaha" meaning "in the business field"—pembauran does not carry the connotation that a distinctive subculture integrates into the larger universal culture. Instead, it simply means mutual cooperation in business between the two racial groups.

Today, many Chinese companies have pribumi as managers or shareholders and vice versa. Admittedly, with nationalist and discriminatory policies still on and off, concerns about expediency could become a major reason for the interracial working relationship. But as I will elaborate in the final section of this article, such policies in the New Order have had little impact upon the big businesses of the Chinese. Thus the recent tendency toward business *pembauran* seems to be an outcome of the new capitalists' conscious realization that both their pribumi and Chinese fractions can benefit from the greater economic share of the pribumi.

This consciousness is displayed in many de facto market cartels formed in the industries developed along the state's import-substitution strategy. The strategy gives significant privileges to the existing companies in these industries by demanding higher costs for the companies that seek new entry. The number of companies operating in these sectors is kept relatively small, which protects inefficient and uncompetitive firms. Although the less competent firms could lose out in limited competition within these sectors, it is also true that the more competent firms have found it harmful to drive out completely their weak competitors, which are often pribumi owned. The existence of these indigenous companies may not only give an appearance of a healthy competition, instead of a Chinese monopoly, but also provide the state with the pretext to maintain its continuous protection of the industrial sectors. The new capitalists may believe that their political weakness can be compensated by increased class cohesiveness and by their deep entrenchment in the economy. To this end, mutual cooperation and interaction among the bigger corporations became increasingly noticeable in the 1980s.

Ideological Role of Elites in Creating the Hegemony of Capitalism

The scheme the new capitalists designed to obtain an *acceptable dominance* has been supported by many elements of the upper class, including high government officials, business people, academicians, and journalists. No doubt, these groups share common interests and concerns behind their near-united support for the scheme. But rather unusual in the 1980s was that the campaign was carried out in exceptionally open ways.

The catalyst was the recession of the early 1980s, which squeezed budgetary resources for public projects and various programs that doled out credit to the already hard-pressed, small, indigenous companies. Facing this plight, the state called on big business, including the Chinese, first, to move the economy out of the recession, and, second, to take over the task of helping the small and medium pribumi-owned companies. During the early 1980s, an *ideological* groundwork was laid to facilitate the state's final abandonment of the racist interpretation of the "weak economic group" in implementing economic policy. Naturally, those who were most affected by, or related to, the economic situation took charge of the ideological task.

I call the concerted effort *ideological* in the sense that all the suggestions and justifications they gave to the policy change remained rhetorical and, in effect, protected the interests of the new capitalists. It was carried out in the form of academic debates, public talks, and official statements. The participants were overwhelmingly united in their intent. Thus it should be called instead a campaign to promote or indoctrinate capitalist ideas. Its core arguments included denunciation of the small pribumi capitalists' lack of entrepreneurial spirit and of their dependence on government projects and racist policies and, at the same time, a eulogy of the free and open market solution to the economic stagnation; the constructive role of Chinese entrepreneurs in the Indonesian economy; the voluntary assistance by big business to small business; and, generally, the efficacy of the private sector and big business. Various associations of indigenous businessmen were in the forefront of the campaign.

The Indonesian Chamber of Commerce and Industry (KADIN) demonstrated the most obvious interest in accepting the enhanced role of the private sector in business affairs. In the early 1980s, the state, in a symbolic gesture, designated KADIN as the only legitimate social institution to provide assistance to small and medium (mostly pribumi-owned) companies. After that, KADIN, which was originally organized to protect pribumi business interests, collected funds primarily from Chinese entrepreneurs and distributed them through its regional offices. Reporting to President Suharto, who called for a consortium for that purpose, KADIN's Vice-Chairman Probosutedjo informed him that Rp. 5 billion had already been collected at the initiation of two leading Chinese entrepreneurs, Liem Sioe Liong and William Soeryadjaya.[7] Each time when they distributed the funds, KADIN representatives did not fail to stress, as the most important means to success, the creativity and hard work of the entrepreneurs themselves rather than outside support.

It was also in this context that a special coordinating body emerged to support the small-scale, pribumi-owned companies. The Indonesian Union of Leading Entrepreneurs (IPPI, Ikatan Pemuka Pengusaha Indonesia), upon its founding in September 1980, declared that its members, consisting of both leading Chinese and indigenous entrepreneurs, would not bid for government tenders valued over Rp. 1 billion.[8] The figure was ten to twenty times higher than the minimum value of government contracts and purchases in which Keppres No. 14/1979 permitted the big pribumi or Chinese-owned businesses to participate. Immediately after its organizational meeting in September, IPPI secured Rp. 3 billion as funds to be credited to small pribumi business people.[9] But because the amount provided to each recipient barely reached Rp. 100,000 and because the funds were given out with no collateral, it seemed obvious that they were aimed to show the good will of big business rather than to make a sincere effort to support entrepreneurial aspirants. These "charity" activities became less publicized after 1980–1981.

At this juncture, various proposals were put forward about how to forge and increase cooperative relationships between big and small business.[10] The so-called *bapak angkat* system was interesting.[11] Because *bapak angkat* means "adoptive father," the idea was patrimonialistic: a big company should help a specially selected group of small companies by giving credit, contracts, management advice, job training, and other assistance. Because the Department of Industry coined the concept, however, no notable progress has been reported beyond interpreting the system to mean whatever links already exist between big and small companies—a usual end for many proposals and debates in Indonesian business.

KADIN has also accelerated its campaign to embrace and involve more Chinese in the organization. For instance, the Executive Board of Directors of KADIN for the term 1982–1985 had at least three Chinese as chairmen or vice-chairmen of its fourteen compartments.[12] Among them, quite revealingly, were the Compartment of Budget and Treasury,

---

[7]*Antara*, July 20, 1980.

[8]*Berita Buana*, October 23, 1980.

[9]*Antara*, October 19, 1980.

[10]See, for example, Kwik Kian Gie, "Pengusaha Kuat Yang Harus Membantu Yang Lemah," *Kompas*, January 22, 1981; and a newspaper article entitled, "Perusahaan Kecil Dimata Konsultan" in *Berita Buana*, February 12, 1979.

[11]*Pelita*, December 30, 1980.

[12]Indonesian Chamber of Commerce and Industry, "Information Guide to the Organization of Kadin Indonesia," Jakarta, 1983, pp. 45–52.

chaired by Mochtar Riady, and that of Small Business Development, chaired by William Soeryadjaya. The compartment led by Soeryadjaya aimed to direct various support from the large (mainly Chinese-owned) industries to the small (pribumi-owned) industries. Its vice-chairman was R. Agung Laksono, the head of the Indonesian Young Entrepreneurs' Association (HIPMI). HIPMI was one of the most outspoken supporters of indigenist public policy.

The most remarkable transformation took place in the Indonesian Indigenous Businessmen's Association (HIPPI: Himpunan Pengusaha Pribumi Indonesia). As its name indicates, it had been an exclusively pribumi organization until 1984. Its head (Ketua Dewan Pembina) was again Probosutedjo and, despite his inconsistent and confusing position, had often made demands and complaints in outright favor of the pribumi business people. But when Benny Moerdani called for a halt to use of the terms pribumi and nonpribumi, HIPPI changed the word pribumi to *putera* (son or prince) in the organization's name.[13] Later Probosutedjo explained that HIPPI has a "broad and big" meaning. The word putera in HIPPI does not mean merely "child" (*anak*) but "a patriot who loves his motherland, its people and country."[14] "Thus," he continued, "for whoever is prepared to serve the nation, regardless of race or size of business, the door to membership is open wide."[15] The only qualification to join HIPPI was "truly having the Pancasila *spirit*."[16] Now he was suggesting precisely what the state wished for. In fact, a week later, Coordinating Minister of Public Welfare, Alamsjah Ratu Prawiranegara, used very similar phrases to second Probosutedjo's idea; "Every Indonesian citizen, regardless of place of origin, religion, or conviction, is an Indonesian *putera* who must be loyal to Pancasila and the 1945 Constitution and has the obligation and responsibility to serve his nation and country."[17] What Probosutedjo quoted Vice-President Umar Wirahadikusumah to have said retained a more concrete recommendation "that the pribumi businessmen can work together *with any group* and *learn* from able and strong businessmen."[18]

Probosutedjo was a man of his word, at least on this matter. When HIPPI reshuffled its leadership one week later, Agus Nursalim, his long-time Chinese business associate, was included in the executive council, and an obscure figure of Chinese name, Nurdani Latif (Lie Hong Wi), was appointed the treasurer. He assessed their spirit of Pancasila by saying, "these people already became good Indonesian putera."[19] A more concrete plan came to life two months later. In November, HIPPI established a company in Medan to implement "*pembauran* in business between big and small entrepreneurs as well as between entrepreneurs of Indonesian origin and those of foreign origin."[20] The company, interestingly named P. T. Asperindo (Asli Putera Indonesia), had two Chinese directors and a Chinese advisor (*penasehat*).

The group that demanded and benefited the most from the nationalist economic policy was the Indonesian Young Entrepreneurs' Association (HIPMI, Himpunan Pengusaha

---

[13] Susumu Awanohara, "The Perennial Problem," *Far Eastern Economic Review*, September 6, 1984, p. 27.

[14] *Antara*, December 22, 1984.

[15] Ibid.

[16] *Sinar Harapan*, October 24, 1984 (emphasis mine).

[17] *Sinar Harapan*, October 30, 1984.

[18] *Merdeka*, October 24, 1984 (emphasis mine).

[19] *Antara*, September 3, 1984.

[20] *Merdeka*, November 13, 1984.

Muda Indonesia). But even in HIPMI, it became more apparent as time went on that the members realized and appreciated the necessity of Chinese support in materializing the government's pro-pribumi programs. They needed more Chinese help than did, probably, any other group of pribumi businessmen because of lack of business experience, shortage of capital, and their excessive dependence on political connections. I learned from interviews with several young pribumi and Chinese businessmen that the younger generation of the two ethnic groups cooperated as much as their seniors did. Before the election of HIPMI's chair due in early 1986, some young Chinese businessmen actively campaigned for a certain candidate with a less racist platform.

HIPMI's anti-Chinese outlook toned down substantially as KADIN became as important a patron as the state in the post–oil boom economy. Its members had to accept Chinese business people as sources of credit and donations and in their role as "bapak angkat," however empty its practical meaning was. Perhaps more important was the polarization of the young indigenous business community, which was precipitated by Keppres no. 10/1980. The presidential decision gave the children around the most powerful group extraordinary opportunities to obtain big government contracts, whereas the immediately ensuing recession drove out numerous less powerful, young business people.[21] In tandem, high government officials—including the so-called nationalists—economists, and journalists launched deliberate all-out attacks on HIPMI. In retrospect, these attacks were only a prelude to what was soon to come. In explaining Keppres nos. 29/1984 and 30/1984, which replaced the previous presidential decrees on small-scale government suppliers and contractors, government officials included in the category of the "weak economic group" "those non-indigenous Indonesians who have assimilated."[22]

Although they chose words cautiously, government officials were clear on what they wished to convey to the HIPMI members. The powerful State Secretary Soedharmono urged them to "apply to their work methods that are pragmatic and practical but are also spirited by the concept of high national idealism."[23] The ambiguity of this statement cleared when he added the following: "You should not accustom yourselves to fiddling around with [government] facilities and living on distributing imported goods. Opportunism and 'protectionist' life-styles, which characterize the attitudes of some HIPMI members, must be thrown away." It is important to notice that it was not the technocrats but the so-called nationalists who led the campaign to undermine the raison-d'être of HIPMI. It implies that because the technocrats would possibly invite backlash, the nationalists acted in this case as defenders of the common interest of the state.

Another minister belonging to the nationalist camp, Minister of Internal Affairs Soepardjo Roestam, declared that the day was gone when "the government helped you with decrees as the mother fed [the baby] with milk,"[24] so "you should not rely on the capacity of others including the government."[25] A less powerful official, Governor of Greater Jakarta R. Soeprapto, spoke in the same vein when he said, somewhat beseechingly, "HIPMI can explore new business areas [rather than government contracting] in an effort to [support the government in tackling] the problem of unemployment" and, "as a government partner, can help the growth of the weak economic group in terms of capitalization, marketing as well as

---

[21]Shin, "Demystifying the Capitalist State," chap. 7, especially pp. 264–74.

[22]Manggi Habir, "Protecting Their Interests," *Far Eastern Economic Review*, May 10, 1984, p. 73.

[23]*Merdeka*, May 8, 1984.

[24]*Kompas*, August 1, 1984.

[25]*Antara*, July 31, 1984.

managerial skills."[26] As an ironical distortion, Soeprapto ignored the fact that HIPMI itself consisted overwhelmingly of "the weak economic group." For example, in the better-off Greater Jakarta (Jaya) branch, 70 to 80 percent of the HIPMI members belonged to this category, whereas the remainder were medium and strong business people.[27]

It seemed that HIPMI also failed to gain sympathy from the parliament, DPR. Receiving a visit by HIPMI's Jaya branch leaders, the chairman of the provincial parliament of Jakarta, Soedarsono, was more straightforward than the bureaucrats in giving advice. He said that "the members of HIPMI Jaya must be capable of developing into self-reliant entrepreneurs without depending on the government, because dependence will bring loss back to them and weaken their activity and creativity as entrepreneurs."[28] Its vice-chairman, H. M. Jufrie, remarked that according to his own observation, most HIPMI Jaya members are active only in the areas of procurement and service and "should be more oriented toward industrial sectors." Another vice-chairman, H. Wim Salamun, ridiculed them by pointing out that "HIPMI should be a little more selective in accepting its members. . . . Do not accept those adventurists *(pengusaha avonturis)* who ruin Hipmi's good reputation."[29]

By the end of 1984, HIPMI seemed finally to give up its effort to mobilize support from outside. Thus the chairman, Agung Laksono, a political aspirant, began to echo what the government officials and business people had suggested to him. In the ceremony officially accepting thirty-four new members, Laksono warned that "government projects should not be the only business area that interests you," adding that "as an entrepreneur, you must be able to create your own business, which will help the government in augmenting employment."[30] Probosutedjo, who used to enjoy the spotlight by repeating statements sympathetic to the pribumi, looked like a born-again entrepreneur when he said, "The buildup of the weak entrepreneurs should not be carried out through state policies."[31] This statement was the best and final summary of the position the policymakers and businessmen wanted to convey to the small pribumi contractors.

In sharp contrast, the morale of big business was boosted by the aggravated situation of the economy and, hence, the credentials it received from various sectors of the society as its savior. If government officials, except the technocrats, were hesitant to acknowledge the state's own responsibility for the country's economic plight, they agreed with those economists who placed their trust in the private sector.

Universities, newspapers, and business organizations organized numerous seminars and symposia to discuss how to develop entrepreneurship and promote exports.[32] Business

---

[26]Ibid. See also, *Antara*, November 10, 1984.

[27]*Berita Buana*, August 2, 1984.

[28]*Merdeka*, October 24, 1984.

[29]Ibid.

[30]*Suara Karya*, November 12, 1984.

[31]*Merdeka*, December 29, 1984. The Indonesian text reads, "Pembinaan atas pengusaha yang lemah hendaknya jangan dilakukan secara politis." It is interesting to note that *politis* in Indonesian can mean either "political" or "in terms of policy." It was clear that Probosutedjo meant the latter from the remark that "if the government continues to give credit, the [weak] businessmen will be dragged in an undesirable direction."

[32]For example, *Suara Karya*, a Golkar-controlled newspaper, organized a huge seminar in February 1984, in which 250 people participated. The participants included most former and present ministers of economic affairs, other ministerial-level government officials, leading business people, economists, and journalists. Two of four panels addressed the issues of "The Business Climate and the Role of the Private Sector" and "Stimulating Non-Oil Exports and Trade Regulations." The papers were published as *Peranan Dunia Usaha Dalam Repelita IV* (Jakarta: Penerbit Suara Karya, 1984). Compare the dominantly "liberal" tones of the proposals to the more or

schools sponsored by the government and the private sector became increasingly popular, and model entrepreneurs were praised and invited to give public talks. The mass media regularly provided forums for debates on economic issues, including monopoly and oligopoly, the Pancasila economic system, development strategy, state interventionism, the weak economic group, and so forth. All these academic activities quickly spread an atmosphere of economic crisis and created a sense that something should be done. In one sense, the consensus was predetermined: that is, the state was an obstacle *(penghambat)* to structural adjustment and was itself an inefficient sector wasting national resources. A solution was easily found, namely, that the private sector should be given the mission of saving the economy from the crisis. This rather obvious conclusion yielded several popular concepts, which, at their core, praised the market economy. While they reflected the changing structure of Indonesian capitalism, they, in turn, contributed to expediting the change. In this regard, the intellectual contribution corresponds precisely to what Hamza Alavi and John Saul saw as the ideological role of the postcolonial state in creating capitalist hegemony.

The key concept summarizing the academic efforts is comparative advantage *(keunggulan komparatif)*. Borrowed from the liberal theory of international trade, this term, when applied to the Indonesian case, stresses the labor-intensive manufacturing industry as the strategic sector for promoting exports. The proponents included most technocrats and liberal economists and, interestingly, some "turncoats" from the nationalist economist group.[33] Inspired by the economic success of the East Asian Newly Industrializing Countries, and pressed by the aggravating balance-of-payments problem, they looked to increasing exports as the solution. But because oil exports proved too inconsistent and because the international prices of other primary exports were also fluctuating violently, the proponents suggested that Indonesia's comparative advantage be based on her cheap and abundant labor. The low quality of Indonesian labor could stand in the way of this solution as well. But because Indonesia's options were extremely limited, economists pushed all the harder in this direction and harshly criticized what was collectively called the "high-cost economy" *(ekonomi biaya tinggi)*. The state is, of course, chiefly responsible for creating and maintaining the high-cost economy.

In the business sector, the comparative advantage school is less refined in its arguments and more supportive of the status quo than its economic gurus. On two occasions, when debates on the issues of monopoly and the weak economic group became heated, the followers of this school lined up to support monopolies and big corporations with some qualifications. And the conclusions from these debates were in near-unanimous favor of them. Therefore, the search by the academicians for an alternative development strategy ended by promoting the interests of the new capitalists, who were strongly represented in the big businesses, monopolies and oligopolies, and the light manufacturing sector.[34] The irony is that most of

---

less indigenist and statist ones of the seminar held nine years earlier on "Strategies to Build up the National Private Entrepreneurs," Seminar Strategi Pembinaan Pengusaha Swasta Nasional, Centre for Strategic and International Studies, May 29–31, 1975 (Malang, Indonesia: Parangan Press, 1975). Numerous workshops and seminars were also organized by *Kompas* and *Sinar Harapan*. See, for example, *Kompas*, August 23, 1985 and September 9, 1985. See also, *Kompas*, September 11 and 12, 1985 for its long summaries of a symposium organized by the Faculty of Economics, University of Indonesia.

[33]Although the quotations that follow in the text are drawn heavily from peranakan Chinese intellectuals, the same ideas were shared by most economists and business observers, not to mention the technocrats. Other evidence hinting at the consensus is the wide and intense coverage the leading newspapers and magazines gave to their criticisms and suggestions.

[34]Therefore, the theoretical supports served as an apologetic justification to the existing and increasing oligopolies that are not necessarily efficient or competitive. As Hal Hill found recently, the enormously high

these big business groups were the creation of the state-initiated strategy of import-substitution industrialization on which the liberal economists launched heavy attacks.

Some economists and business observers were quick to argue that export promotion requires the development of equivalents to the general trading companies, *sogo shosha*, of Japan.[35] To compete with the multinationals in the international as well as domestic markets, they contended, Indonesia, too, needs big corporations that have an advantage in productivity, costs, and marketing. An evident twist in this proposal is that they emphasized only the size of the Japanese general trading companies while avoiding mention of their outward orientation and remarkable cost-saving efficiency in production and marketing, which Indonesian big business corporations largely lack. Attentive to the guiding role of the Japanese state in leading exports, they also argued that the Indonesian state must assume the same role in creating favorable environments and providing infrastructures. Yet considering the precisely opposite role the Indonesian state has played, the idea of "Indonesia Inc." again would be too wishful a concept to materialize.[36]

Wibisono also maintained that two types of monopolies and oligopolies should be distinguished.[37] One he called command monopoly, which is enforced "from 'above,' with political 'backing' and a 'command' mechanism."[38] This type, mostly found in the public sector, is the one at which the criticisms of monopoly should be directed. But the other type, the "market oligopolies," must be encouraged, because they are "the outcome of healthy, honest, free, and open competition, reflect efficiency, productivity, and creativity, and benefit consumers by providing positive services for consumers' needs." In a somewhat convincing article, he gave specific examples of the market oligopolies, which were almost exclusively controlled by, in my term, the new capitalists. As industries in which free competition created an oligopolistic situation, he listed batteries, clove and regular cigarettes, milk, film, toothpaste and detergents, polyester and rayon synthetic fibers, paint, motorcycles, flat and safety glasses, monosodium glutamate (MSG), and such auto parts as tires, batteries, and spark plugs. Although he took into account neither "nonprice competition" and government protection as crucial factors in creating the oligopolies[39] nor their negative effects on consumer prices and employment,[40] his notion of market oligopoly contributed effectively to justifying the role of big business.

"seller concentration" of Indonesia is not related to efficiency but to government protection. In addition, Indonesia remains, perhaps, the most concentrated economy that Hill knew of in the developing countries, although he found it declining slightly between 1975 and 1983. See Hal Hill, "Concentration in Indonesian Manufacturing," *Bulletin of Indonesian Economic Studies* 23 (2) (1987): 80–82, 98.

[35]"Trading House Nusantara, Seperti Apa?" *Informasi* 12 (1981): 12–20; "Jaringan Sogo-Shosha," *Informasi* 5 (1982): 3–23; Christianto Wibisono, *Kearah Indonesia Incorporated*, 2 vols. (Jakarta: Yayasan Management Informasi, 1985).

[36]Christianto Wibisono borrows from "Japanese Inc." to conceptualize "Indonesian Inc.," in which the national economy can be run as if it were an incorporated company with the state as the management and the private sector as the production line. Ibid.

[37]Christianto Wibisono, "Oligopoli Pasar dan Monopoli Komando," *Kompas*, January 31, 1985; see also, "Anatomi Tiga Kelompok Industri," *Informasi* 3 (1985): 5–19.

[38]Wibisono, "Oligopoli."

[39]For details of this criticism, see H. M. T. Oppusunggu, "Semedi Ekonomi," *Sinar Harapan*, February 14, 1985. According to Oppusunggu, nonprice competition refers to various "means of competition [other than low prices] such as service, warranty, credit, advertisement, packing, and so forth," which weaken the competitiveness of new, mainly small, producers.

[40]For details, see Hasibunan, "Oligopoli di Indonesia: Kasus Sektor Industri," *Prisma* (April 1985): 21–33.

Kwik Kian Gie went further than Wibisono to defend monopolies. He argued that most critics are not consistent if they blame only the privately owned monopolies while accepting the state monopolies. If the state monopolies are justified on the grounds of their public service, the private monopolies should also be given credit for their pioneering contribution to developing capital-intensive industries and meeting consumer needs. In his view, it was not economic reasoning but "social jealousy" (*kecemburuan sosial*) that stirred up discontent with monopolies. He was extremely straightforward to point out that social jealousy is inflated because most privately owned monopolies involve non-pribumi business people. To be fair, he suggested, the issue should be the general question of rich and poor or of big and small capital, instead of a racial one. He then concluded, "In a stable and well-ordered country, the absence of monopolies is ideal. . . . [But] when can Indonesia reach this situation?"[41] He thus suggested clearly that monopolies will be inevitable and necessary until the Indonesian economy becomes sufficiently industrialized.[42]

Another term that surfaced in the economic and business circles was "national assets" (*kekayaan nasional* or *asset nasional*). In Panglaykim's definition, "[t]he development of national businesses in Indonesia, which consist of family-owned groups, and which place themselves in the world of the national and the international economy, can be termed national assets." He went on to argue that "[i]n the process of their growth, they not only increase employment opportunities but also act as implementers of development programs if the business climate is enticing."[43] Now, the stress was placed on the contribution big business people could make toward creating jobs, paying taxes, earning dollars, promoting entrepreneurship, and, in general, developing the national economy.

Indirectly criticizing the government-proposed bapak angkat system, the economist Thee Kian Wie, whose concern for economic equality was well known, joined to caution that big companies may help small ones by giving subcontracts but that this should not be considered a long-term solution. Thee suggested that the best and final means to achieve economic equality was education and management training. He pointed out that "Indonesian society should instead be oriented toward *an economy that is not spiritual[ly based]*," and that "[t]hey [small-scale pribumi businessmen] should be able to behave as the *nonpribumi group* does now."[44] No doubt, by the "economy that is not spiritual *(ekonomi bukan spiritual)*" he meant a capitalist economy and expressed it only circuitously because of the widespread suspicion of the latter term in Indonesia. His direct reference to the Chinese as rational economic actors is surprising but, considering that Thee is himself a peranakan Chinese, such negative perception of pribumi entrepreneurs may well have been shared, widely and regardless of ethnicity, by the business community.

The rejuvenated mood of private capitalism is also evident in a blooming of the business press, which has been a phenomenon since the early 1980s. Several business newspapers and magazines have come into being, escalating such a mood. Probably its most marked

---

[41] Kwik Kian Gie, "Monopoli dan Kecemburuan Sosial," *Prisma* (April, 1985): 48.

[42] As an active member of the opposition Indonesian Democratic Party (PDI), Kwik is an outspoken critic of the New Order state's authoritarian rule, corruption, development strategy, and cultural policy. His consistently liberal position on these issues is rare among peranakan Chinese. He is also famous for a direct and logical style of debate. For his strong defense of Chinese capital and big capital, see Kwik Kian Gie, "Non-Pribumi, Dominasi Ekonomi dan Keadilan Sosial," *Kompas*, June 23, 1978 and idem, "Kapitalis dari Gang Ribald," *Tempo*, August, 1986, respectively.

[43] Panglaykim, *Bisnis Keluarga: Perkembangan dan Dampaknya* (Yogyakarta, Indonesia: Andi Offset, 1984), p. 3; see also *Tempo*, March 31, 1984, p. 66.

[44] *Sinar Harapan*, October 3, 1980 (emphasis mine).

consequences are opening up Indonesian business and, thus, implicitly promoting a capitalist value that business is also a virtue. Not only the business press has a professional interest in an open business atmosphere but also its major owners themselves are tied to business interests. Although such sensationalist magazines as *Jurnal Ekuin*, *Fokus*, and *Expo*, were closed by the government, several economic and business dailies, magazines, newsletters, and journals, such as the *Business News, Bisnis Indonesia, Neraca, Eksekutif, Swasembada, Forum Ekonomi, Indonesian Commercial Newsletter*, and *Informasi*, have flourished with a professional approach to economic and business issues.

For all the rhetoric, new concepts, and apparent changes in journalism, it is too soon to predict that the ideological campaign will have a significant and marked impact on the precapitalist culture of ordinary Indonesians, particularly in the numerically dominant rural sector. Capitalist hegemony in Gramsci's sense will be established only by the fundamental transformation of the economic and social structures of Indonesia. A long and intense struggle between new and old ideologies will be waged in the process. It is also premature to conclude that the Indonesian state has already committed itself fully to the capitalist pattern of economic growth in that capitalist development undermines the state's own dominance and autonomy. The New Order state's support for the new capitalists and their mouthpiece, intellectuals, could be seen as its temporary accommodation to the economic recession and the consequent fiscal crisis facing the state. These doubts and cautions notwithstanding, it is safe to argue that the Indonesian state has begun to perform one mission of the postcolonial state, namely, *creating* the hegemony of capitalism—instead of waiting idly for, as John Saul says, "an ideological cement for the capitalist system . . . [to] evolve slowly and surely."[45]

The Failure of Indigenist Policies and Its Implication

A more substantive move has been the increasingly evident determination of the policymakers create a "national capitalist class." This position is ironically reflected in the various policies the New Order state initiated in the name of helping the "weak economic group" *(golongan ekonomi lemah)*, which the government defined[46] as the small and medium companies in which pribumi either own at least 50 percent of shares or comprise the majority of the management with capital less than Rp. 25 million for the trading and other service sectors and Rp. 100 million for the construction and industrial sectors. The policies, summarized in table 1, are far more modest, inconsequential, and ineffective than the ones carried out by Suharto's predecessors.

Most of the policies that came out continuously and under various names after 1971 revolved around what Ralph Anspach called credit indigenism.[47] Anspach characterized the pre-Suharto economic policy making as a frustrating process of increasingly radicalized nationalism. The earlier policies under Parliamentary Democracy were failures, followed by the more radical and more disastrous ones. The earlier policies oscillated between "credit indigenism" and less moderate "decree indigenism." The former method favored the "subsidization of indigenous business without further restrictions upon existing or even new alien enterprises," whereas the latter used "the police power of the state to intervene directly in the market for the benefit of indigenous business" by either allowing "only entry

---

[45]Saul, "State," p. 170.

[46]Reported in *Antara*, June 7, 1979.

[47]Ralph Anspach, "Indonesia," in *Underdevelopment and Economic Nationalism in Southeast Asia*, ed. Frank H. Golay, Ralph Anspach, M. Ruth Pfanner, and Eliezer B. Ayal (Ithaca, N.Y.: Cornell University Press, 1969). See also, Dorodjatun Kuntjoro-Jakti, "The Political-Economy of Development: The Case of Indonesia under the New Order Government, 1966–1978" (Ph.D. diss., University of California, Berkeley, 1981), pp. 225–38.

Table 1

The New Order State's Policies to Promote Pribumi Entrepreneurship

Year	Institution/Program	Implementing Agencies	Content
1971	P.T. Askrindo[a]	Bank Indonesia	Insurance on bank loans to the small and medium firms
1972	P.T. Upprindo[b]	Bank Indonesia/Dutch government	Financing small and medium firms
1973	P.T. Bahana	Bank Indonesia	Equity financing (to 12.5%) and managerial assistance
1973	KIK/KMKP[c d]	Bank Indonesia; state banks; regional development banks	Small fixed investments and financing working capital
1974	DSEN decision[e]	None	Restriction on foreign investment and earlier transfer of PMA shares to pribumi partners
1974	Kredit Mini	Bank Indonesia; state banks; regional development banks	Small credit to small rural enterprises (up to Rp 100,000)
1975	Proyek BIPIK[f]	Bank Indonesia; World Bank; Department of Industry	Management training to small entrepreneurs
	Pegal[g]	Department of Trade; universities	Management training to small entrepreneurs
1976	KCK/Inpres Pasar[h]	Budgetary allocation via BUUDs[i]	Small credit to rural traders
1977	P.T. Danareksa		Promotion of equity participation by pribumis in PMAs
1977	DSP[j]	Department of Industry/BKPM[k]	Restriction on PMA and PMDN investments
1979	Keppres no. 14	Government agencies; public companies	Giving priority to small pribumi suppliers and contractors to the government
1980	Keppres no. 14A	State banks	Credit to the Keppres no. 14/1979 recipients

Notes: Abbreviations:

[a] Askrindo (Asuransi Kredit Indonesia): Indonesian Credit Insurance Ltd.

[b] Upprindo (Usaha Pembiayaan Pembangunan Indonesia): Indonesian Development Finance Company

[c] KIK (Kredit Investasi Kecil): Small Investment Credit

[d] KMKP (Kredit Modal Kerja Permanen): Permanent Working Capital Credit

[e] DSEN (Dewan Stabilisasi Ekonomi Nasional): National Council for Economic Stabilization

[f] Proyek BIPIK (Proyek Bimbingan dan Industri Kecil): Small Industry Guidance and Development Project

[g] Pegal (Pengusaha Golongan Ekonomi Lemah): Weak Economic Group Entrepreneur

[h] KCK (Kredit Candak Kecil): Small Trader Credit

[j] BUUD (Badan Usaha Unit Desa): Village Working Unit

[i] DSP (Daftar Skala Prioritas): Investment Priority List

[k] BKPM (Badan Kordinasi Penanaman Modal): Capital Investment Coordinating Board.

into a sector to members of the indigenous group," or more extremely, by excluding "all aliens from a sector by licensing arrangements."[48] The most extreme form of decree indigenism in the pre-Suharto era was best illustrated by the Benteng program. It designated certain categories of commodities (increased from about 10 percent of total imports in 1950 to 85 percent in 1954) to be imported only by *bangsa Indonesia asli* (native Indonesians). Although this program was supported by bank credit, it created a large number of "briefcase importers" and a very limited number of bona fide importers.[49] It faded out by 1957. In frustration arising from a series of failed programs, Sukarno mobilized nationalist forces to turn to the most radical form yet. This extreme radicalism was epitomized in the nationalization campaign of 1958. But the nationalization, in Anspach's words, simply "reflected the priority goal of indigenism rather than socialism."[50]

In the New Order, most policies were in the line of credit indigenism. Typically, the government set up companies and sanctioned state banks to finance, coinvest in, or provide cheap loans to small and medium companies owned by pribumi (P.T.'s Askrindo, Upprindo, and Bahana). Otherwise, it introduced education programs to train managers and entrepreneurs (Proyek BIPIK and Pegal). Between 1973 and 1976, several credit systems were created to provide part of the capital financing needed by pribumi businessmen to set up and run new companies (KIK and KMKP) or to help the rural enterprises and traders compete with the Chinese middlemen (KCK and Inpres Mini). By no means, however, did these institutions and programs directly infringe upon the dominance and vested interest of the big businesses.

In the past two decades, the New Order state's pribumi-supporting policy was closely associated with the condition of the national economy. More precisely, it is largely the affordability of the economy and the state budget that have determined the course of the state's action in responding to "nationalist" demands by small pribumi capitalists and their political supporters. In other words, economic recessions and fiscal difficulties of the state that must have doubled the hardship of small industries, in fact, brought about few meaningful policies despite their louder complaints and greater demands. For the first few years of the New Order, while the economy was busy recovering from the consequences of Sukarno's mismanagement and laying groundwork for full-fledged development, small capital received little attention, and, in fact, few protests were heard. Since 1982, the sense of economic crisis felt by both the state and the business community has overwhelmed the outcries of the desperate small capitalists. The mood certainly has favored moving toward antistatism and a free-market economy, as discussed.

It was, thus, during the best years of the Indonesian economy, the 1970s, that the state worked on the demands of the indigenous entrepreneurs. The latter half of the 1970s witnessed the revival of decree indigenism, although on a far smaller scale than that of the sweeping Benteng program of the early 1950s. The catalyst was the Malari affair of 1973–1974, which made an issue of economic domination by foreign capital and corrupt associations between the leadership and the Chinese cukong. The decision in early 1974 by the Board for the Stabilization of the National Economy (Dewan Stabilisasi Ekonomi Nasional) yielded a guideline for restricting foreign investment and speeding up the foreign investor's transfer of the majority shares to the domestic partners. But real action did not follow until

---

[48] Anspach, "Indonesia," pp. 123, 124.

[49] Ibid., pp. 167–79. See also, John O. Sutter, *Indonesianisasi: Politics in a Changing Economy, 1940–1955*, 4 vols., Data Paper no. 36 (Ithaca, N.Y.: Department of Far Eastern Studies, Cornell University, 1959), chap. 24.

[50] Anspach, "Indonesia," p. 126.

1977 when P. T. Danareksa, a national trust fund, was established. Danareksa would function as "an issuing house and underwriter as well as one of the most important stockholders."[51] But because the scheme counted on Jakarta's dormant stock market and because no antimonopoly regulations were yet in effect in Indonesia, its failure was guaranteed.

If there has been any notable success with decree indigenism, it was achieved by the more forceful Keppres no. 14/1979 and its ensuing Keppres no. 14A/1980, which were later superseded by Keppres nos. 29/1984 and 30/1984. The presidential decisions gave the weak economic group a priority or exclusive status to receive certain government contracts. For government projects and purchases valued under Rp. 25 million, only the weak group would be allowed to participate in its tender. For the range between Rp. 25 million and Rp. 50 million, the government would give a 5 percent premium on the price bid by the contractor belonging to this category. Although this program recorded modest success for the first few years, the ill timing of its launch just before the post–oil boom recession diminished its effectiveness. Furthermore, the typical problems with government-sanctioned policies, such as corruption, confusion of interpretation, lack of interdepartmental coordination, Ali-Baba firms, and abuse by big companies, were widely reported in the first year of the program.[52] Yet the most telling fact is that this policy did not and was not intended to discourage the growth of the big business sector. Suharto himself underscored that Keppres no. 14A/1980 did not mean to discourage "the role of the strong economic group" but only to "give the weak economic group opportunities and guidance to become strong."[53] In fact, the economic sectors that benefited the most from the policy were contracting and construction, which had long been congested by small and medium firms and were represented quite strongly by state-owned and a few indigenously owned companies.

As the foregoing evidence indicates, the significance of the New Order state's pribumi-promotion policy has been undercut by its preference for credit indigenism and by the minimal impact of decree indigenism on the dominance of big business. My second argument to the same effect is based on the almost negligible government spending and bank credit allocated to the colorfully titled programs. For example, the KIK/KMKP credit was awarded to 377,529 cases totaling Rp. 203,285 million for the first four years since they were implemented.[54] If one considers that the credit took the forms of fixed investments and working capital, it is doubtful that slightly over 500,000 rupiah (about US $1,000) per case ever made a significant difference in the overall structure of Indonesian capitalism. For the first six years (as of the end of the fiscal year 1979/80), Rp. 571 billion was allocated in the form of KIK/KMKP and Rp. 20.5 billion in the form of Kredit Mini against Rp. 2.5 trillion of the total bank credit for 1979/80 alone.[55] Kuntjoro-Jakti gives a similar figure: "By the end of 1978 the total cumulative value of KIK-KMKP-Kredit Mini represented only 6.4% of the total cumulative value of approved PMDNs."[56]

Other programs were even more trivial in their achievements. Kuntjoro-Jakti also found that for the first six years of implementation, P. T. Askrindo provided insurance on a total Rp. 219 billion or Rp. 482,585 per client while P. T. Upprindo carried out only eighty projects

---

[51] Kuntjoro-Jakti, "Political Economy," p. 233.

[52] See, for example, *Kompas*, October 11, 1979; *Antara*, August 11, 1979; *Pelita*, October 24, 1980; *Kompas*, March 29, 1980.

[53] Quoted in *Kompas*, July 11, 1980.

[54] Kuntjoro-Jakti, "Political Economy," p. 239.

[55] *Antara*, June 26, 1980.

[56] Kuntjoro-Jakti, "Political Economy," p. 235.

with the Rp. 11.5 billion of equity financing.[57] The case of P. T. Bahana clearly indicates that the institution was nothing more than a showcase; only ten projects were implemented with Rp. 600 million between 1973 and 1976. Kredit Candak Kulak amounted to Rp. 87.6 billion by September 1980.[58]

My additional sources of evidence point to the New Order state's soft stance on indigenism. Various problems nullified and distorted the policy objectives, if taken seriously at all, in the implementation stage. Corruption, incompetence, confusion over policies, and abuse besetting both the implementers—government agencies and state banks—and the beneficiaries continued to undermine the cause of such programs. Even if the policy makers were seriously committed at the beginning, the dismal outcome of almost every program that was implemented weakened the position of its advocates. Because no alternatives have been found and because more radical policies had a catastrophic history, the extent and degree of future pribumi-promotion policy are very likely, at most, to remain at the existing level.

In fact, no more policies have been initiated to support the small pribumi business people since the collapse of oil prices. The Keppres nos. 29/1984 and 30/1984 were the last of the ill-fated indigenist programs. Instead, the state's commitment to them have strictly remained within the boundary of pure rhetoric. The cooperative spirit declared in ARTICLE 33 of the Constitution *(UUD'45)*[59] has often been stressed but how this ambiguous and declamatory statement could be materialized interested few policy makers, economists, and business people. By 1985, the decision and opinion makers appeared to lean toward the final conclusion that the growth of small pribumi capitalists should be achieved by market forces and submitted to the free will of the business people involved, or to put it more appropriately, the mercy of the strong economic group.[60]

This development now clarifies what purposes the numerous policies actually served. The making of the "unsuccessful" policies was an *ideological* project the New Order state carried on to cushion the effects of a rapid restructuring of the Indonesian economy in which the new capitalists, along with the military-dominated state, rose to dominance. The policies, which achieved little progress over time, nevertheless had to be created repeatedly, only to make the state appear neutral and above class interests. In the meantime, the repetition of failures demoralized the advocates for such programs and alternative forms of the Indonesian economic system while assuring the new capitalists of the state's commitment to

---

[57]Ibid.

[58]*Business News*, January 29, 1980.

[59]The extremely short and ambiguous article of the Constitution invited the persons involved to use their full imagination in interpreting it to their liking. Clause 1 of ARTICLE 33 reads: "Economy shall be organized cooperatively" (official translation). The original text in Indonesian has space for more controversies, which is roughly translated as, "Economy shall be organized as a joint venture on the basis of the family spirit" (Perekonomian disusun sebagai usaha bersama berdasar atas azas kekeluargaan). This clause, especially the phrase "joint venture" *(usaha bersama)*, is the only reference to the constitutional foundation of the private sector. Less obscure and more words are instead given to the public enterprise in clauses 2 and 3 of the same article. They read respectively as: "Branches of production which are important to the State and which affect the life of most people, shall be controlled by the State" and "Land and water and the natural riches therein shall be controlled by the State and shall be exploited for the greatest welfare of the people."

[60]From the long-term perspective, however, this conclusion might well be seen as tentative. Unless the ideological project the elites were carrying out in the 1980s leads to the creation of a capitalist hegemony in its truest sense, indigenist demands will continue to surface. Policy makers, the condition permitting, may yield to such demands. The state's fiscal capacity and the ability of the economy to afford the discriminatory policy meet the condition.

their continued growth. If the state is still in the driver's seat in Indonesia's modernization, the industrial strength the capitalists have already accomplished, the economic predicament that requires a further procapitalist restructuring, and the steady growth of capitalist ethics in Indonesian society all indicate that the formation process of a capitalist *class* will accelerate, at least, in the foreseeable future.

CHINA AND INDONESIA MAKE UP: REFLECTIONS ON A TROUBLED RELATIONSHIP

Michael Williams

In February 1989 I was in Jakarta covering JIM II, the second Jakarta informal meeting on Cambodia, for the BBC World Service. Like so many other peace initiatives on that troubled country in recent years, the meeting ended in dismal failure on the night of February 22. Feeling weary and despondent I retired to my hotel. To my surprise, there was a message to telephone a long-standing contact in the foreign ministry. We spoke about the failure of the peace talks, my contact ending the conversation by saying cryptically, "Be prepared for a big story tomorrow." In the morning, before an early flight to Singapore, I rang a friend on *Suara Pembaruan*. After coaxing, she told me that President Suharto would meet that day in Tokyo with Qian Qichen, the Chinese foreign minister. On reaching Singapore, I filed the story, pleasing editors in London when the BBC was the first to break the news that Indonesia and China had agreed to normalize their relations after a break of almost a quarter of a century.

The meeting between Suharto and the Chinese foreign minister against the backdrop of the funeral in Tokyo of Emperor Hirohito came as a surprise to observers. In a decisive fashion, it ended years of hesitation and doubt over one of the most basic matters between states, the establishment of diplomatic relations. Once before I had been in Indonesia, in April 1985, when it seemed that the ice was about to break between the two countries. On that occasion, then Chinese foreign minister Wu Queqian became the first Chinese minister to visit Indonesia since 1965, when he attended the thirtieth commemoration of the 1955 Bandung Afro-Asian solidarity conference. An expected meeting with President Suharto failed to take place, in circumstances that have never been properly explained. The visit of Mr. Wu had highlighted the deep divisions between the Indonesian foreign ministry and the military over the question of relations with China. Only two weeks before the Chinese minister's visit, the Indonesian armed forces commander Benny Murdani invited Vietnamese Defense Minister, General Van Tien Dung to town with timing that could not have been accidental. And to the embarrassment of the foreign ministry and of Indonesia's ASEAN partners, Benny reiterated his well-known thesis that Vietnam was not a threat to regional security and suggested that Indonesia and Vietnam could cooperate militarily.

That episode underlined the divisions within the New Order establishment that have been evident ever since 1966 over relations with China. Every foreign minister of the Orde Baru—Adam Malik, Mochtar Kusumaatmadja, and Ali Alatas—has pronounced in public in favor of the restoration of diplomatic ties. It was Malik in 1967 who tried to avoid a complete rupture in diplomatic relations by using the term "frozen," a coinage absent in the normal diplomatic lexicon. As early as 1972, he was advocating the restoration of links with China on certain conditions, but it was to be almost two decades later before this was to be realized. Even after three of Indonesia's ASEAN partners—Malaysia, Thailand and the Philippines—recognized China in the mid-seventies, President Suharto showed no inclination to join the flock of pilgrims to Peking in the wake of China's new "Open Door" policy. Indeed, the outbreak of hostilities between China and Vietnam in 1979, preceded by Peking's intervention on behalf of ethnic Chinese in Vietnam, reawakened for Indonesia old fears about China's role in Southeast Asia. The fact that by the early eighties China and ASEAN were making common cause in backing the anti-Vietnamese resistance in Cambodia did little to persuade Indonesia that its best interests were served by restoring ties with the People's Republic. Almost alone in ASEAN, Indonesia insisted on the need to keep open a dialogue with Vietnam which was not confined to diplomatic channels. In 1984, Benny Murdani became the first non-Communist military commander to be received with considerable acclaim in Hanoi. That visit served to underline not only the foreign policy role played by the Indonesian military but also its continuing suspicion and hostility toward China.

But laying the blame on the army for the absence of diplomatic relations between Indonesia and China for almost a quarter-century, an extraordinary state of affairs in the modern world, is to tell only part of the story. Suharto himself is believed to have shared the military's apprehension about China. When I was in Indonesia in 1985, the assumption was widespread that although the reopening of direct trading links was only a matter of time, restoring diplomatic ties would have to wait until Indonesia's third president took office sometime in the 1990s. As it came to pass, however, full restoration of diplomatic ties did take place in 1990 with the visit of Indonesian Foreign Minister Ali Alatas to Peking in July and a reciprocal visit by Chinese Prime Minister Li Peng to Jakarta in August. The reasons for this somewhat sudden volte-face will be explored later.

Historical Antecedents

Since China and Indonesia established diplomatic relations in March 1950, their relationship has been inherently unstable. Although still a poor country, China by virtue of its vast territory, population, ideology, and military might has consciously sought great power and status for itself since the founding of the People's Republic in October 1949. Indonesia, on the other hand, is the largest country in Southeast Asia and under both its presidents, Sukarno and Suharto, has sought to play a role as a regional power. The conflict between the power ambitions of the two states has been exacerbated for Indonesia by the fact that China for decades has not simply been a potentially threatening state but has also symbolized revolution and posed as the protector of ethnic Chinese in Southeast Asia.[1]

Following the complete Dutch withdrawal from Indonesia in December 1949, most countries were quick to open diplomatic relations with the Indonesian Republic. The Soviet Union, for example, did so in January 1950. It was the end of March, however, before China recognized Indonesia, and not until 1953 did an Indonesian ambassador take up residence

---

[1] Ruth McVey, "Indonesian Communism and China," in *China In Crisis*, ed. Tang Tsou, (Chicago: University of Chicago Press, 1968), 2: 357.

in Peking. (Vice-President Hatta, in fact, sent a cable to the Chinese government on January 11, 1950, requesting the opening of diplomatic relations. That the cable was sent via the Netherlands embassy in Peking may have confirmed Chinese suspicions of the Indonesian government.)[2] Although it might have been expected that both countries shared common ground as republics newly emerged from protracted armed struggles, both states viewed each other with considerable apprehension. For the new revolutionary authorities in Peking, the suppression of the Indonesian Communist party (PKI) revolt in Madiun, in East Java, in 1948 was clear evidence of the reactionary nature of the Indonesian government led by President Sukarno. In view of their own earlier experience in dealing with bourgeois nationalist movements like the Kuomintang, for the Chinese Communists certain parallels seemed to be obvious in Indonesia. For Indonesia, early proof that the Chinese could not be trusted not to interfere in Indonesian politics seemed to come in August 1951. Following a clampdown, or *razzia*, against the PKI, a prominent party leader, Alimin, took refuge in the Chinese embassy in Jakarta.[3]

It was hardly a promising start to the modern history of relations between Indonesia and China. It illustrated only too well the cagey attitudes that each country harbored toward the other, which have continued to bedevil their relations over the past four decades. These attitudes have deep historical roots that have served until modern times to keep the two countries apart. Unlike Vietnam, or even Thailand to some extent, Indonesia had never been part of the Chinese cultural sphere of influence in Southeast Asia. The coming of first Hinduism and then, more importantly, Islam gave Indonesia a very separate and particular identity, further distancing it from China. Indonesian Moslems, who soon formed the vast majority of the archipelago's inhabitants, looked to the Middle East and not northward to China. The arrival of the Dutch from the seventeenth century onward separated the two countries even further. Even in the early twentieth century, when many Indonesian nationalists did look for Asian examples, Japan, rather than poverty-stricken and divided China, seemed to represent the wave of the future. Inevitably, Indonesian perceptions of China were also shaped by the arrival of Chinese immigrants who soon occupied typical middle roles in the colonial economy. The Chinese, more than the Dutch, may have lived among Indonesians, but they retained their own cultural identity and even separate legal status in colonial days. Frequently, they became the targets of popular social unrest. And in the independence struggle against the Dutch after 1945, the Chinese community seemed at best lukewarm in its support for the republic and, at worst, to be active fifth columnists for the colonial power.

The new Chinese government's attitude toward the Indonesian republic can best be described in the early fifties as one of revolutionary militancy, if not outright hostility. Quite apart from the republic's suppression of the Madiun revolt, the war in Korea, the struggle of the Viet Minh against the French in Vietnam and of the Malayan Communist party against the British, convinced the ruling Communist party in China that a revolutionary wave was sweeping East Asia and little was to be gained from fostering close ties with bourgeois governments. Moreover, China's rulers probably had less experience and feel for Indonesia than for any other Southeast Asian country. Sadly, the passing of time was not necessarily going to repair this deficit.

---

[2]D. Mozingo, *Chinese Policy toward Indonesia, 1949–67* (Ithaca, N.Y.: Cornell University Press, 1976), p. 87.

[3]Herbert Feith, *The Decline of Constitutional Democracy in Indonesia* (Ithaca, N.Y.: Cornell University Press, 1962), pp. 192–93, and Mozingo, *Chinese Policy*, pp. 94–101; see also "Sebuah Puncak, Setelah Jurang Terlewati," *Tempo*, March 4, 1990.

Nevertheless, by the mid-fifties the regional context had changed considerably. The Korean War had ended and the Geneva agreement of 1954 had brought at least a temporary respite from war to Indochina. Furthermore, unlike Thailand or the Philippines, Indonesia did not have an attitude of outright hostility to China and had avoided involvement in security arrangements with the United States, such as SEATO. The way was, therefore, set for Chou En-lai's historic visit to Indonesia in 1955. In the space of a few weeks, Chou transformed Sino-Indonesian relations from the distinctly cool to something resembling reasonable friendship. The Chinese prime minister's role at the Bandung Afro-Asian solidarity conference, where he espoused the principles of peaceful coexistence and noninterference, made a distinct impression on the Indonesians and helped to contribute significantly to the success of the conference. Prior to the conference, Chou had signed the Sino-Indonesian Nationality Treaty, under which China made several concessions to Indonesia. Under the terms of the treaty, Indonesian Chinese were obliged to choose between Indonesian or Chinese nationality. In the aftermath of Chou's visit, President Sukarno paid his first visit to China in October 1956. Two years later, in April 1958, China offered Indonesia significant political and financial support during the PRRI-Permesta rebellion, including for the first time a $16 million loan for the purchase of rice and textiles.

The 1959 Crisis

The goodwill generated by these measures, however, was almost totally lost during the crisis that beset Sino-Indonesian relations in 1959. In a series of discriminatory measures, President Sukarno's government revoked the trading licenses of Chinese in rural areas. In West Java, the army followed this measure by ordering all Chinese to evacuate to the major towns. Chinese diplomats in Jakarta openly criticized the measures and tried to advise the local Chinese of their rights. Relations between Peking and Jakarta became severely strained, and China sent ships to Indonesian ports to evacuate more than 120,000 local Chinese. The crisis in relations lasted almost a year and was only prevented from becoming a disastrous diplomatic rupture for two reasons. First, China itself steadily retreated on all the major points of issue, and second, the Indonesian army effectively overplayed its hand. The damage to bilateral relations, though, was considerable. Moreover, the incident dramatically reinforced the Indonesian military's suspicion and hostility toward China. Indeed, this may have been the most lasting effect of the incident.

Some time elapsed before Sino-Indonesian relations recovered from the crisis of 1959. In April 1961, Chinese Foreign Minister Chen Yi visited Indonesia, and in June Sukarno paid his second visit to China. But when Sukarno stepped up his campaign over the Netherlands occupation of West New Guinea (Irian Barat), the Soviet Union rather than China was his principal foreign backer. Moscow provided Jakarta with considerable financial and military assistance as well as diplomatic support. At this stage in its development, China almost certainly was not in a position to render aid on this scale. In October 1961, it did loan $30 million for building textile factories. But Indonesia was also reluctant after the 1959 crisis to move too close to China.

During 1962 to 1963, matters were to change considerably. The resolution of the Irian campaign and the territory's incorporation into Indonesia was soon followed by another external crisis prompted by the formation of Malaysia. This time, support from the Soviet Union was not so forthcoming, especially as Moscow had only just emerged from the trauma of the Cuban missile crisis.[4] Like Indonesia, however, China viewed the creation of Malaysia with considerable suspicion, seeing it as an attempt to bolster the position of West-

---

[4]Michael Leifer, *Indonesian Foreign Policy*, (London: Allen and Unwin, 1983), pp. 69–70.

ern imperialism in Southeast Asia. Peking's longtime patronage of the Malayan Communist party also led it into opposition to the new federation. At the same time, from 1963 the PKI began to move significantly closer to the Chinese Communist party ideologically and lent support to Peking's denunciations of Soviet revisionism. Increasingly, Peking and Jakarta shared a common platform of militant opposition to Western imperialism. But beneath this platform, there remained considerable unease in the army at the emerging Peking-Jakarta axis. Indeed, military support for the anti-Malaysia campaign was premised on hostility to China. Many in the army feared that a Malaysian federation was not viable and that the new state would be dominated by ethnic Chinese and possibly, eventually by China itself.[5]

"Gestapu" and the Break in Relations

The diplomatic culmination of Sukarno's campaign against Malaysia came in December 1964 when Indonesia became the only state ever to withdraw from the United Nations. This bold gesture left Sukarno with nowhere to go internationally except into China's arms. He apparently had already recognized this when in November 1964 he flew to Shanghai for talks with Chinese Prime Minister Chou En-lai. Sukarno's sudden visit to China followed Indonesia's failure to secure the backing of the Nonaligned Movement for its anti-Malaysia campaign at a meeting in Cairo the same month. At the end of November, Chinese Foreign Minister Chen Yi visited Jakarta for a week-long visit and granted Indonesia a $50 million loan. The burgeoning political axis between the two countries was cemented in January 1965 when Foreign Minister Subandrio led a large delegation to Peking that concluded an agreement on political principles. Throughout 1965, contacts between China and Indonesia increased markedly. In May, Peng Chen, a Chinese Communist party politburo member, visited Indonesia to attend the 45th anniversary celebrations of the PKI. In the same month, President Sukarno, in an address to the National Defense Institute, endorsed a PKI proposal for the creation of an armed militia, adding that the idea had also been proposed to him by Chou En-lai.[6] In August, at an Independence Day rally attended by Chinese Foreign Minister Chen Yi, Sukarno again took up this idea and formally proclaimed the existence of an anti-imperialist alliance between Indonesia and China.[7] The announcement of these two initiatives thoroughly alarmed senior figures in the army and undoubtedly contributed to their feeling that drastic political change was necessary if Indonesia was not irrevocably to move to the left and fall into the Chinese camp.

The September 30 incident (Gestapu), involving an attempted leftist coup and a counter-coup led by General Suharto, provided the *casus belli* for a military offensive against the Indonesian Communist party, the overseas Chinese, and China itself. For most senior military figures these were three elements of the same security problem. The floodgates were now open, and the pent up frustrations and hostilities of two decades burst forth. In the process, Indonesia was the scene of one of the worst bloodbaths in modern Asian history. The political map of the country was effectively redrawn in the eighteen months after October 1965, eliminating the world's third largest Communist party and leading to the eventual replacement of President Sukarno by General Suharto.

Although evidence existed that PKI leaders were at least apprised of the leftist Untung coup of September 30, 1965, little or no indication was found of Chinese involvement. In one

---

[5]See George McT. Kahin "Comments," in Tang Tsou, *China in Crisis*, 2: 353; also Mohammad Hatta, "One Indonesian View of the Malaysia Issue," *Asian Survey* March 1965, cited in Leifer, p. 73.

[6]Harold Crouch, *The Army and Politics in Indonesia*, rev. ed. (Ithaca, N.Y.: Cornell University Press, 1988), p. 89–90.

[7]Mozingo, *Chinese Policy*, p. 13; Leifer, *Indonesian Foreign Policy*, p. 105.

sense this did not matter. For just as the military were deeply suspicious of local Chinese, whom they considered to be pro-Communist and loyal to Peking, given the PKI's ideological orientation and Sukarno's proclamation of a Peking-Jakarta axis, it was axiomatic that the military would accuse China of involvement in the coup. China, the PKI, and local Chinese were inextricably linked in the military mind. Moreover, the existence of an externally inspired plot lent credibility to the military's desire for a break in relations with China and justified their own dominant position in politics after 1965.

For China, needless to say, the events of September and October 1965 were a debacle. Almost overnight what had looked like the most spectacular achievement of Chinese foreign policy had turned into a dramatic reverse. So spectacular was this reversal that the Chinese leadership appears to have taken weeks and months to digest it. As late as early 1966 they seem to have clung to the hope that although the PKI had been liquidated, Sukarno might yet be able to pull off some political miracle and contain the right-wing generals.[8] It was only in May 1966 that China withdrew its ambassador from Jakarta.

Following President Sukarno's handover of effective power to General Suharto on March 11, 1966, pressure grew from within the military for a complete break in relations with China.[9] New Order Foreign Minister Adam Malik, anxious that Indonesia should retain a nonaligned profile in its foreign policy, was able for many months to keep these pressures at bay. In April, however, Djawoto, the Indonesian ambassador in Peking, asked for and was granted political asylum in China. For its part, China, realizing that Sukarno had failed to regain the political initiative, was increasingly critical of the New Order regime. China's criticisms were mostly directed at the mistreatment of ethnic Chinese; it showed less concern over the fate of the PKI or the reorientation in Indonesian foreign policy.[10] But as in the 1959 crisis in Sino-Indonesian relations, Peking's belated defense of its friends and allies in Indonesia played into the army's hands. By early 1967, the military pressure on Malik to break with China had become intense. In April, the Chinese chargé d'affaires in Jakarta was expelled. A renewed outbreak of anti-Chinese rioting in Jakarta coincided with the takeover of the Foreign Ministry in Peking by an ultra-left group. As the Cultural Revolution gripped China, Peking spent little effort in trying to maintain relations with Indonesia. In July, it gave public backing to the now underground PKI and called for a "people's war" against the "Suharto Fascist regime." Daily demonstrations outside the Indonesian embassy in Peking emphasized that it was only a matter of time before a final break came. It is a testimony to the influence Adam Malik exercised over Suharto that even at this stage he was able to avoid a total rupture, declaring instead on October 9, 1967 that relations with China were frozen.

Back from the Brink

Almost a quarter-century was to pass before normal diplomatic relations between Indonesia and China were restored. This despite the fact that by the end of the 1970s Indonesia was one of the few major countries in Asia, if not in the world, that had not normalized relations with China in the wake of the "Open Door" policy. In the immediate years after 1967, both countries maintained a policy of outright hostility toward each other. At least until 1971, Peking lent its full support to the underground PKI, offering shelter to a number of

---

[8]Mozingo, *Chinese Policy*, p. 234.

[9]Crouch, *The Army and Politics*, pp. 331–34; A. Nadesan, *Sino-Indonesian Relations 1950–67* (Paper submitted to the 25th Annual Meeting of the Midwest Conference on Asian Affairs, University of Minnesota, October 15–16, 1976), pp. 23–5.

[10]Sheldon Simon, *The Broken Triangle: Peking, Djakarta and the PKI*, (Baltimore: Johns Hopkins, 1969), pp.126.

Indonesian Communist exiles and reiterating its call for armed revolt in Indonesia.[11] On the other side, Indonesia continued to see China as a major external threat and a promoter of domestic instability. Military concerns about security meant that with regard to China, the considerations of the generals often far outweighed those of the foreign ministry in Jakarta. Thus, in 1971 when China at last gained admission to the United Nations, Indonesia voted for a United States–sponsored resolution requiring a two-thirds majority to sanction Taiwan's expulsion and then abstained on the decisive vote to allow Peking entry to the world body.[12]

On China, more than any other issue, the ministries of Foreign Affairs and Defense have been at odds. A reluctant participant in the 1967 decision to freeze relations, Malik as early as 1972 pronounced in favor of the restoration of diplomatic relations. Intermittent ministerial contact was resumed at this time, the first meeting taking place in Paris. For many years Indonesia was to hold to a position that Peking would have to apologize for its alleged role in the events of 1965 and cut its connections with Southeast Asian Communist parties, especially the PKI. Fears were deeply ingrained that China would seek to manipulate the political loyalties of the economically powerful Chinese minority. After 1965, the New Order government had gone to considerable lengths to purge local Chinese of their ethnic identity, closing Chinese schools and even banning all materials written in the Chinese language. Moslem groups, along with the military, have been prominent in voicing their opposition to restoring ties with China. And although President Suharto's government has not generally been noted for its concessions to the Moslem opposition, it has usually avoided offering them any leverage to criticize the regime.

The cumulative effect of these objections was that relations with China remained frozen even when in 1974–1975 three of Indonesia's partners in ASEAN—Malaysia, the Philippines, and Thailand recognized China and opened diplomatic relations. For its part, China had by the mid-seventies considerably muted its criticism of the Suharto government. Anti-Chinese riots in Bandung in 1973, for example, and again in Jakarta in January 1974 drew no real response from Peking.[13] But after the triumph of communism in Indochina in 1975 and the withdrawal of the United States from mainland Southeast Asia, Indonesia was forced to rethink its strategic priorities. Not having diplomatic relations with China at a time when Peking was emerging as one of the most powerful players in Southeast Asia seemed to be taking unnecessary risks.

This logic seemed to be behind President Suharto's announcement in March 1978 that Indonesia was moving to prepare the way for restoring diplomatic links.[14] In September 1977, the Foreign Minister, Adam Malik, had met with his Chinese counterpart, Huang Hua, at the United Nations in New York, the first such meeting since the freezing of relations in 1967.[15] In May, a delegation from the Indonesian Chamber of Commerce (KADIN) visited China and reached an agreement on the resumption of direct trading ties.[16] But President Suharto's move drew a critical response from the Moslem Development Unity party. In parliament it was critical not only of any move to resume diplomatic ties but also to direct

---

[11] Wayne Bert, "Chinese Relations with Burma and Indonesia," *Asian Survey*, 15 (6) (June (1975): 483–4.

[12] Leifer, *Indonesian Foreign Policy*, p. 127.

[13] Bert, "Chinese Relations," p. 484.

[14] Leifer, *Indonesian Foreign Policy*, p. 180; Wayne Bert, "Chinese Policy towards Burma and Indonesia: A Post-Mao Perspective," *Asian Survey* 25 (9) (September 1985): 971.

[15] "Malik bicara dengan Menlu RRT Huang Hua," *Merdeka*, October 3, 1977.

[16] "Sudah Disetujui, Hubungan Dagang Langsung Indonesia-PRC," *Kompas*, May 19, 1978.

trading links.[17] For the Islamic factions, opposition to China stemmed from economic as well as ideological motives. Many Islamic leaders, who were also business people, resented the dominant economic position of the ethnic Chinese; they argued that only when there was a strong indigenous middle class should Indonesia think of reestablishing relations with China.

Suharto had scarcely made his announcement when developments in Indochina once again shifted to the advantage of conservatives in the Indonesian military establishment. In the spring of 1978, relations between China and Vietnam deteriorated rapidly over Hanoi's treatment of the ethnic Chinese in what had formerly been South Vietnam. Peking protested vociferously and dispatched ships to Saigon to evacuate Chinese.[18] For Indonesians, the parallels with their own experience with China in 1959 were all too obvious. And even Vietnam's invasion of Cambodia to topple the Khmer Rouge in December 1978 was offset for many Indoneian generals by China's punitive attack on Vietnam in February 1979. China, rather than Vietnam, seemed to many figures in the Indonesian military establishment to be the real threat to Southeast Asia in the long run.[19] Increasingly, any moves toward normalization were to become the subject of ill-concealed spoiling operations by the military. In December 1981, for example, an Indonesian trade mission to China that had been planned for several months had to be cancelled following a surprise visit to Jakarta by Taiwan Prime Minister Sun Yun-hsuan.[20] To add salt to China's wounds, the Taiwan premier was received by President Suharto himself.

The Debate in the Eighties

Despite some faltering initiatives in the 1970s, the outlook for Sino-Indonesian relations in the early eighties scarcely looked any better than it had a decade or so earlier. Fundamental distrust of China, especially by the military, remained as deeply entrenched as ever. Nor was this picture changed by Vietnam's 1978 invasion of Cambodia and attempt to establish political hegemony over Indochina. The establishment of a Soviet military presence at the former American bases at Da Nang and Cam Ranh Bay did not ring the alarm bells in Jakarta that it rang in Bangkok and Singapore. Even Foreign Minister Dr. Mochtar Kusumaatmadja downplayed the significance of the Soviet military bases in Vietnam. On the contrary, Vietnam was seen as a strong bulwark to Chinese encroachment in the region, and the long-term military perception of China as the main threat to stability in Southeast Asia remained unchanged.

This point was driven home dramatically in February 1984 when to the delight of Vietnam, General Benny Murdani, the commander-in-chief of the Indonesian armed forces, visited Hanoi. Not only was Murdani the most senior ASEAN official to visit Hanoi since its invasion of Cambodia but he was the first non-Communist military commander to hold extensive military consultations with the Vietnamese.[21]

---

[17] See *Antara*, May 25, 1978 for comments of Amin Iskandar, Chairman of the Islamic PPP.

[18] See Nayan Chanda, *Brother Enemy: The War After the War*, (New York: Macmillan, Collier Books, 1988), pp. 231–47; see also Leo Suryadinata, *China and the ASEAN States The Ethnic Chinese Dimension*, (Singapore: Singapore University Press, 1985), p. 1.

[19] These views were not confined to the military; see, for example, the opinions of the Golkar Secretary General Sarwono Kusumaatmadja, "RI Harus Hati-Kati Amati RRT," *Merdeka*, January 10, 1985; see also, Harold Crouch, "No Enemy in Sight," *Far Eastern Economic Review*, February 14, 1985, pp. 32–34.

[20] Bert, "Chinese Policy towards Burma," pp. 971–72; Leifer, *Indonesian Foreign Policy*, p. 171.

[21] Nayan Chanda, "ASEAN's Odd Man Out," *Far Eastern Economic Review*, March 1, 1984, p. 8.

Moreover, a new irritant in Sino-Indonesian relations had arisen following Jakarta's annexation in 1976 of the former Portuguese colony of East Timor, an action that was described by Peking as "a naked act of aggression."[22] At the United Nations, China backed up its condemnation by voting until 1982 for a resolution calling on Indonesia to withdraw its forces from East Timor and allow its people to decide their own fate. (No vote on this matter has been taken at the General Assembly since 1982.)

China has waited patiently for Indonesian attitudes to change. From the early 1970s, Peking rarely commented critically on events in Indonesia. East Timor was something of an exception; not to have condemned Indonesia might have lost China considerable support elsewhere in the Third World, especially in Africa where other former Portuguese colonies galvanized opposition to Indonesia's move. China could also take some consolation from the fact that although Jakarta was more sympathetic to Hanoi than was any other ASEAN capital, after 1982 Indonesia and China shared common ground in supporting the opposition Coalition Government of Democratic Kampuchea led by Prince Sihanouk. Other issues, such as the Soviet military intervention in Afghanistan, also indicated a shared point of view between China and Indonesia on an important international matter. Another more vital issue for Jakarta that received Chinese support was Indonesia's initiative for legal recognition of its declared archipelagic status, which was finally included in the draft convention of the Law of the Sea Conference in 1982.[23] Peking's support showed China's willingness to conciliate Indonesia, the most important power in Southeast Asia, as long as Jakarta did not develop close ties with the Soviet Union or actively oppose China on major issues.

That patience began to show some sign of success by the mid-eighties. Adam Malik, freed of the constraints of the offices of foreign minister and vice-president, seemed increasingly critical of official policy toward China. He stated bluntly in 1984 that there had been no indication of Chinese involvement in subversion in Indonesia since the mid-sixties and that normalization of relations was necessary if Indonesia wanted to pursue a more active policy on the international stage. Even before normalization, Malik urged that Foreign Minister Mochtar should travel to Peking on behalf of ASEAN for discussions of the Cambodian conflict.[24] Although Mochtar himself was quick to say that the time was still not ripe for normalization of relations with China, Malik's intervention had placed the issue firmly on the public agenda again.[25]

The first real breakthrough in Sino-Indonesian relations since 1967 came in 1985 when Chinese Foreign Minister Wu Xueqian was invited to Indonesia for the thirtieth anniversary of the 1955 Bandung Afro-Asian solidarity conference. The presence of a Chinese minister in Indonesia for the first time in two decades added interest to an otherwise painfully lackluster conference, which only served to underline the failure of the "Orde Baru" to generate anything like the support that President Sukarno had enjoyed in the Third World.[26] But if Wu's visit did at least succeed in breaking the ice, there was to be no dramatic reconciliation. At the end of the visit in an embarrassing incident, Wu was apparently offered a meet-

---

[22]S. Kim, *China, the United Nations and World Order*, (Princeton, N.J.: Princeton University Press, 1979), p. 222–23.

[23]G. W. Choudhury, *China in World Affairs: The Foreign Policy of the PRC since 1970* (Boulder, Colo.: Westview, 1982), p. 240.

[24]Bert, "Chinese Policy," p. 973; *Kompas*, March 1 and March 9, 1984.

[25]*Sinar Harapan*, March 9, 1984.

[26]Conspicuous by their absence, although invited, were Rajiv Gandhi, Pham Van Dong, and Prince Sihanouk; see Richard Nations and Lincoln Kaye, "Repeat Performance," *Far Eastern Economic Review*, May 2, 1985.

ing with Suharto after his scheduled time of departure. The meeting never took place, and both sides blamed each other for a lost opportunity.[27] Behind this gaffe, Indonesian officials indicated their displeasure at China's continued unwillingness to apologize for the events of 1965 and to break its ties with Southeast Asian Communist parties.[28] And to emphasize its continued lack of any shared strategic interests with China, the Indonesian armed forces chief Benny Murdani invited Vietnamese Defense Minister Van Tien Dung to Jakarta only one week before Wu's historic visit.

But if the Wu visit had not led to any dramatic breakthrough in political relations between the two states, it did lead to Jakarta giving the green light to the resumption of direct trading links between Indonesia and China. The logic for doing so was inescapable. By the mid-eighties, Indonesia was running a substantial deficit in its indirect trade with China. Indonesian business people were increasingly irked at the substantial cut made by traders in third countries like Singapore and Hong Kong. KADIN, the Indonesian Chamber of Commerce and Industry, was vocal in its demands that direct trading to be resumed. Fortunately, its vice-chairman, Probosutedjo, was also Suharto's brother-in-law. In April, Probosutedjo had visited Peking with a group of Indonesian businessmen, anxious that they were missing out on a China market that was only too accessible to other ASEAN business. Indonesia's efforts to boost its non-oil exports also underlined the need to find new markets. In July, a memorandum of understanding between KADIN and the China Council for the Promotion of International Trade (CCPIT) was signed in Singapore.[29] An exchange of trade delegations was carried out within two months after the agreement to resume direct trade. Although this move, coming so soon after the Wu visit, was the most concrete manifestation by Indonesia in many years of its desire for better relations with China, the acute sensitivity of Jakarta was once again only too obvious. The memorandum that the two countries' trade organizations signed was remarkable for omitting any mention by name of either the Republic of Indonesia or the People's Republic of China. The Indonesian government had insisted on deletion of the names from the text to amplify the unofficial nature of the agreement. The requirement for both Chinese and Indonesian business executives to handle visa procedures either in Singapore or Hong Kong, and not in each other's capitals, further reflected Indonesia's continuing caution toward China.

Important though the agreement to resume direct trade was, no real breakthrough on the diplomatic front occurred. Indeed, the caveats the Indonesian authorities had made about even the resumption of trading relations, the failure of Suharto to meet with Wu Xueqian, and the Vietnamese defense minister's visit to Jakarta all emphasized the ambivalence with which Indonesia continued to regard China. But throughout the late 1980s, it became increasingly obvious that Indonesia was paying a considerable political price because of the absence of diplomatic relations with China. Its ambitions to play a greater role within the Nonaligned Movement and even to chair the movement and its efforts to find a solution to the Cambodian conflict through the Jakarta Informal Meetings (JIMS) were all hampered by the absence of diplomatic relations with China. The two meetings that Indonesia hosted

---

[27]Richard Nations, "Wu-ing Suharto," *Far Eastern Economic Review*, May 23, 1985; "Tampaknya Masih Lama Lagi," *Merdeka*, April 29, 1985. For critical reactions from the Islamic United Development party to the visit see comments of Amin Iskandar, "Harus Dibuktikan Tak Ada Hubungan PKC dengan Komunis Indonesia," *Sinar Harapan*, April 26, 1985.

[28]There was an expectation in official circles that Wu had brought a letter from Deng Xiaoping for Suharto; see the interview with Mochtar in *Tempo*, April 27, 1985, p. 18.

[29]*Sinar Harapan*, July 4 and July 5, 1985; *Kompas*, July 5, 1985; see also the interview with Moerdiono, the Cabinet Secretary who was in charge of managing reestablishment of relations on Indonesian side, *Tempo*, May 25, 1990.

on Cambodia were handicapped by the noninclusion of China, the principal diplomatic and military backer of the Cambodian resistance, and gave Vietnam a greater opportunity to dominate the proceedings. Growing indications that the two superpowers were disengaging from Southeast Asia also made Indonesia feel that it had to position itself to take a more active part in the processes of detente. Rapprochement between the Soviet Union and China showed only too clearly that detente was not limited to the superpowers and illustrated that the balance of power in Asia was undergoing radical change. Indonesia could no longer afford to be isolated from one of the key players in East Asia.[30]

The final breakthrough came on February 23, 1989, in the Imperial Hotel in Tokyo when President Suharto met with Chinese Foreign Minister Qian Qichen. In a move that took observers by surprise, the two countries agreed to move toward normalizing their relations at an early date.[31] Qian repeated assurances that China would not meddle in Indonesian domestic affairs at either state or party levels. In separate talks with Indonesian State Secretary Moerdiono, Qian also said that exiled members of the PKI in China would not henceforth be allowed to carry out political activities. (As chairman of the coordinating body set up by presidential decree after the trade agreement of 1985, Moerdiono was the only senior official closely involved in the Tokyo negotiations. Although negotiations with the Chinese have taken place since 1985 at the United Nations in New York, they have been handled exclusively by the State Secretariat.[32]

In looking at the reasons why such a major change in Indonesian foreign policy took place, it is clear that external factors, and especially changes in East Asia itself, had a major impact on revising Indonesian attitudes towards China. By early 1989, the increasing tempo of superpower detente was already indicating strongly that the Cold War era was drawing to a close. Inevitably, the shock waves from this change were beginning to be felt in East Asia. In the weeks before Suharto's meeting with Qian Qichen in Tokyo, Soviet Foreign Minister Eduard Shevardnadze had visited Peking, laying the ground for the historic summit between President Gorbachev and Deng Xiaoping in May 1989 that was to signal Sino-Soviet rapprochement. Elsewhere, the Soviet Union was indicating its desire to open relations with South Korea, and Vietnam was preparing to announce a military withdrawal from Cambodia after a decade-long involvement, while Thailand's new Premier Chatichai Choonhavan was declaring his desire to see Indochina transformed from a battle zone into a marketplace. By contrast, Indonesian foreign policy seemed to be in a rut. A second major initiative on Cambodia, "JIM II," had ended in failure while Indonesia's ambitions to chair the Nonaligned Movement seemed nowhere near success. Jakarta seemed unable to shake off its image in the Third World as being too closely tied to the United States and Japan. The attractions of at last normalizing relations with China, and the dangers of even greater isolation if Indonesia did not do so, had become all too evident.

Quite apart from the external factors that pushed President Suharto to undertake such a reversal in foreign policy, a reversal that few observers expected, domestic factors militating against normalization had by 1989 become less serious than they had been earlier. It is significant that the move came after the 1987 elections and after Suharto's own reelection as

---

[30]See "Satu Lagi, Hubungan Diplomatik antara RI dan RRT," *Merdeka*, June 11, 1990; Richard Borsuk, "Indonesia's Resumption of Ties to China Signals Desire for More Regional Clout," *Asian Wall Street Journal*, August 13, 1990.

[31]Hamish McDonald, "Breaking the Ice," *Far Eastern Economic Review*, March 9, 1989, pp. 10–11; "Berjabat Tangan Dengan Cina," *Tempo*, March 4, 1989, pp. 14–22, see especially interview with the Foreign Minister, Ali Alatas.

[32]Michael Vatikiotis, "Another Step Closer," *Far Eastern Economic Review*, November 30, 1990, p. 36.

president in 1988. By recognizing China after the elections, Suharto avoided having the matter become an election issue and a potential vote winner for the Islamic United Development party (PPP). More interesting for what it says about the politics of the New Order was the absence of anything other than muted response from the military and security authorities. On several occasions in 1989, Yoga Sugama, the former chief of Bakin, the powerful state intelligence agency, did urge the government to slow the normalization process, and in July the governor of the National Defense Institute, Major General Soebiakto, warned that China remained a threat to Southeast Asia.[33] But there were no overt manifestations of military displeasure such as occurred in 1981 when the Taiwanese prime minister visited Jakarta, or again in 1985 when the military invited the Vietnamese defense minister to visit Jakarta only one week before the Chinese foreign minister.

Economic arguments may well have helped sway the president's mind. In the eighties, Indonesia became increasingly concerned about diversifying its economy away from oil and gas and boosting other exports. The attraction of a billion strong market was as great for Indonesian traders as it was for business people elsewhere. Although direct trade with China had been resumed in 1985, as a country that still did not have diplomatic relations with China, Indonesia's goods were subject to 10–30 percent import levies. Moreover, many of the business people heavily involved in the China trade were either close to Suharto or members of his own family. Two of the three Indonesian banks that are correspondents for the Bank of China, Bank Umum Nasional and Bank Central Asia, are controlled by Liem Sioe Liong, who has long been closely identified with Suharto. KADIN's China trade committee is run from the offices of a company that is 40 percent owned by one of the president's sons, Bambang Trihadmojo, and Suharto's half-brother, Probosutedjo, has long been an advocate of closer trading ties with China.

Perhaps most importantly, by the end of the eighties the government seemed to be more confident of the loyalties of Indonesia's Chinese community. Although suspicion and resentment of the Chinese remains rife in many quarters in Indonesia, the government itself seems convinced that despite the continued existence of three hundred thousand "stateless" Chinese, the assimilationist policies of the New Order have worked.[34] Despite many shortcomings, a new liberal policy on naturalization that was introduced in 1980 and does seem to have had a considerable impact on what had been a long-running sore in Sino-Indonesian relations.[35]

Within eighteen months of the Tokyo meeting, Indonesian Foreign Minister Ali Alatas had visited Peking and Chinese Prime Minister Li Peng had visited Jakarta. Diplomatic relations were officially restored on July 8, 1990.[36] For China, the resumption of ties with Indonesia represented a major diplomatic triumph at a time when much of the rest of the world had shunned contact with Peking after the bloody suppression of the democracy movement in June 1989. By a grim irony, massacres marked the freezing of relations between the two countries in 1967 and their unfreezing in 1990.

---

[33] See *Far Eastern Economic Review*, October 26, November 16 and November 30, 1989.

[34] Leo Suryadinata, "Indonesian Policies towards the Chinese Minority under the New Order," *Asian Survey*, 16 (8) 1987: 770–787.

[35] Rum Hardjono, "Antara Normalisasi dengan Penyelesaian Hoakiao," *Kompas*, September 22, 1978.

[36] Michael Vaikiotis, "Red Carpets, Red Flags," *Far Eastern Economic Review*, August 23, 1990, pp. 8–9; Michael Williams, "In Asia, Two Giants Bury the Ax," *International Herald Tribune*, June 29, 1990; see also "Communique of the Government of the Republic of Indonesia and the Government of the People's Republic of China on the Resumption of Diplomatic Relations between the Two Countries," United Nations document, NV/90/21, July 6, 1990.

Appendix 1
Annotated Chronology of Sino-Indonesian Relations

1910	The Netherlands East Indies government allows China to open consulates in Indonesia for the first time.
March 28, 1950	The People's Republic of China recognizes Indonesia. Two months after the Soviet Union does.
July 20, 1950	The first Chinese ambassador, Wang Jen-Shu, arrives in Indonesia.
January 21, 1951	Indonesian chargé d'affaires, Isak Mahdi, arrives in Peking.
March 1951	The PRC is allowed to open consulates in Medan, Banjarmasin, and Makassar.
August 1951	The Chinese embassy gives refuge to communist leader Alimin during clampdown on PKI (Sukiman razzia).
October 1953	The first Indonesian ambassador, Arnold Monontu, arrives in Peking.
April 22, 1955	In the Sino-Indonesian Dual Nationality Treaty, China makes important concessions. Agreement is not ratified by the Indonesian parliament until 1958.
April 1955	Chinese Prime Minister Chou En-lai attends the Bandung Conference of Afro-Asian nations and outlines principles of peaceful coexistence as the basis of relations between non-Western states.
October 1956	President Sukarno pays his first visit to China at the end of a world tour. His impressions of China contribute to the adoption of Guided Democracy in 1951.
April 1958	China offers political and financial support during the PRRI-Permesta rebellion—a $16 million loan for the purchase of rice and textiles.
May 1959	A major crisis in Sino-Indonesian relations follows measures revoking trading licences of Chinese in rural areas. The army in West Java orders all Chinese to be evacuated to major towns.
October 1959	Indonesian Foreign Minister Subandrio flies to Peking for talks on the crisis.
May 1960	Indonesia and China are on the verge of a diplomatic break. China eventually backs down.
April 1961	Chinese Foreign Minister Chen Yi visits Indonesia, reestablishing good relations.
June 1961	Sukarno visits China for the second time.
October 1961	China lends Indonesia $30 million for building textile factories.
April 1963	Chinese President Liu Shao-chi visits Indonesia.
November 1964	Sukarno makes a surprise visit to Shanghai for talks with Chou En-lai. His visit follows the failure of the Cairo nonaligned meeting to back Indonesia's opposition to Malaysia.

November 27, 1964	Chinese Foreign Minister Chen Yi arrives in Jakarta for a week long visit and announces a $50 million loan for Indonesia.
January 1965	Subandrio visits Peking at the head of a large Indonesian delegation. A Sino-Indonesian declaration of diplomatic and political unity is issued.
May 1965	Chinese CP politburo member, Peng Chen, visits Jakarta for the 45th anniversary celebrations of the Indonesian Communist party (PKI).
August 17, 1965	Sukarno announces the Sino-Indonesian alliance.
October 1, 1965	The Untung coup attempt is defeated by the military under General Suharto.
October 16, 1965	The army enters the offices of a Chinese commercial counselor in Jakarta, which begins a rapid deterioration in Sino-Indonesian relations.
April 1966	The Indonesian ambassador in Peking, Djawoto, asks for political asylum.
May 1966	The Chinese ambassador is recalled from Jakarta. All Chinese economic aid is suspended.
September 1966	Indonesian Foreign Minister Adam Malik accuses China of being involved in the Untung coup attempt. The trial of Subandrio opens with allegations that Chinese arms were supplied to coup plotters. Demonstrations occur outside the Chinese embassy in Jakarta.
April 24, 1967	Chinese chargé d'affaires is expelled from Indonesia. On the following day, China expels the Indonesian chargé d'affaires.
July 7, 1967	China endorses the new PKI revolutionary line and calls for a people's war against the "Suharto fascist regime" three months after Sukarno is stripped of all remaining power.
August 1967	Demonstrations and attacks occur on the Indonesian embassy in Peking.
October 7, 1967	Indonesia announces the freezing of diplomatic relations with China.
April 1985	The Chinese foreign minister visits Indonesia for the commemoration of the 1955 Bandung conference. An expected meeting with President Suharto fails to take place.
February 23, 1989	President Suharto meets with Chinese Foreign Minister Qian Qichen in Tokyo at the funeral of Emperor Hirohito. An agreement is reached on normalizing relations.
September 1989	Talks take place in New York between Ali Alatas and Qian Qichen.
July 1, 1990	Ali Alatas visits China, the first visit by an Indonesian minister in a quarter-century.
August 8, 1990	Diplomatic relations between China and Indonesia are officially restored.

SOUTHEAST ASIA PROGRAM PUBLICATIONS
Cornell University
East Hill Plaza
Ithaca, New York 14850

Studies on Southeast Asia

Number 1   *The Symbolism of the Stupa*, Adrian Snodgrass. 1985. Rep. with index, 1988. 469 pp. $16.00.

Number 2   *Context, Meaning, and Power in Southeast Asia*, ed. Mark Hobart and Robert Taylor. 1986. 156 pp. $16.00.

Number 4   *In the Center of Authority: The Malay Merong Mahawangsa*, Hendrik M. J. Maier. 1988. 210 pp. $14.00

Number 5   *Southeast Asian Ephemeris: Solar and Planetary Positions, A.D. 638–2000*, J. C. Eade. 1989. 171 pp. $15.00.

Number 6   *Trends in Khmer Art*, Jean Boisselier. Ed. Natasha Eilenberg. Trans. Natasha Eilenberg and Melvin Elliott. 1989. 124 pp. $15.00.

Number 7   *A Malay Frontier: Unity and Duality in a Sumatran Kingdom*, Jane Drakard. 1990. 215 pp. $15.00.

SEAP Series

Number 2   *The Dobama Movement in Burma (1930–1938)*, Khin Yi. 1988. 160 pp. $9.00.

Number 2A   *The Dobama Movement in Burma: Appendix (Documents in Burmese)*. 1988. 140 pp. $16.00.

Number 3   *Postwar Vietnam: Dilemmas in Socialist Development*, ed. Christine White and David Marr. 1988. 264 pp. $12.00.

Number 4   *Independent Burma at Forty Years*, ed. Josef Silverstein. 1989. 118 pp. $10.00

Number 5   *Japanese Relations with Vietnam: 1951–1987*, Masaya Shiraishi. 1990. 174 pp. $12.00.

Number 6   *The Rise and Fall of the Communist Party of Burma (CPB)*, Bertil Lintner. 1990. 124 pp. $10.00.

Number 7   *Intellectual Property and US Relations with Indonesia, Malaysia, Singapore, and Thailand*, Elisabeth Uphoff. 1991. 67 pp. $8.00.

Translation Series

Volume 1   *Reading Southeast Asia*. 1990. 188 pp. $12.00.

* * * * *

In the Mirror, Literature and Politics in Siam in the American Era, ed. and trans. Benedict R. Anderson and Ruchira Mendiones. 1985. 303 pp. Hardcover. $10.00.

Data Papers

In Print

Number 18 *Conceptions of State and Kingship in Southeast Asia,* Robert Heine-Geldern. 1956. (6th printing 1987) 14 pp. $3.50.

Number 75 *White Hmong-English Dictionary,* compiled by Ernest E. Heimbach. Linguistics Ser. 4. 1969. (2nd printing 1979) 497 pp. $6.50.

Number 92 *Feasting and Social Oscillation: A Working Paper on Religion and Society in Upland Southeast Asia,* A. Thomas Kirsch. 1973 (4th printing 1990). 67 pp. $5.00.

Number 102 *No Other Road to Take,* Memoir of Mrs. Nguyen Thi Dinh, trans. Mai Elliott. 1976. 77 pp. $6.00.

Number 111 *Cambodia's Economy and Industrial Development,* Khieu Samphan, trans. and with an intro. by Laura Summers. 1979. 122 pp. $5.75.

Indonesia, a semiannual journal, devoted to Indonesia's culture, history, and social and political problems.

No. 16, October 1973, No. 17, April 1974, No. 20, October 1975, $4.50
No. 21, April 1976, No. 22, October 1976, No. 23, April 1977, $5.00
No. 32, October 1981, No. 34, October 1982, $6.50
No. 37, April 1984, No. 40, October 1985, $7.50
No. 41, April 1986, No. 42, October 1986, $7.50 each, $14.00 both
No. 43, April 1987, No. 44, October 1987, $8.50 each, $16.00 both
No. 45, April 1988, No. 46, October 1988, $8.50 each, $16.00 both
No. 47, April 1989, No. 48, October 1989, $8.50 each, $16.00 both
No. 49, April 1990, No. 50, October 1990, $9.50 each, $18.00 both
No. 51, April 1991, No. 52, October 1991, $9.50 each, $18.00 both

STUDY AND TEACHING MATERIALS

Obtainable from Southeast Asia Program Publications
Cornell University, East Hill Plaza, Ithaca, New York 14850

Thai

Thai Cultural Reader, Book I, by Robert B. Jones, Ruchira C. Mendiones and Craig J. Reynolds. 1970. (2nd rev. ed. 1976) 517 pp. $7.50.

A.U.A. Language Center Thai Course, J. Marvin Brown, Books 1, 2, 3, $9.00 each. Tape supplement for Books 1, 2, 3, $4.00. Small Talk (dialogue book A), $9.00. Getting Help (ddialogue book B), $9.00. Book R (reading), $9.00. Book W (writing), $9.00.

Indonesian

Beginning Indonesian through Self-Instruction, John U. Wolff, Dédé Oetomo, and Daniel Fietkiewicz. 1984. 900 pp. 3 vols. $27.00/set.

Indonesian Readings, John U. Wolff. 1978. (3rd printing 1988) 468 pp. $16.00.

Indonesian Conversations, John U. Wolff. 1978. (2nd printing 1981) 297 pp. $14.00.

Formal Indonesian, John U. Wolff. 1980. (2nd printing 1986) 446 pp. $16.00.

Vietnamese

An Intermediate Reader, Robert M. Quinn. 1972. 200 pp. $3.50.

Intermediate Spoken Vietnamese, Franklin Huffman and Tran Trong Hai. 1980. 401 pp. $12.00.

Khmer

Cambodian System of Writing and Beginning Reader, Franklin E. Huffman. (Originally published by Yale University Press, 1970.) Reissued by Cornell Southeast Asia Program, 1987. 365 pp. $14.00.

Modern Spoken Cambodian, Franklin E. Huffman, with the assistance of Charan Promchan and Chhom-Rak Thong Lambert. (Originally published by Yale University Press, 1970.) Reissued by Cornell Southeast Asia Program, 1984, 1987. 451 pp. $16.00.

Intermediate Cambodian Reader, ed. Franklin E. Huffman, assisted by Im Proum. (Originally published by Yale University Press, 1972.) Reissued by Cornell Southeast Asia Program, 1988. 499 pp. $16.00.

Cambodian Literary Reader and Glossary, Franklin E. Huffman and Im Proum. (Originally issued by Yale University Press, 1977.) Reprinted with permission by Cornell Southeast Asia Program, 1988. 494 pp. $16.00.

Accessions List of the John M. Echols Collection on Southeast Asia, compiled monthly by John H. Badgley, ed. Annual subscription $20.00.

Language Tapes

Order tapes from: The Language Laboratory, Dept. of Modern Languages, Morrill Hall, Cornell University, Ithaca, NY 14853-4701. Tel: (607) 255-7394.
(Make checks out to "Cornell University.")

(For A.U.A. tapes,, institutions should order a master set directly from A.U.A. Language Center, 17 Rajadamri Road, Bangkok 5, Thailand. Cassettes sold in sets only.)

A.U.A. books: Books 1, 2, 3, $48.00 per set (8 cassettes/book);

Beginning Indonesian through Self-Instruction, Lessons 1–12, $180.00; Lessons 13–25, $168.00; complete set $348.00; $6.50 per individual cassette;

Indonesian Conversations, complete set of 20 cassettes, $120.00;

Modern Spoken Cambodian, set of 26 tapes available for $126.00; $6.50 per individual tape.

CORNELL UNIVERSITY
MODERN INDONESIA PROJECT PUBLICATIONS

102 West Avenue
Ithaca, NY 14850-3982

In Print

Number 6 *The Indonesian Elections of 1955*, Herbert Feith. 1957. (2nd printing 1971.) 91 pp. $3.50. (Interim report.)

Number 7 *The Soviet View of the Indonesian Revolution*, Ruth T. McVey. 1957. (3rd printing 1969.) 90 pp. $2.50. (Interim report.)

Number 25 *The Communist Uprisings of 1926–1927 in Indonesia: Key Documents*, ed. and with an intro. by Harry J. Benda and Ruth T. McVey. 1960. (2nd printing 1969.) 177 pp. $5.50. (Translation.)

Number 37 *Mythology and the Tolerance of the Javanese*, Benedict R. Anderson. 1965. (6th printing 1988.) 77 pp. $5.00. (Monograph.)

Number 43 *State and Statecraft in Old Java: A Study of the Later Mataram Period, 16th to 19th Century*, Soemarsaid Moertono. 1968. (Rev. ed. 1981.) 180 pp. $9.00. (Monograph.)

Number 45 *Indonesia Abandons Confrontation*, Franklin B. Weinstein. 1969. 94 pp. $3.00. (Interim report.)

Number 46 *The Origins of the Modern Chinese Movement in Indonesia*, Kwee Tek Hoay. Trans. and ed. Lea E. Williams. 1969. 64 pp. $3.00. (Translation.)

Number 48 *Nationalism, Islam and Marxism*, Soekarno. With an intro. by Ruth T. McVey. 1970. (2nd printing 1984.) 62 pp. $4.00. (Translation.)

Number 49 *The Foundation of the Partai Muslimin Indonesia*, K. E. Ward. 1970. 75 pp. $3.00. (Interim report.)

Number 50 *Schools and Politics: The Kaum Muda Movement in West Sumatra (1927–1933)*, Taufik Abdullah. 1971. 257 pp. $6.00. (Monograph.)

Number 51 *The Putera Reports: Problems in Indonesian-Javanese War-Time Cooperation*, Mohammad Hatta. Trans. and intro. William H. Frederick. 1971. 114 pp. $4.00. (Translation.)

Number 52 *A Preliminary Analysis of the October 1, 1965, Coup in Indonesia* (Prepared in January 1966), Benedict R. Anderson, Ruth T. McVey (assisted by Frederick P. Bunnell). 1971. 174 pp. $9.00. (Interim report.)

Number 55 *Report from Banaran: The Story of the Experiences of a Soldier during the War of Independence*, Major General T. B. Simatupang. 1972. 186 pp. $6.50. (Translation.)

Number 56 *Golkar and the Indonesian Elections of 1971*, Masashi Nishihara. 1972. 56 pp. $3.50. (Monograph.)

Number 57 *Permesta: Half a Rebellion*, Barbara S. Harvey, 1977. 174 pp. $5.00. (Monograph.)

Number 58 *Administration of Islam in Indonesia*, Deliar Noer. 1978. 82 pp. $4.50. (Monograph.)

Number 59 *Breaking the Chains of Oppression of the Indonesian People: Defense Statement at His Trial on Charges of Insulting the Head of State, Bandung, June 7–10, 1979*, Heri Akhmadi. 1981. 201 pp. $8.75. (Translation.)

Number 60 *The Minangkabau Response to Dutch Colonial Rule in the Nineteenth Century*, Elizabeth E. Graves. 1981. 157 pp. $7.50. (Monograph.)

Number 61 *Sickle and Crescent: The Communist Revolt of 1926 in Banten*, Michael C. Williams. 1982. 81 pp. $6.00. (Monograph.)

Number 62	*Interpreting Indonesian Politics: Thirteen Contributions to the Debate, 1964–1981.* Ed. Benedict Anderson and Audrey Kahin, with an intro. by Daniel S. Lev. 1982. 172 pp. $9.00. (Interim report.)
Number 63	*Dynamics of Dissent in Indonesia: Sawito and the Phantom Coup,* David Bourchier. 1984. 128 pp. $9.00. (Interim report.)
Number 64	*Suharto and His Generals: Indonesia's Military Politics, 1975–1983,* David Jenkins. 1984. 300 pp. $12.50. (Monograph.)
Number 65	*The Kenpeitai in Java and Sumatra.* Trans. from the Japanese by Barbara G. Shimer and Guy Hobbs, with an intro. by Theodore Friend. 1986. 80 pp. $8.00. (Translation.)
Number 66	*Prisoners at Kota Cane,* Leon Salim. Trans. Audrey Kahin. 1986. 112 pp. $9.00. (Translation.)
Number 67	*Indonesia Free: A Biography of Mohammad Hatta,* Mavis Rose. 1987. 252 pp. $10.50. (Monograph.)
Number 68	*Intellectuals and Nationalism in Indonesia: A Study of the Following Recruited by Sutan Sjahrir in Occupation Jakarta,* J. D. Legge. 1988. 159 pp. $8.00. (Monograph.)
Number 69	*The Road to Madiun: The Indonesian Communist Uprising of 1948,* Elizabeth Ann Swift. 1989. 120 pp. $9.00. (Monograph.)

Contributors

Leonard Blussé is professor of History at the University of Leiden.

Daniel S. Lev is professor of Political Science at the University of Washington, Seattle.

Jamie Mackie is professor of Political Science and Social Change at the Research School of Pacific Studies, the Australian National University, Canberra.

H. M. J. Maier is professor of Malay and Indonesian Language and Literature at the University of Leiden.

Dédé Oetomo is chairman of the Department of Language and Literature, Faculty of Social and Political Sciences, Airlangga University in Surabaya.

James Rush is with the Department of History, Arizona State University, Tempe.

Claudine Salmon is senior researcher at the National Centre for Scientific Research, Paris.

Yoon Hwan Shin is assistant professor of Political Science at Sogang University, Seoul.

Mély G. Tan is a senior researcher at the Centre for Social and Cultural Studies at the Indonesian Institute of Sciences.

Michael Williams was a Luce Visiting Fellow at Cornell in 1990 and is a senior commentator with the British Broadcasting System Far Eastern Service, London.

www.ingramcontent.com/pod-product-compliance
Lightning Source LLC
Chambersburg PA
CBHW080635230426
43663CB00016B/2881